WHEN WE WERE ARABS

WHEN WE WERE ARABS

A JEWISH FAMILY'S
FORGOTTEN HISTORY

MASSOUD HAYOUN

THE
NEW
PRESS

NEW YORK
LONDON

Lines from "Those Who Seek Life" and "Bint el-Aarab" used with permission.

All photos courtesy of the author.

Requests for permission to reproduce selections from this book should be made
through our website: https://thenewpress.com/contact.

Published in the United States by The New Press, New York, 2019
Distributed by Two Rivers Distribution

ISBN 978-1-62097-458-2 (ebook)

LIBRARY OF CONGRESS CATALOGING-IN-PUBLICATION DATA

Names: Hayoun, Massoud, author.
Title: When we were Arabs : a Jewish family's forgotten history / Massoud
    Hayoun.
Description: New York ; London : New Press, [2019] | "A vivid account of
    Massoud Hayoun's grandparents' lives in Egypt, Tunisia, France, Palestine,
    and Los Angeles, in which he reclaims his family's Jewish Arab
    identity"--From the publisher. | Includes bibliographical references.
Identifiers: LCCN 2018055994 | ISBN 9781620974162 (hc : alk. paper)
Subjects: LCSH: Mizrahim—Biography. | North Africans—Egypt—Biography.
    |
    Cultural fusion—Egypt. | Jews—Identity. | Hayoun, Massoud—Childhood
and
    youth.
Classification: LCC DS113.8.S4 H39 2019 | DDC 305.892/40620922--dc23
LC record available at https://lccn.loc.gov/2018055994

The New Press publishes books that promote and enrich public discussion and
understanding of the issues vital to our democracy and to a more equitable
world. These books are made possible by the enthusiasm of our readers; the
support of a committed group of donors, large and small; the collaboration
of our many partners in the independent media and the not-for-profit sector;
booksellers, who often hand-sell New Press books; librarians; and above all by
our authors.

www.thenewpress.com

Book design and composition by Bookbright Media
This book was set in Bembo and Alternate Gothic

Printed in the United States of America

For our youth

إذا الشعب يوما أراد الحياة

فلا بدّ أن يستجيب القدر

ولا بد لليل أن ينجلي

ولا بد للقيد أن ينكسر

When common people seek life,
Destiny will verily respond,
And the darkness will surely pass,
And shackles will surely shatter.

——الشابي أبو القاسم / Abou el-Kacem e-Chebi from 1933
poem الحياة إرادة / "Those Who Seek Life," adopted as
part of the national anthem of Tunisia in 1987

آنا عربية, آنا بدوية

وآنا بنت العرب!

I am Arab, I am Bedouin
And I am a daughter of the Arabs!

—From العرب بنت / "Bint el-Aarab" (Daughter of
the Arabs), written by composer Salah el-Mahdi,
performed by legendary Jewish Tunisian singer لويزا
سعدون / Louisa Saadoun (known by stage name لويزا
تونسية / Louisa Tounsia / Louisa the Tunisian), record
released in 1961

CONTENTS

WHEN WE WERE ARABS

INTRODUCTION

I am a Jewish Arab. For many, I'm a curiosity or a detestable thing. Some say I don't exist, or if I did, I no longer do.

I reject these ideas. My rejection demands that I paint for you a lost world to prove that we existed. Sadly, many of the faces, sounds, and moods of the last days of chez nous, of my grandparents' world, are totally gone. And only so much can be reconstructed here in writing, without the help of the film and song with which my grandparents recalled to me our civilization and its decline.

In the minds of many non-Jewish Arabs who remember us fondly, we are preserved in the cinema of a colonial era—the so-called Golden Age of Egyptian cinema that flourished from the 1940s to the 1960s.[1] My grandparents' generation, portrayed in those old films, drips with poetry and grace. The films star Jewish Arab actors and singers but aren't about Jewish Arabs; rather, they recall a society in which we existed without question. We are a reminder of the cosmopolitanism, the pluralism, and the colonial degradation of that time—a time of fresh-pressed suits and tarbooshes, of singing about our anguished feelings as we walk along the Nile.

Others view Jewish Arabs this way too. Once, a European American journalist—an enthusiast of our region, you know the sort—who knew I was Arab but not that I was Jewish, told me of *The Man in the White Sharkskin Suit*, Lucette Lagnado's memoir of her Egyptian Jewish family's departure from Egypt. I'd already read it, but I didn't say so; I was keen to hear what he'd have to say. He told me the Jewish Egyptians are forever part of a bygone era of romance and poetry. Difficult as it was to nod and smile at this, a compliment is "better than a kick in the teeth," as my grandfather would say when he heard people suggest, for example, that Arabs are more given to passion (in other words, barbaric) and that Jews are good with money (so, cheap).

Maybe we are trapped in a cinematic or historical Golden Age. Maybe we, the Jewish Arabs, have indeed ceased to exist in real time. In my grandparents' home in Los Angeles, I was raised on recollections, some more faded than others, of a lost world that had existed for as long as we could remember only to end suddenly in my grandparents' generation. My grandparents' Arabic—which my grandfather tried to teach me every summer at our kitchen table—was the dated colloquial Arabic of those films. In some respects, we share the experience of many other American immigrants, our heads often turned back toward a far-flung past. On Saturdays, we watched *Arab American Music*

Television for an hour on the all-purpose foreigner channel, Channel 18, between Indian American and Korean American programming. That was our slot. But they must have been reruns. The Armenian Lebanese man in Glendale from whom we bought the CDs we liked said that Egyptian pop star Amr Diab and Lebanese pop star Nawal al-Zoghbi had already come and gone in popularity in the Middle East. He knew better than we did. Unlike the shop owner, we didn't regularly return to our homelands. Our exile was a fait accompli.

Because I was raised by my maternal grandparents, Daida and Oscar, and am obstinate like them, my instinct is to refute unequivocally the suggestion that I am of the past, a stillborn. Whether or not that's true, this book is intended to breathe life into my grandparents and to avenge their lives, which multiple incarnations of imperialist white supremacy truncated and warped to political ends at so many turns. This book is also a wholesale rejection of the sentimentality, well-meaning as it is, that sets the Jewish Arab in the imagined past of our at once enjoyable and insidious classic movies. It is ironic, then, that these very same films are among the little that was left to my family after we left our homes and that they became indispensable to us in our struggle to remember who we were.

When Oscar left Egypt in 1950, around the same time as the vast majority of Jewish Egyptians, there was a limit to what he could bring; the rest was claimed by the Egyptian government. He brought some clothes, a few books, and some records of songs from films—they were all musicals. He brought with him, too, a gold bangle that he had intended to sell. Even at his poorest, he never did, and today I wear it around my wrist. Some of the records cracked on the journeys from Egypt to France to the early Zionist State back to France, then to the Bronx, and to the more familiar Mediterranean climes of Los Angeles. He had a superhuman power to see the good in everything—to take the good and leave the bad, as he said. Even damaged records from Egypt were better than nothing.

In Paris, in the early 1960s, these records were even more valuable for my grandparents. Oscar, of Jewish faith with an Arabic-language surname and a North African countenance, for all his education in Egypt and fluency in five languages, couldn't find a regular job in Paris to support his wife and two daughters. So he sold textiles door-to-door in the first real winter he'd experienced and with no great success. The wind "cut the skin," he'd recall. He felt he was living on the edge of civilization in the end of times, the superficial beauty of Paris's facades a mockery as the war for Algerian independence raged and young white Frenchmen died killing countless Algerians to defend what French politicians had convinced much of the world was their just presence in North Africa. The white deaths fanned the flames of white resentment against Arabs and other newcomers who had traveled to France to subsist on the fruits of the empire's blood-drawing expansionism. For Oscar's family, there was no hope for survival in this France.

At the time, Oscar and Daida frequented an Arabic movie house in the Parisian neighborhood of Barbès, which remains one of the city's postcolonial immigrant enclaves. Go there today, and you'll see that not much has changed. Facing the tides of populism and failed integrationist policies, the people cling to each other in these neighborhoods, in Barbès, in Belleville, and Porte de Clichy, and in the suburban ghettos of the likes seen in the 1995 film *La Haine*. Young men, of the age my grandfather was when he was there, stand on the roadside, waiting for a chance to be the breadwinners of their family—to feel like what they're taught men should be. These are the parts of town where French people of color are made to languish in poverty. It was in these parts that Théo Luhaka was sodomized by police with a baton in 2017, a presidential election year when the populist National Front made unprecedented strides onto the political stage. But these neighborhoods are not pockets of misery so much as of resilience. As my grandparents did in their time, people go to these Arab, African, and Asian neighborhoods to watch movies, smoke shisha, drink fresh fruit juice or tea, and survive the loneliness of exile and forget a system that has willfully forgotten them.

Films offered my grandparents respite in those cold Parisian winters. Even when there was no money, there was enough for escapist movies. Daida and Oscar would sit in the dark and watch stars like Mohammed Abdel Wahab, the Muslim composer of one of Egypt's revolutionary awakenings, and Leila Mourad, the Jewish Egyptian starlet he brought to prominence, who became an icon of her nation's cinema and song.

Oscar never told me that Leila Mourad and her brother Mounir Mourad, a sort of Egyptian Gene Kelly, were Jewish. I don't know why he didn't. Perhaps it was because the two of them had converted to Islam in order to marry. Women in our family had done that, and we never spoke of them except to say that they had done something unthinkable: they had ceased to be Jewish. Or maybe the music was so good that Oscar didn't care about their religious identities.

In *Ghazal al-banat* (The Flirtation of Girls), which was shown at the Arabic movie house in Barbès, Leila Mourad portrays an Egyptian governor's daughter who flirts cruelly with her physically unattractive, emotionally generous classical Arabic tutor. At the close of that film, Oscar's beloved Abdel Wahab makes a cameo, strumming a mandolin and singing a song he's written that would have meant so much to many people sitting in that theater in Paris: "Aasheq el-rouh" (Spiritual Love) is about a life lived yearning for a bygone happiness. Imagine what it was for my grandfather, my grandmother, and the rest of the audience to see their perilous wandering from a place of familiarity and from their loved ones reflected on the silver screen, in a song sung by the greatest composer and male performer of contemporary Arabic music.

Daida's favorite film was *Gharam wa Intiqam* (Love and Revenge), the second and last movie to star the diva Asmahan, a Syrian Egyptian actress who wore Western dresses and styled her jet-black hair in the fashion of Western pinup girls. Photos of my grandmother in Paris at the time show that she'd modeled herself on her—an Arab woman trying to present as European. In those times, as in ours, the standards of beauty were white.

It was through a bootlegger in Los Angeles that we found these films, and they were impressed on me when I was small. Oscar found the bootlegger—another Armenian Lebanese, not to be confused with our music vendor—through one of his Egyptian Jewish friends from our synagogue deep in the San Fernando Valley. The vendor rented out the blockbusters of the day and kept VHS tapes of old Egyptian movies—recorded from an Arabic cable channel—in a cabinet behind the cash register.

My favorite of these bootleg films was the 1957 classic *Bnat el-Youm* (Girls These Days), in which the handsome so-called Brown Nightingale Abdel Halim Hafez sings the song "Ahwak" (I Breathe You). "I breathe you," the song goes, "And I wish I could forget you." Fingers dance across the piano as the Western orchestra crescendos to an Arabic *tarab*, a frenetic confluence of percussion, heart-rending strings, and a honeyed voice. The lyrics express this small corner of the human experience so acutely and with such beauty in a way that no other language but Arabic can convey.

That era of film is one that most non-Jewish Arabs I've encountered in my life—mostly female friends—recall wistfully. They compare that chivalrous, poetic time with the present, the men who don't call the next day and the freeze-dried feelings of a digital age.

These films were absent from my life for a while. After my grandfather died, I didn't know where to get them, or how. The movie rental place we used to frequent had become a Quiznos. It seemed I had lost everything, and yet I found myself occasionally recalling fragments of those films. They'd come back to me, songs without names, melodies I could hum. And then, years later, with the internet, I rediscovered my grandparents' films online. I returned to Egypt, where I found something of my grandfather and, in the Cairo opera house and at the video stores in Heliopolis, a small slice of what I had relegated to memory.

There are elements of the Arab world that you carry with you even when generations of colonialism have made you feel that you must let it go. Film and song were how Arabness was transmitted to me. The debonair men and stately women in those films were Arabness, as told to me by my grandparents. They were who we were meant to be, had history panned out differently. I walk down the street today, a Jewish Arab guy, and in my mind's eye, I'm not wearing whatever generic Urban Outfitters plaid I have on; I'm wearing a fine-pressed suit and a tarboosh, like Mohammed Abdel Wahab and his fan, Oscar.

To breathe life into the Jewish Arab is to redefine the Arab, insofar as the Jewish Arab is one small corner of a large and proud Arab nation. There is an internationalism inherent in the Arab experience, conveyed in the seminal *Muqadimmah* (Prolegomena), the introduction to the study of history by Ibn Khaldoun that despite a certain xenophobia to be expected from a text penned in 1377 moves beyond Western concepts of race. "The Arabs are a fierce people, their character having been thus molded by the rough life they lead, until roughness has become a second nature to them. In fact, they positively enjoy a rough life, because it enables them to shake off the yoke of authority and to escape political domination," he writes. For Ibn Khaldoun, Arabness isn't a bloodline; it is the weathering of harsh elements, a defiance of subjugation. Ibn Khaldoun's is one in a series of definitions of Arabness, but it is one that continues to manifest itself throughout history.

Like my ancestors for as long as my family can remember, I am Arab. Of Jewish faith. I am not Sephardi or Mizrahi. Those are two fairly recent but popular polite-society terms for what I am. They are certainly better than slurs, but I won't settle for them.

The term *Sephardi*, Hebrew for "Spanish," describes Iberian Jews who fled during the Spanish Inquisition that began in 1492, when they were told to convert or leave. Many ended up scattered across North Africa and the Middle East, where they were treated—by the authorities and their indigenous coreligionists—as outsiders, in some quarters until my grandparents' generation. *Sephardi* has often been used as a catchall term for all non-European Jews, a whitewashing of Jewish Arabs that ignores the well-documented fact that a great many of us have no known historical roots in Spain and that even the Jews expelled from Spain to North Africa and the Middle East in the Inquisition had ancestral roots in North Africa. I have also frequently heard it used to describe not just Arab but Persian, Desi, and other Asian and African Jews.

Elsewhere, it is popular to refer to Jewish Arabs as *Mizrahi*, the Hebrew term for "Eastern." This emerged in response to resounding criticism over the misuse of *Sephardi* to describe Jewish Arabs and other Jewish non-Europeans without any apparent roots in Spain. Much as it has the flavor of respect toward a community that Jewish Europeans have intermittently called a host of racial epithets—for example, *schwartze*, a derogatory Yiddish term for people of color that literally means "black"—*Mizrahi* echoes the colonial European term *Oriental*. The term denotes people and things of the East as envisioned in colonial Western imaginations, the opposite of Occidental. I am not an Oriental, in English or in Hebrew. My family is not from east of somewhere. To us, where we are from in North Africa is not in an imagined East of an imagined West; it is the center of our world.

What's worse, these terms exist in deference to Jewish people of Arab origin who have rejected Arabness after generations of inculcation against it. French, British, and Israeli administrations have repeatedly cautioned us against and punished us for being Arab. Many of us appear to remain convinced that being Arab is a disgraceful, barbaric, and ultimately condemnable thing. For self-preservation and dignity, it became essential for Oscar and Daida and people like them to view themselves as something—anything—other than Arab. As Sephardi or Mizrahi, for instance.

In large part, I identify as Arab because reclaiming my place in a broader Arab world—an aspirational Arab world, in solidarity with itself—scares our foes who have, for so long, taught us to fight against ourselves. I am an Arab because that is the legacy I inherit from Daida and Oscar. It is how they remain, for me, immortal. My Arabness is cultural. It is African. My Arabness is Jewish. It is also retaliatory. I am Arab because it is what I and my parents have been told not to be, for generations, to stop us from living in solidarity with other Arabs.

Why would I claim Arabness in this way right now? Large swaths of North Africa and the Middle East have been devastated by war and dictatorship, and the majority of the countries that the Donald Trump White House sought to ban from entering the United States are Arab. In this context, to revive the Jewish Arab is to demand dignity for an Arab people continuously derided by the West's self-fulfilling prophecies for the East. America simultaneously funds dictatorship in and drops bombs over much of the Arab world, only for Thomas Friedman and other non-Arab intellectuals empowered to tell our stories to use our chronic struggles with governance and infrastructure to dehumanize us to a Western public. I choose Arabness, because Arabness in reality is as diverse as the many characters in this book. There are dark- and light-skinned Arabs, Arabs of many and no faiths, Arabs who further colonialism and Arabs who stamp it our wherever they see it. I find the internationalism of Arabness enormously useful to reverse the tides of populism and neoliberalism, of which Arabs are made to bear the brunt. It is to choose solidarity over the division wrought by white colonialism. To quote the tomb of leftist Jewish Egyptian activist Shehata Haroun, the father of Magda Haroun, the current president of the few remnants of the Jewish community who remain in Cairo: "Every human being has multiple identities, I am a human being, I am Egyptian when Egyptians are oppressed, I am Black when Blacks are oppressed, I am Jewish when Jews are oppressed, and I am Palestinian when Palestinians are oppressed."[2]

The fact that I say I am a Jewish Arab will upset many people. It will upset some non-Jewish Arabs because I am complicating and, in their minds, weakening the monolithic Arab-Muslim identity. Jewish Arabs will also be upset; they'll recall how *Arab* was used by European Jews in early Israel to undermine our faith and our humanity. They'll point to differences engineered by generations of white supremacist colonial administrations and try to disprove my existence.

If some people are upset by reading these things, that's a necessary evil. In acupuncture, the practitioner often presses different pressure points on the body and inserts a hair-thin needle where the patient hurts the most, sometimes causing shock or pain but with the objective of releasing any obstruction of blood and energy and setting the patient on a course of healing. That is my purpose here.

There are several ways for me to prove to you the existence of the Jewish Arab. I could endeavor to prove to you, using DNA, that Jewish Arabs are related to Arab non-Jews. But I won't, because racial science—for that's what it is that AncestryDNA and other DNA-testing products are peddling—should terrify you, as it does me. Not only have we seen emerging concerns over how that data is stored and used by companies, but the data also serves to popularize what academia agrees are false and potentially eugenic concepts of race.

I could also observe that Jewish Arabs are often physically indistinguishable from their Muslim and Christian Arab counterparts. My opponents will disagree—even if Jews from Arab countries are frequently darker than their European counterparts, it's a different sort of dark, they'll say, from Muslim and Christian Arabs. The fact is, our flawed, subjective human experience of color—white, yellow, brown, black—is absolutely useless most of the time. What skin tone conveys to different people is never consistent: where a darker person in Los Angeles is often presumed to be Mexican or Salvadoran or Persian—all ethnic identities with dark- and light-skinned people—in Paris that person becomes Algerian. So-called white people are very often more pink or olive in hue. What color do we ascribe to the Arab? Internationally, the image of the Arab is brown, but in calling Arabs brown, we ignore countless Arabs who identify as both Arab and black. Do we claim Syria and Lebanon for Europe because it is often observed—without any meaningful survey of those populations—that there are many light-skinned people there?

Most anthropologists agree that categorizing humans by racial phenotype, particularly our imperfect experiences of color, is an entirely unscientific way of observing the genetic development of humankind.[3] Studies have shown that there is a greater degree of genetic differentiation within perceived race categories than there is among them; there is a consensus that it is more useful to study experiences with racism than flawed human perceptions of race.[4] The results of these arbitrary categories have been eugenic and racist public policies, with which we are still contending in the United States and around the world.

There are a great many academics who have made arguments for the existence of the Jewish Arab premised on distant history. There exist arguments that Jews—despite being prohibited by faith from proselytism—did indeed convert North African Imazighen (Berbers, to use the more popular pejorative term) and others to Judaism to bolster their ranks in the aftermath of the destruction of the Second Temple in 70 c.e., when the Jews felt under siege.[5] The Imazighen are themselves often heralded as the original inhabitants of North Africa, who before converting first to Judaism and then to Islam practiced a pantheistic faith that endures in their syncretic belief systems. Today, many of the people who identify as Imazighen do so to distinguish themselves from Arabs, divisions exacerbated by French colonial rule that sought to divide and conquer. But the fact that many

Imazighen were once Jewish is proof of the centrality of the Jews to a land that became part of the Arab world. I could very well use these arguments to make the case for the existence of Jewish Arab as a race. But I don't need to employ a flawed history of "who came first" to prove to you the validity of my identity.

Academics have also argued for the existence of Jewish Arabs by claiming a bond solely based on language—if our families spoke Arabic in the home as a native tongue, that's proof enough that we were Arab, they say. Arabic language is indeed central to the Arab people, but there is no one Arabic. I have often encountered Levantine Arabs who consider their Arabic to be more standard than North African forms of Arabic, which are mostly incomprehensible to nonnative speakers. Ask Moroccans about their dialect of Arabic, though, and many will brag it is rooted in the language of the Quran. Arabic, in its many forms—the uniqueness of its expressions and the history of its poetry and literature—is certainly a unifier. But what of Arab Americans like me, whose parents endeavored to teach them formal Arabic every summer and were manifestly frustrated that they were not born speaking it? Language is, indeed, important, but in the diaspora, do I cease to be an Arab because I will in all likelihood never write in Arabic, much less write a book in the language? No.

The fact is, humankind's very definitions of race and ethnicity are nebulous. This book is an unbraiding of the colonial manipulations of identity, first in my family's homelands in North Africa under the French and the British, then in Israel, and ultimately in their search for home in France and the United

States. It is a recollection of the lives and worlds of two Jewish Arabs: my grandfather, an Egyptian of Moroccan, Amazigh, and Jewish origin, and my grandmother, a Jewish Tunisian. Through their lives, I will delve into the definition of Arabness and the celebration of that identity in which I recognize my family and myself.

1

الأصول / Origins

There are many potential origin stories for the Jewish Arab—a tiny fraction of humanity at the nexus of so much that's wrong with the world. The recollection of my grandparents' lives is itself an origin story, but before we embark on that, I'll convey to you what may have come before them: a perfidy of beginnings, real and imaginary. Some of these stories my grandparents passed to me as a child, in Los Angeles, in their anecdotes and tall tales. Others I learned much later, filling in the gaps.

There are no conclusive origin stories or absolute answers. Not to the Arab identity, or the Jewish one, or the North African one. Not to the mix of the three that I claim here. I hope you take heart in the imperfections of my account. Absolute answers are the first signs of a sinister political project brewing beneath the surface.

My grandparents' stories began and ended where they found

energy to tell them and meaning in their retelling. They had
an agenda. Implicit in their stories of goodly women and men
in our family was the demand that I not fuck it all up by being
undignified. Origin stories often come in the form of bedtime
stories. But they serve a political purpose. They give us a mandate to live in solidarity with or in opposition to each other.
Like previous origin stories, this book has a political agenda.
The main difference is that I'm telling you, upfront: my intention is to reclaim the Jewish Arab identity for me and to recuperate it as a stolen asset of the Arab world.

There are many imagined origin stories offering clues to
the antecedents of the Jewish Arab and, more specifically, my
grandparents. I'll lay out a few for you here, in this chapter, but
it is important to note that, even with all the legitimate history
interspersed with these stories, the consensus in academia is that
many of these accounts are totally inaccurate and ultimately useless to a scientific understanding of world civilizations. But that
doesn't mean they're devoid of meaning. We decide for ourselves what counts.

Many Arabs—my grandparents and non-Jewish Arabs I've
encountered—speak of the Arab people that exists today as one
descended from specific Arabic-speaking tribes in the Arabian
Peninsula, mostly polytheists until the Prophet Mohammed
introduced Islam.

But if the view of a homogenous Arab nation—one nar-
rowly descended from the Arabian Peninsula without significant intermarriage or evolution from the first Arab arrivals
in North Africa—holds, then how does one explain the cul-

turally diverse Christian and Jewish Arabs, the many people of Amazigh and Phoenician descent who identify as Arabs, Iran's ethnic Arabs? What of Arabs whose ancestors arrived more recently, escaping the Armenian genocide to join pre-existing Armenian communities in the Arab world? Reality itself runs counter to the concept of Arabness prevalent among Arabs today. And yet that doesn't nullify the importance of an abstract belief in the Arabs' roots in the Arabian Peninsula. If the first Arabs aren't my blood ancestors, they founded a civilization of which my ancestors since time immemorial became a functioning part.

By the same token, many Jews—who in reality are of all skin colors and ethnicities, Argentine and northern Chinese—speak of themselves as a singular Am Yisrael, a Nation of Israel—as though, despite their apparent Ethiopian-ness, Iraqi-ness, Russian-ness, German-ness, and so on, their ancestors were the ethnically homogenous descendants of that ancient Kingdom of Judah who magically morphed into distinct nationalities. Does the global Jewish faith community possess superhuman powers of phenotypic assimilation? No. And yet, in the practice of Judaism, it is inarguably useful to imagine our faith community's forebears as a single community that suffered slavery under pharaohs and emerged, delivered by the hand of God, together. In the abstract. In spiritual stories, of immeasurable value but still not firmly rooted in this world.

Amid these origin stories is a murky place where documented history and faith intersect. Implicit in these piecemeal retellings of origins is a perhaps sobering truth: our concepts of self

and of history are much less an exact science than we've been
led to believe. The past is shrouded in imperfect narratives. We
can choose, as I do, to both ascribe meaning to and realize the
practical limits of origin stories, like the Jewish Arab's imagined
roots in the Arabian Peninsula and in a Biblical Nation of Israel
emerging from Egypt. And that's good. We can still wrench
our histories back from the hands of people once exclusively
empowered, often by colonial conquest or class dominance, to
write them.

Conquest is a running theme of the many origin stories for North
Africa, which I use in the most physically broad and inclusive
sense to mean the region that stretches atop the continent from
Egypt to Mauritania. Before the Common Era, North Africa
had already seen conquest by the Phoenicians, the Greeks, and
the Romans. The physical landscape of North African cities was
likely built and razed several times over before the construction of what became the Roman ruins that dotted the landscape
of my grandparents' hometowns. In the seventh century C.E.,
the Arab conquest swept the region, bringing with it Islam. In
the sixteenth century, Ottoman wars of conquest wrested control of North Africa from a host of indigenous and European
controllers. Finally in the nineteenth and twentieth centuries,
the region fell to colonial European, mainly French and British,
control.

Of course the question becomes, Why would I choose to
identify with one particular element of these conquests? The
answer is that Arabness is what ties me to people from Mar-

rakech to Manama who share a similar legacy and, in my experience with them, recall to me things I know of my family and self
in the way that they live their lives today. That Arabness does
not, to my mind, negate the sacred things that came before, in
which I also take great pride, namely my Amazigh-ness and my
Judaism. I can feel Arab, first and foremost, without forgoing or
denigrating other simultaneous identities.

The Amazigh people (the Berbers) who predated all the suc-
cessive conquests are themselves a diverse group of people of
different dialects, skin tones, and cultural practices. My grandparents never spoke to me of the Amazigh people as a child. We
had left our region long before the Amazighist movement of the
late twentieth century fought for greater recognition of North
Africa's earliest antecedents. It wasn't until long after my grandfather's death that I realized that the strange community and the
language separate from Arabic to which he referred occasionally
when talking about his ancestors was the Amazigh community
and the Amazigh language, Tamazight. For my grandparents,
in their stories from North Africa, there were more often two
classes of humans: there were North Africans and there were the
Europeans. The stories they told involved Muslim and Jewish
and Arabic-speaking and Tamazight-speaking characters, but all
of those were part of a society defined in contrast to the European
invaders. In my later conversations with my grandmother, unless
I asked, the religious and ethnic identities of the North African
people in her stories were rarely evident.

As an adult, attempting to fill the gaps in the stories they'd
told, I was especially captivated by one Amazigh origin story

that sits squarely at the intersection of fact and fiction, the story of Queen Dihiya.

In North Africa, before all these carefully measured nations with borders and the paper permits needed to cross them, there was a region from the Atlantic to the eastern Mediterranean called Tamazgha, and the people that lived there were called Amazigh—Imazighen in the plural—Free People. Among them were many different tribes—the Irifyen, the Shleuh, the Iqvayliyen, for example. Many of the communities that existed then endure in some form; many don't. The Imazighen were a matriarchal society that predated the arrival of monotheism on the continent of Africa. Before the Arabs arrived in Tamazgha, there was a warrior queen who was from what historian Ibn Khaldoun described in the fourteenth century C.E. as the Jewish Amazigh Djeouara tribe. She was named Dihiya—"gazelle" in Tamazight. The Arab invaders called her the Kahena, the priestess. The history, as recounted by Ibn Khaldoun, describes her as a witch with the power to foresee marauding invaders from hundreds of miles away. (This is when the Imazighen began to be known as Berbers: the Arabs called them that because Tamazight sounded to them like a babbling brook, *berberberber*, and the name, forged in misconception, stuck.)

In the time of the Ummayad Caliphate, the Islamic empire that reigned over the Arab world and Spain in the seventh and eighth centuries C.E., Dihiya is said to have battled the Arab invaders three times.[1] In the first two battles, the Arab army outnumbered Dihiya's and their weapons were far more advanced, and still the Ummayad faced great difficulty defeating her. Finally, the Ummayad army sent her head to the caliph,

Abd al-Malik ibn Marwan, in far-off Damascus, an assurance that North Africa had been won.

Countless questions emerge from this origin story that purports to explain how North Africa became Arab. Does the contemporary North African call the Amazigh our ancestor? Or does the North African call the Arab invader our ancestor? Or was a new people forged from a generation's violence?

Dihiya's story—the facts and the creative embellishments that emanate from it—has been used by a host of political actors in North Africa. To the French who conquered the region over the course of the nineteenth century C.E., she would serve as a symbol of the otherness of the Arab. The Arab too had invaded and conquered, the French would teach, attempting to legitimize their own conquest over an Arab majority they simultaneously classed as indigenes. Imazighen who continue to fight socioeconomic and political marginalization in their countries today often conjure Dihiya as a symbol of their age-old resistance to Arab dominion. North African women's rights activists of all ethnic and religious identifications have also used her as proof that North Africa is, at its base, a society of women who know how to fight. Often, in the Jewish North African telling of this story, Dihiya underlines that the Jewish North Africans have longer-running roots in North Africa than their Muslim compatriots. And in the same way that the story has been used in French histories of North Africa to establish a world in which people identifying as North African Arabs and Imazighen are eternal adversaries, it pits Jews against Muslims. In teasing out long-forgotten divisions, Dihiya's story, one that prefigured the French invasion of North Africa by centuries, was manipulated

to suit the colonial politic of divide and conquer that guided
France's conquest of our region.

The Jewish Bible, or Tanakh, is an origin story that Oscar
told me when I was a child, as was, in Oscar's own way, the
Quran. Our Judaism was often defined in contrast to the Islam
and Christianity Oscar had learned from Muslim and Christian
friends and instructors and in the French schools of his youth,
and so to our minds, the elements of Judaism echoed in Islam
and Christianity seemed to have the air of indisputable fact.

Islam establishes a divine mandate through origin stories
involving divine genealogies. Similarly, Jewish texts portray the
Jews as a Chosen People, bound not just by faith but blood; early
Islamic theologians tie the Prophet Mohammed to several key
figures within both the Judeo-Christian canon and also Arab
history.

As Oscar and Judaism told it, Abraham had two sons born of
two women—Isaac, born of his wife, Sarah, and Ishmael, born
of Sarah's handmaid, Hagar. Ishmael and his mother, Hagar,
were cast out into the desert, and their descendants eventually
became the Muslims—and the Arabs. Isaac fathered the Jews.
In the oral history surrounding the Quran and as Oscar taught
me, Hagar (Hajer in Arabic) and her son Ishmael (Ismail) feature
more prominently. With them, Abraham (Ibrahim) travels to
Mecca, where he constructs the Kaaba, Islam's House of God.

In both Islam and Judaism, the Abrahamic brothers are divided by Sarah's bitterness. Oral histories emanating from both the
Quran and Torah maintain the division of the Jews and Muslims. What's more, the two traditions seem to tie Arabness to
the Islamic faith.

The Torah announces that Ishmael's firstborn was called Nevaiot, who, according to fourteenth-century Damascene Islamic theologian Ismail Ibn Kathir, is Nabit—an Arabic version of the same name.[2] From there, Ibn Kathir writes that Nabit was the grandfather of Yarab, the historic namesake of the Arabs. Yarab's direct descendent was Adnan, an ancestor of the Prophet Mohammed.

What Ibn Kathir does in his account of the Prophet Mohammed's ancestry is imbue him with not just the sacred bloodline of the first Judeo-Christian humans, prophets of God, but also the bloodline of the Arab people. In perhaps the same vein as Ibn Kathir, in the Tanakh, Yitzhak (Isaac), Abraham's younger son, is portrayed as the grandfather of Judah—forefather of a kingdom of the same name that existed from the ninth to the sixth centuries B.C.E.[3] Judah is, of course, the namesake of Judaism and the Jewish people.

Theological origin stories across Islam and Judaism observe that holy people are not holy by virtue of their interactions with God. They are holy by virtue of their families, or rather a noble bloodline. These stories are about inheritance and tribalism. In both faiths, what we are is forcibly better—more sacred—than others. In Judaism, Jews are often portrayed as superior to Muslims. In Islam, Muslims are often portrayed as superior to Jews. The Biblical origin stories can serve, particularly in the genealogical analyses of theologians studying sacred texts, to separate, to elevate, and to debase.

The Biblical origin stories and their divisions and suggestions of sacred or elevated blood are part of but do not comport with the Judaism of my youth. My grandparents never told me I was a chosen person, even if that is codified in our religion, or more likely to go to heaven because of who we were; on the contrary, I was frequently punished for exhibiting any form of pride and it was drummed into me that good and compassionate people went to heaven, regardless of their chosen or inherited spiritual path. For my grandparents, God was sacred. No divine families, no divine human blood. We all had to strive to be better than the deeply flawed characters of Biblical and Quranic stories. That was the point of retelling them.

For us, the line between Isaac and Ismail was blurred, more than in other families, perhaps, because we took nothing but God very seriously. When we said things like *insha'Allah* ("God willing" in Arabic) or *HamdelA* ("thank God"), we tacitly acknowledged that the Allah of Islam is the same Allah we serve in our Judaism.

My family half believed in the origin story that is race—that I'd inherited how we were by birth. The identity claimed in this book is indeed an inherited one, but to my mind, the inheritance didn't come down to me by blood. If, theoretically, I were adopted, my adoptive parents would have transmitted this legacy of Jewish Arabness to me. And yet, for many, race has become the most valid and immutable expression of that familial and communal inheritance, despite the fact that origin stories based on race—stories premised on the belief that our ethnic identities exist along biologically determined color lines—have been used for the most repugnant purposes this century and the last.

Growing up, my grandparents made comments contrasting us with Ashkenazi or Jewish European Americans and European Americans more broadly—especially in moments of injustice against communities of color, newer immigrants, and others, as if to say, look at the cruelty and misplaced arrogance of these people. These comments would indicate they believed in race—that whites have a biological proclivity toward racism and megalomania. This is of course not universally true, much as it may sometimes seem so.

More delightful to me but equally wrong was my grandparents' assumption that I, born in Los Angeles, had biologically inherited certain Arab manners from them. My grandfather, in our Arabic lessons, was confounded to the point of breathlessness to find that I couldn't pronounce the throaty *h* sound in *hummus*, in *Hamas*, and *Hizbollah* (these were the words he used to teach me that letter since they were names often spoken in our kitchen and on our TV). There was a moment where he threw his hands up and left the kitchen table. How could I be his grandson?

On another occasion, when we were visiting my grandmother's relatives in Paris, we went to a "Mediterranean" restaurant—couscous, tagine, and pizza—and they ordered two desserts from a tray of traditional Arabic sweets. One, *kataifi*, was a kind of baklava with stringy dough, the other *zlabia*, a bright orange, sweet, syrupy fried pretzel. My grandmother and grandfather watched while I ate. The *kataifi* was meant to represent Egypt and eastern Arabia, and the *zlabia* Tunisia and North Africa (in actuality, *zlabia* is quite international—an identical sweet is known as *jalebi* in South Asia, for instance), and they'd hoped to see which flavor was more to my taste as a means of determining whose child I was. The understanding in this instance—only half serious, as was everything in

our family—was that our language and culture are transmitted
in the DNA and that simple syrup and crushed pistachio run
through my veins.

History books seem to corroborate Oscar and Daida's more or
less universally shared belief that an Arab is a person with origins in the Arabian Peninsula and that the Jews—or the spiritual practice of Judaism—have roots in Biblical Canaan. But
from there, at least for the Jewish Arab, the narrative is more
complicated—and nuanced. It may well be that the person
called Yarab was truly an ancestor of the Prophet Mohammed
and a father of both the Arab and Muslim peoples. But then it
is important to recall too that Yarab was also the forefather of a
great many Jews—an entire kingdom of Jews.

Yarab exists at the intersection of historical fact and religion.
He is, in addition to Mohammed's ancestor, also a historical
character described in ancient Yemeni historical accounts as the
first man to speak Arabic—some say as the Arabs' first poet.
Embedded in Yarab's own origin story is the centrality of
not just the Arabic language but of its use as an art form that
became—and remains—an expression of Arab identity.

Yarab's genealogy is laid out in early Islamic histories that
describe him as the great-grandfather of Himyar, king of the
eponymous kingdom that existed in what is now Yemen from
the second century B.C.E. to the sixth century C.E. Around 380,
the Kingdom of Himyar abandoned polytheism for Judaism,
at a time when the Byzantine Empire and the nearby Kingdom of Aksum (in what are now Ethiopia and Eritrea) had also
begun to embrace monotheism, but in the form of Christianity.

Historians say it was likely that the Himyari kings began to profess Judaism out of a need to distinguish themselves from the expansionist Christian Aksum and Byzantium, and that despite artifacts showing that Himyari prayer used Hebrew words, referring to a single God as "the Compassionate One," the mundane aspects of Himyari—proto-Arabian—culture remained relatively unchanged.

Arabs begin to identify as "Arab" a few centuries before the arrival of the Prophet Mohammed and Islam on the peninsula. The exact origins of the several tribes of Arabia professing Judaism at the time of the prophet remain uncertain, but some are perhaps the descendants of the Himyari Jewish Arabians. In Ibn Khaldoun's recollection of the earliest days of the Arab identity and of Islam, in his 1377 C.E. *Muqadimah*, he offers an amply broad, explicitly inclusive definition of Arabness. "Islam originated as an Arab sect, with an Arab founder," he wrote, recognizing that Islam began as the faith of a fragment of a longer-running, more diverse Arab whole, "distinguished by common habits and characteristics as well as descent." The exact origins of the several Arabian tribes of Jewish faith, including the Banu Qaynuqa and the Banu Nadir at the time of the prophet and mentioned in Islamic texts, remain uncertain. Some are perhaps the descendants of the Himyari Jewish Arabians. My grandmother, in her old age, sitting in a mechanical recliner in our home in Los Angeles, was very surprised and indeed excited to hear that there were actually several Jewish Arabian tribes at the dawn of Arab identity.

Jewish American historians, particularly those who speak positively of the Zionist project, have endeavored to downplay the

Jewish Arab identity of these historical communities. For instance, Romanian-born Israeli historian Élie Barnavi, who is uncritical of modern Zionism, is the editor of a comprehensive history of the world's Jewish communities from Mexico to China entitled *A Historical Atlas of the Jewish People*. His book says resolutely that Himyar was "not Jewish, and its monotheism was but an expression of Himyarite independence." This runs counter to findings published in Oxford University's *Oxford Handbook of Late Antiquity* and other prominent scholarship on Himyar, including Jewish scholarship, that maintain that Himyaris professed Judaism, however unorthodox that Judaism may have been in practice.[4] To cast doubt on the faith Himyaris are shown to have professed is to figuratively reach into history and rip from the Jewish proto-Arabians a faith that they, by all signs, felt in earnest.

The Arabness of the Jewish Arabian tribes that existed by the time of the Prophet Mohammed has also been called into question. The tribes professing Judaism enjoyed a "high degree of assimilation into Arabian society," writes historian Norman A. Stillman, whose work often focuses on Jewish Arabs.[5] Stillman clarifies that this means they feuded and partnered with other tribes and wrote Arabic poetry, among other things. However, they "were still viewed as a separate group with their own peculiar customs and characteristics," which included Jewish rites like the Sabbath. "The same could be said with regard to the Christians of Arabia who, like the Jews, formed a distinct religious community while at the same time being highly assimilated," Stillman adds. This reading of history begs the question: What exactly constitutes assimilation, in the context of people with less than a couple of centuries self-identifying as Arabs?

To assimilate indicates, at least in my contemporary American reading of the term, the submission of a smaller, less-dominant culture to broader, more mainstream, or more dominant social norms. With an Arab identity still developing, it appears to me that the Jews and Christians weren't assimilated but that the Arabs were still developing a civilization that in its ensemble was Arab.

When the Prophet Mohammed introduced Islam to the Jewish tribes of Arabia, some rejected him. Violence ensued. Many Jews converted or fled, historians say, to the farthest reaches of what would become the Arab world today. That, perhaps, offers a kind of origin story about a Jewish Arab identity in North Africa and the Sham regions. But no one in my family ever told me a bedtime story about our distant ancestors in the Arabian Gulf, and very little of it factors into how I understand myself or live my life now.

My family found some of these origin stories interesting, certainly. But my grandparents were hardheaded people. Just because Oxford University scholars say there was a Jewish kingdom in ancient Arabia, for instance, doesn't mean that the tectonics of our identities shift underneath us. In my childhood, our origin stories were found in more immediate, concrete things. We identified with our names, our birthplaces, and our family retellings of the past. For me now, it is those details that are paramount.

Oscar's family were native Jewish Egyptian on his mother's side—the Levy family, a Hebrew surname indicating that some of their ancestors had performed certain religious rites in the

Temples of Canaan. His father's family were Moroccan émigrés to Egypt called Hayoun, which means "the living ones" in
Arabic. With few exceptions, Hayoun is a Jewish North African
name, and the fact that it is a Judeo-Arabic-language surname
separates my family from North African Jewish families with
Spanish- and Italian-language surnames like Aragon or Sonci-
no. Close to half of North African Jews bore Arabic or Amazigh
surnames, according to a Jewish French study on Jewish North
African origins in the 1930s.[6]

When I first discussed the meaning of our family name with
my grandfather, we were on our way home from our synagogue.
We and several other congregants parked a few blocks away,
since our synagogue did not believe in the European-led reform
movements that maintain one can drive on the Sabbath. It was
in the darkness of that walk to our car and then the drive home
that my grandfather discussed with me our name and its approx-
imate meaning in Arabic: Hayoun, the living people. And it
illuminated a pathway for me going forward. Many of our origin stories were of suffering and of death and of sorrow; our
name, to my young mind, was a mandate to really live, adroitly
and with purpose.

What my grandfather never told me, since he had never bothered to ask his own grandfather, is that Hayoun is the name of
a hamlet in eastern Morocco, a few hours south of Fez, abandoned around the time of the Industrial Revolution, historians
say, after the artisans—jewelers mostly—had left. The original residents of this town would have spoken Tamazight, the
Amazigh language, but by the time my grandfather was born
in Alexandria, Egypt, our family no longer spoke the language.

Today, the Jewish Moroccan dialects of Tamazight are dying out, as the few émigrés from those parts of Morocco age in cities like Montreal and Tel Aviv, where Tamazight is essentially useless. The same, of course, is true of Jewish Arabic dialects, now spoken almost exclusively by only the most eccentric linguists.

Oscar identified as Moroccan—in his time in Egypt and among other Jewish Moroccans and Egyptians at our synagogue in Los Angeles. But to everyone, he spoke in Egyptian-accented Arabic. In middle school, when I was studying Islam in social studies class, I learned that the Arabic word for mosque is *masjid*. My grandfather was adamant that I pronounce it the Egyptian way: "masgid." He then said that almost everyone—in almost every country except parts of Yemen—pronounces it "masjid," but we say "masgid." "Because it's better," he explained. For all his Moroccan-ness, he never in his life visited Morocco, although he spoke its dialect in the home with his father and grandfather. He also conceived of himself as superior in many ways for having been born in Egypt, even as a half Egyptian in a culture that mandated that his father's was the predominant bloodline in his veins. He was very much a proponent of the obnoxiously patriotic adage that *Masr oum adounia!* (Egypt is the mother of the world!), a concept boosted by the dominance of Egyptian film and music in all Arab countries.

The rest of his stories about his family involved his amply problematic, yet sincere impressions of the two sides of his family. His maternal grandmother, Messaouda, was Egyptian. She was relatively fair-skinned, beautiful, and militantly tidy, by his estimation; his paternal grandmother, Maryam, from the Moroccan side, was the opposite, he said. She was dark ("black" in his description, since Oscar didn't seem to recognize the American difference between black and dark people), and less beautiful, and not as clean. This description, to my mind, tells me more about my grandfather than our ancestors.

Beyond his maternal grandmother's complexion, little was conveyed to me about his maternal line. Oscar called himself Moroccan, despite only being part Moroccan and physically distant from that country. Morocco remained, for him and for me, a sacred land, more the country of our origin than Egypt, the land of his mother Rosa's family. Oscar did say that Rosa's parents' families were native to Egypt—a kind of family referred to as "indigenous" in the literature of my grandfather's generation, of which there is a great deal. In Oscar's generation, the Jewish community of Alexandria was a diverse and robust faith group, comprised of Jewish émigrés from Morocco, Syria, Lebanon, and places much farther afield in southern and even eastern Europe, as well as indigenes like his mother. There were around 20,000 of them living among a diverse Alexandrine population of over 920,000.[7] There were multiple Arabic-language newspapers for the Jewish Egyptian community with deeper roots in the Arab world—the main one was *Al-Chams* (The Sun)—and at least one publishing house, Les Editions Juives d'Egypte (The Jewish Editions of Egypt).[8]

To understand who Rosa, Messaouda, and Oscar's Egyptian foremothers may have been, we have only to look to the histories written by their community. A key resource for me is a history book that Oscar brought from Egypt to the United States called *Les Communautés Israélites d'Alexandrie: Aperçu Historique, depuis les Temps des Ptolémées jusqu'à nos jours* (The Israelite

Communities of Alexandria: A Historical Overview from the
Ptolomaic Period to the Present Day), by Bension Taragan.
Taragan describes himself as an amateur historian of the local
Jewish community and, by profession, a Hebrew professor in the
community's schools. My grandfather's copy of Taragan's book
is falling apart, and on the cover, in rough cursive, someone has
written in blue ink "hotchimin" (Hồ Chí Minh). Oscar arrived
in Paris during the twilight of the French empire and then in the
United States during the Vietnam War.

According to Taragan, there is Biblical evidence of a Jewish
community in Egypt, their emigration the subject of the book
of Exodus, and there is evidence of a Jewish Alexandrine community dating back as far as the fourth century B.C.E., when
Alexandria was the capital of the Ptolemaic Kingdom.[9] Under
Christian domination, many Jewish Alexandrines were violently expelled from the city.[10] After the Arab Conquest, they
were permitted—albeit with higher taxes—to return to the city
to live in the peace and dignity that Islam guarantees Jews and
Christians, the Ahl al-Kitab (People of the Book). "The Jews
began to breathe the air of liberty, for the Caliph Omar had
returned to them their rights that had been taken" in the time
of Cyril of Alexandria, the Ptolemaic theocrat, Taragan writes.

In 1171 [C.E.], Saladin rose to the throne of Egypt
and successfully conquered Syria and Palestine. His
successors were known for their tolerance toward
other religions in a measure greater than their pre-
decessors. It was under his reign that Maimonides
established himself in Egypt. This goodly Jew was

named doctor of the court and elected Grand Rabbi
of Egypt. Despite several occupations, Maimonides
found the time to direct the affairs of the Community and all Egypt, and to write his famous books.

During the Arab period, Egyptian Jewish theology thrived
under the communal leadership of Maimonides, who was born
in Andalusian Cordoba, Spain, with the Arabic name Moussa
bin Maimoun, commonly referred to in Jewish studies now by
the Hebrew acronym Rambam.

The Jewish Alexandrines of this time looked a great deal like
their Muslim neighbors, other sources say. In 1481, Messulam
de Voltera, a Jewish Italian visitor to Egypt whose travel log is
cited by Taragan, wrote, "The habits of the [Jewish Alexan-
drines] are naturally identical to those of their Muslim compatriots. They dress as [Muslims dress], they sit on the floor and
enter their synagogues barefooted."[11] De Voltera is careful to
note that these Jews are "Rabbinic" Jews—Jews who believe in
the sanctity of theological literature produced by pious men—as
opposed to the Karaites, many of whom were Jewish Egyptians
who accept only the Tanakh, or Jewish Bible, as binding expressions of Jewish law. Today the Karaite synagogue is characteristically without seating. The Karaite Jews prostrate themselves
on the floor in a style not unlike the *soujoud*, the prostrations
of Islamic prayer.[12] Rabbinic Jewish Egyptians have in recent
centuries adopted the foreign custom of putting pews in their
synagogues.

Jewish emigration from Spain to Egypt predated the Spanish Inquisition by centuries. Maimonides, for instance, arrived in the twelfth century C.E. The major influx of Spanish or Sephardic Jews that arrived as exiles around the time of their expulsion in 1492 were subject to the governance of the Jewish Egyptian "prince" or governor of the Jewish community, named Isaac Cohen Sholal, a close confidant and devotee of the Egyptian sultan of that period.[13] Taragan, whose name suggests possible origins in the Spanish city of Tarragona, remarks that the arrival of the Ottomans in Egypt in 1517 "assured for the Spanish Jews a supremacy over their indigenous coreligionists." A large Sephardic community already established at the Ottoman Empire's helm in Istanbul, and Abraham de Castro, "a Jew of Spanish origin," had been selected by the first Ottoman sultan, Selim I, to reign over Egypt, to participate in Egypt's new administration and, in particular, the administration of the Jewish community.[14]

But the history of the indigenous Jewish Alexandrines continues, even if it becomes secondary to that of their Ottoman Sephardic Jewish community leaders. In the 1700s, Taragan writes, "a group of Jewish fishermen originally from Damietta (Damyat) and Rosetta (Rashid) established themselves in Alexandria, close to the sea. They established themselves at the Street of Souk el Samak el Kadim (the old fish market) that until our times comprises the Haret el Yahoud (the Jewish Quarter)."[15]

For lack of anything more substantive in Oscar's journals and oral history, I have only to believe that Rosa's family existed somewhere among these histories. Rosa's ancestors were maybe fishermen from Damyat or Rashid, who entered their synagogues barefooted like Muslims and whose political representation to Egyptian authorities was dominated by the Jewish Spanish—or Sephardic—Alexandrines whom the Ottomans designated as their ruling class.

My grandmother Daida identified staunchly as being from Tunis. She left Tunis in her late teens, never to return, but if asked, she underlined that she was a Tunisian from Tunis. She felt that gave her more sophistication than being from her father's relatively small, coastal hometown of Mahdia, despite our custom of aligning ourselves with our patrilineal hometowns. There were 100,000 Jews in Tunisia in Daida's generation, and they were scattered throughout the country.[16] Although there were large Jewish communities in most major Arab cities—Baghdad was 40 percent Jewish before the chaos over Israel's inception, for instance—much of my family had originated in small towns or villages and found themselves traveling to large cities as economic migrants.[17]

Daida's mother, Kamouna, was a daughter of the Shemama family. *Shemama* is the name of a mountain in the southwest of Tunisia. Maybe the mountain is important to our family's history, but our branch of the Shemamas have lived in Tunis since time immemorial. Other North African genealogical analyses say the name comes from a type of scented plant used to make a kind of Arabic incense. Alternatively, the name *Shemama* can also mean "butter maker" in our dialect of Arabic, which is cute, since Daida's father's family were the Boukhobzas, which means "son of the bread baker." Daida was made of bread and butter. Her father, Sami, was a very tall, lithe man who worked at her maternal grandfather Yaqoub's small olive oil factory; her mother, Kamouna, was a squat, voluptuous sort of woman, considered attractive in those times, who was fond of shisha (a taboo for Tunisian women of all faiths at the time), cards with friends (also taboo), and salty jokes (also taboo). In other words, Kamouna was a good time and strong enough to stand up to the relatively low tides of Tunisian patriarchy.

The Shemamas and Boukhobzas, as their names illustrate, were indigenous, Arabic-speaking Tunisians of Jewish faith. In Tunisia, the ethnic division between Jewish Europeans residing in Tunisia and indigenous Jewish Arabs with Arabic surnames who spoke a dialect of Tunisian Arabic in the home was especially pronounced. The Jewish Tunisians and the newer arrivals they absorbed from neighboring Arab lands were called Twansa (Tunisian in Arabic), and the Jewish Italians—from the northwestern Italian town of Livorno—and other Jewish Europeans were called Grana, an Arabic slang term meaning Livornese. Grana, considered to have remained ethnically European over generations, were for much of Tunisia's feudal era not beholden to the same laws as Twansa. The Twansa were subjects of the king, or bey, while until the 1800s, just before the French conquest, the Grana, even those whose families had resided in Tunisia for generations, were not. They were exempt from paying jizya, the tax on non-Muslims that was imposed throughout the Arab world on Jews and Christians alike. That tax was only abolished for the indigenous Jewish community in the mid-1800s, decades before the French arrival.

Some separation persisted into the twentieth century. Daida recalls there were separate synagogues for indigenous Tunisian

Jews and the Livornese Italian, Spanish, or Portuguese Jews, who began arriving at the time of the Spanish Inquisition. "If they had a synagogue, I wouldn't know where it was," she says, throwing some characteristic shade. But the construction of the Grand Synagogue of Tunis near Daida's childhood home, completed in 1937, a few years after she was born, brought all the Jews together, regardless of their provenance. It had been uncommon, historically, to see the two groups intermarry, Daida said, but those divisions were shifting in Daida's generation, under the French, although only in cosmopolitan Tunis. Outside of the capital, for instance, in her father's more conservative hometown of Mahdia, interethnic marriage would never, to her knowledge, have been permitted. There existed a preference to keep things as close to the family as possible, which one might rightfully call xenophobia. In many quarters of the Arab world, especially at the time, it was considered preferable to marry someone not just from your own country but, where possible, from your hometown, your neighborhood, your street, and even your family.

The apparent divisions that persisted between Twansa and Grana were not without nuance. There were a number of Grana who contributed generously to Tunisian and more specifically Jewish Tunisian civilization. Raoul Journo, for instance, an icon of Jewish Tunisian music born in 1911, bore an Italian family name that derived from the Italian *giorno* (day). He famously sang the patriotic Tunisian ballad "Sellemt ana fik ya bledi" (I Found Peace in You, My Homeland).

My grandmother had never heard the term *Sephardi* until long after she had left Tunisia and come to the United States.

She learned it in the 1970s and '80s, when many people of our background appeared to identify as Sephardi, apparently for lack of a way to distinguish themselves from the Jewish Europeans who dominate the American consciousness of Judaism. Until I began to discuss this book with her, she had never once been told that this Hebrew-language word meant "Spanish." If she had known, she says, she would have found it absurd to suddenly associate us with a country with which we have no known tie.

The stories told by our names, coupled with our sense of geographic belonging, are significant to my understanding of my identity. But they are in no way definitive. I have never been to the mountains of southwestern Tunisia or the mountains of eastern Morocco. Nor have my grandparents. And I write this without any *Namesake, Joy Luck Club, Everything Is Illuminated*–inspired travel plans to reconnect spiritually with an abstract past in a place my grandparents never told me about. All my family's surnames tie us to finite places, but that doesn't mean that my family necessarily arose from the earth there. It is possible that there are infinite more origin stories that precede my family's arrival at those namesake towns. Or maybe I will return there, and my life in America is but a momentary blip in a historical trajectory that takes me homeward.

Some origin stories are shameful to me, but they are inextricable from this primordial *shakshouka* of origins. Daida's maternal family line is studded with Tunisian historical notables. El-Banat Shemama (the Shemama Sisters) were a music trio considered to have beguiled much of Tunis before the French conquest in the late nineteenth century with their crooning and their precolonial, curvaceous, unibrowed beauty. They were likely our distant relatives. And for centuries before their arrival on the scene, and for reasons totally unclear to me and the historians and texts I've consulted, Shemama men occupied a variety of posts in the Tunisian royal government. Daida's grandfather Yaqoub was the great-grandson of a qaid or Tunisian royal dignitary, Ibrahim Shemama, and the first wife of his three simultaneous wives, Sultana, which means queen in Arabic. The other two wives were called Rahmouna and Ghozala, elegant Arabic-language names meaning "compassionate" and "gazelle," respectively. I note the names because they are also important to our understanding of our ethnic origins. At a glance, my family tree—on my grandmother's and grandfather's sides, which span almost all of North Africa and therefore a lot of cultural and geographical landscape within the Arab world—shows that with few exceptions, men bore either Hebrew-language first names or names that exist in both Hebrew and Arabic, like Moshe in Hebrew, which is Moussa in Arabic, and women often bore exclusively Arabic-language names. It appears it was more important for our men to have Godly or potentially Godly names and for women to have whimsical, poetic, or cultural names. This comports with our traditional practice of religion; men prayed for their families, while women prepared Shabbat or holiday meals at home. Males interceded to God on behalf of women in the way that priests represent Catholics to God. Only there are no intermediaries in Judaism, or there aren't meant to be.

The government dignitaries of the Shemama family, who frequently bore the Arabic title of qaid, or governor, found themselves among a ruling class detached from the overwhelming problems faced by the Tunisian public—Jewish, Muslim, and otherwise. Where other Jewish Tunisians paid the infamous jizya tax on non-Muslim subjects, dignitaries of the Shemama family were frequently in charge of collecting it. At a moment in Tunisian history when Tunisian Muslims were allowed to wear a red chechia, the traditional Tunisian cap, and Tunisian Jews were required to wear a black chechia, the Shemama family's dignitaries wore red.[18]

Qaid Nassim Shemama, who family histories indicate was likely my ancestor Ibrahim's first cousin, lived from 1805 to 1873 and amassed an enormous fortune at a time when poverty and famine had most Muslims and Jews in their grip. Nassim was the director of public finances, and, while in that position, he is said to have embezzled vast sums of money, estimated to have amounted to more than the nation's entire annual revenue. According to a French traveler, Armand de Flaux, who met him, Nassim "lent the government 20 million pilasters in one fell swoop, and the honorable man asked for nothing more than 12 percent interest, the title of general, and the cross of the commander of the Nishan i-Ftikhar (Order of Glory)."[19] Granted, he wasn't alone; he was one of several rotten cogs in the feudal leadership, although he had the distinction of being the only one of Jewish faith at the time. I say this with immense reverence for my family and with a culturally compulsory respect for the dead: his greed and malfeasance weakened Tunisia as France, buoyed by its recent conquest of neighboring Algeria, began to search for the first signs of weakness.

In 1863, provoked by the doubling of a crippling tax on major cities, the Tunisian people rose in revolt. The Ottomans helped the bey effect calm by injecting gold into the nation's economy, staving off the uprising at home as well as creditors from abroad.[20] Still, Qaid Nassim feared for his life and for the fortune he had siphoned from public funds. He looked to France, and the following year, married a second wife. His first wife was his cousin Elmaya Shemama. His second wife, Esther Lellouche, was a French national of Jewish Arab origin. Through her Nassim sought French citizenship. By then, according to de Flaux, Qaid Nassim was "a little old man, very conservative, somewhere between sixty and seventy years old."

Very disturbingly, although not at all atypical of this sort of Orientalist travel log, de Flaux writes of Qaid Nassim, "When I left Tunis, he was awaiting a young fiancée, coming to him directly from Paris, who must have seen but sixteen or seventeen springtimes in her life. It is only the Orientals who commit such imprudences. In his place, I would have preferred a Tunisian woman. She would have brought to the bedroom her habits of submission that form the primary qualities of the women of the Orient, and that would seem strange to a Parisian woman."

Qaid Nassim left first for France, and then, finding no luck there, for Livorno, Italy, where he stopped short of seeking full Italian naturalization. He renounced his domicile in Tunisia but never renounced his Tunisian nationality before Italian authorities.[21] Until his death, he exchanged letters with former allies in the Tunisian government that suggest some regret at having left Tunisia and a desire to return. His contemporaries viewed him not as a Jewish other who had committed a crime against their nation, but as a compatriot who had committed an act of treason. Nonetheless, Mohammed Bakkoush, a fellow general in Qaid Nassim's circle, entreated him to "return to your homeland . . . the homeland needs its children who are intelligent like you."[22]

Indeed, how Qaid Nassim felt and what he did in life are nowhere near as important as his death, when both his descendants and the Tunisian government made competing claims to the Italian government over his ill-gotten estate. To recuperate its assets, Tunis was forced to define Tunisian-ness—to Italian authorities, yes, but also for itself. "On the eve of the French occupation, a debate on nationality, on identity and the belonging of Tunisians to their country was also happening in courtrooms and official correspondences," Fatma Ben Slimane, professor of history at Tunisia's University of Gabès writes in her oft-cited study on Nassim Shemama, "Defining Tunisianness."[23]

Nassim's will, composed in Judeo-Arabic (written in Hebrew letters that form Arabic-language sounds in a dialect specific to Jewish Tunisians), was found not to have been drawn up by a traditional notary and was invalidated. After the will was nullified, the question became whether Nassim Shemama should be considered by Italian authorities to have been Tunisian or Italian at the time of his death. If he was Tunisian, his estate would be divided among his male descendants according to Jewish law, since in Tunisia inheritance was governed by communal religious law. The Tunisian government would then be able to pursue a legal challenge to recuperate what had been stolen from the public. If he was Italian, Elmaya and her inheritors, living in the Tunisian coastal town of Sousse, would have become the main beneficiaries of the estate.

Elmaya and her inheritors, together with the support of an Italian diplomat in Tunis, made several colorful long-shot arguments against Qaid Nassim's Tunisian identity. At one juncture, they pointed to the jizya, the tax on non-Muslims, in an attempt to claim that Nassim, who had been in the Tunisian government, was never a full-fledged Tunisian citizen. But the tax had long since been abolished in the 1857 Fundamental Pact, a guarantee of the equal rights of non-Muslim Tunisians. At another point, they produced a document claiming that Qaid Nassim's father—unlike other branches of the Shemama family—was originally from Tuscany, a document later invalidated by indigenous Twansa rabbis with extensive records attesting to Nassim's exclusively Tunisian lineage. Elmaya, her inheritors, and their supporters went as far as to produce a fatwa solicited from Tunisian Muslim clergy in Sousse claiming that according to Islamic law, a subject of a Muslim nation—Muslim or Jewish—loses their nationality if they are absent from their homeland in excess of three years.[24] The fatwa was found not to have been based on a single Quranic verse of Islamic liturgical precedent; rather it was an arbitrary decision of a Muslim theologian either friendly with or paid off by the Shemamas.

General Hussein, a high-ranking government official charged with advocating for the Tunisian government in the Qaid Nassim affair, based his argument on a family tree that showed that Qaid Nassim was not at all Italian, but "Tunisian and the son of a Tunisian." Tunisian identity within this argument was inherited. General Hussein also established the parameters of Tunisian identity in a letter to Italian legal authorities. According to Islamic and therefore erstwhile Tunisian law, Hussein wrote, nationality is intertwined with religion, so a renunciation of one's nationality is tantamount to blasphemy; for non-Muslims living in a Muslim state, citizenship is tantamount to a pact with the state and to Islam.[25] Muslims and non-Muslims are equally bound to their nation.

In other words, a Tunisian is defined as such by a divine rite or pact, familial inheritance, and an intent to remain Tunisian and therefore, by extension, Arab. In sum, I am the son of a family that helped to colonize and temporarily destroy Tunisia. I am also the son of the family that unwittingly defined its people.

Much as I have had to fill in the gaps of these bedtime stories, an abundance of people these days are doing the work of considering or reconsidering the Arab, what she was, what she will be. Osama Abi-Mershed, a professor of Arab history at Georgetown University, tells me that the Arab identity has always been nebulous to allow people to accept or reject it. Abi-Mershed points to the time before the Prophet Mohammed. The first so-called Arab Arabs were said to have been the Qahtanis from the south of the Arabian Peninsula. After them, adopting their language and customs, came the Adnanis, often referred to as "Arabized Arabs." "So, from the very origins, there have been contending definitions of Arabness: the narrow ethnolinguistic notion of the Qahtanis and the broader cultural understanding of the Adnanis. Adnanis considered themselves just as Arab as the Qahtanis, based on their adoption of the language, customs, and oral traditions of Arabia," he explains.[26]

Arabness was broad enough to include a larger population of people who claim Arabness as a unifying culture and language and sense of place. From the seventh to the ninth centuries C.E., the Arab identity spread with Islam in wars of conquest that swept across vast swaths of land to the east and west of Arabia. In North Africa as elsewhere, the conquered began to identify with the culture of the conquerors in order to be closer to the culture of the "new elites," until "their cultural understanding of Arabness became ascendant," Abi-Mershed says. Even generations after conquest, there was an "impulse to 'Arabize' and invent an Arab genealogy" that was not necessarily linked to Islam, he argues. "One could adopt Arabic speech and manners, but still identify primarily with Christianity or Judaism." For instance, Christian Arabs have—more consistently than the Jews, in the modern day—professed the Arab identity and contributed to the building of Arab societies while maintaining their religious beliefs.

In the nineteenth century, Arabs were again in the process of reconfiguring the Arab identity, Abi-Mershed says. "Beginning in the 1860s, the redefinition of a secular Arab identity that is religiously, ethnically, and historically plural became the cornerstone of the modernizing reform movement known as An-Nahda," the rebirth. This new "national" definition included three components: "Arabs share a common language and history; identify with the cultural legacies of Arab civilization; and finally, voluntarily accept that this secular identity supersedes other makers of identity, especially religious affiliation."

The pan-Arabist project gained momentum in the mid-twentieth century, its aim to unify the diverse peoples of the Arab world and to cast off the Western imperialist yoke. There were strains of Arabist thought that instead of celebrating religious and ethnic difference among Arabs sought to silence it in the interest of creating a new monolithic Arab identity. To rebuild what had been smashed by the colonists, Arabists employed Western conceptions of race to prop up their imagined Arab identity. Governments throughout the Middle East and North Africa jockeyed for dominance over a massive united Arabia in the style of the Soviet Union, while the inability of early Arabism to fully embrace difference and pluralism disillusioned supporters such that today, to profess Arabism in some Arab intellectual circles has become taboo, if not a joke.

There are many in the Arab world who don't voluntarily identify as Arab. In Tunisia, for example, "there are an increasing number of people—especially intellectuals, I'm not talking about everyone as a whole—who claim an identity more historically and geographically complex and not exclusively Arab or Muslim," says Ben Slimane.

The Tunisians who are moving away from Arabness are part of an uptick in people moving away from the Arab identity, or otherwise struggling with it. The Arab identity, at least as one separate from Islam, is "going the way of the dodo," Abi-Mershed warned. In part, he argues, this is because of the creation of Israel, which convinced many Arab nationals of the power of religious-national movements as opposed to the mostly secular Arabist movement. Arabism ran counter to the theocracy of Zionism. The creation of a modern state premised on faith proved to many in the region that a guiding principle for politics was a unity premised not on history, language, and culture, but on God and holy texts.

The Arabist project persists, albeit disempowered, in the hearts

of some Arabs throughout the world. Arabism is a movement of
hope that persists despite what befell the Arab Spring, which
had driven so many Arab nationals into the streets. It is separate
from the Islamist project that aims to empower the Arab and the
broader Muslim world on religious terms, even though Arabness
informs and is informed by Islam and to argue for Arabness is
by no means to argue against Islam. I love Islam. Islam is me,
although it is not my religion. It is the faith of my friends and
loved ones. It is a faith that belongs to me, if only culturally. It
has influenced the manners and the sense of justice that guides
my family. It professes an equality that the Western concept of
socialism has failed to instill in the world. It is possible to love
the secularist project of Arabism and the cultural and social
impact of a religion that is about love and justice—one that, like
Judaism and Christianity, has also been used to perpetrate some
devastating carnage.

Sion Assidon is a stalwart champion of Arabism. He is a
seventy-year-old Moroccan human rights activist and orga-
nizer of Morocco's chapter of the international, Palestinian-led
movement against the Israeli occupation known as Boycott,
Divestment, and Sanctions (BDS). And he is Jewish. Assidon's
ancestors—at least the fraction of them from which he inher-
its his surname—hailed from the Andalusian city of Sidonia in
Spain. At one point, Assidon's ancestors had been Sephardi in
earnest, but his ancestors from Sidonia themselves traveled there
from the Amazigh tribe of Ait Sadden, located not far from Fez,
in Morocco's east, he says. Amazigh roots, in turn, are often
determined—by the majority of the world Amazigh commu-

nity, it would seem—to be mutually exclusive from Arab roots, given the socioeconomic marginalization Imazighen sometimes face at the hands of Arab-led administrations.

Assidon is indeed Amazigh and Sephardi, but he is also Arab. His experience illustrates the centrality of choice to the Arab identity. He chooses Arabness and practices it in his activism for the survival and the dignity of his fellow Arabs. For him, an Arab is "an individual who by culture, belongs to the large ethnic ensemble that stretches from the Atlantic to the Arabian Gulf, with particularities according to the North African, Levantine, and Gulfi regions. This grouping includes the Imazighen. This is to highlight that the language and the culture [of Arabs] are not uniform." Other distinct ethnicities within the scope of Arabness include the Druze and the Circassians in the Levant, he notes.

For Assidon, one's Arabness "is evident in the language, the poetry, the music, the song, the clothes, the sense of humor even," but he adds, "In my opinion, there is a difference between proclaiming oneself an Arab Jew and a Jewish Arab. The first puts the accent on a communal (Jewish) belonging, as superseding belonging to a large group of humanity: the Arabs." To be an Arab who is Jewish is to choose to stand firmly against the tribalism that dictates modern politics and in solidarity with the largest possible swaths of humanity. Above the din. Across the globe.

Arabness is a personal identity; it is my politics, my inheritance, how I was raised, my relationship and bond to others who share in that legacy, the soil from which I emerge. Judaism is my faith and my understanding of metaphysical things. Matters of the here and now are more urgent in this dour moment of history than matters of the spirit. I do pray for the deliverance of humanity from so much injustice but realize that isn't nearly enough. In this world, I am Arab first and last. Judaism is an adjective that modifies my Arabness. Like me, Oscar and Daida were nuanced enough people to have multiple identities—to have at once professed a religion in the spirit and to have simultaneously belonged to a soil and to a people, when and where they were Arabs.

2

الوطن / The Nation

Oscar was a diabetic who loved sweets. When his relatives came to visit, they took coffee with what I once counted to be five generous spoons of sugar. I enjoy knowing that; there's no point living a life of bitterness. That's how it still is in Egypt, without our family. I saw for myself when I went for the first time, alone. People stop the car at a café, hand a busboy a glass, and wait for him to return it filled with tea, often Lipton, often with a lost world of sugar in the bottom of the glass.

I felt as though I spent my childhood in hospital waiting rooms and cafeterias, as Oscar fought diabetes and heart disease, to prolong his life. He had an immense and often unrequited love of life. I didn't understand why until I read his autobiography, written in three Price Club notebooks, but Oscar's life had been especially full. He had been fond of roller coasters and women. He had relished risk.

We weren't to say the word *death* around him, such was the
fervor of his lust for life. Perhaps typical for a North African of
his generation—caught between our origins and a sort of psychological colonialism that taught us to reject those origins—he
felt our superstitions were silly, but he could not escape them. If
by mistake we did speak of death, Oscar replied with a frantic
"God forbid." In my experience as a visitor and a returning son
to Egypt, perhaps more than in Oscar's ancestral homeland of
Morocco and Daida's homeland of Tunisia—it is compulsory to
say "God forbid," "Astaghfir Allah" in Arabic—one of a number of invocations that transcend the borderlines of the three
Abrahamic religions there.

Finally in 2004, in lieu of a long-shot second quadruple bypass,
Oscar's doctor gave him a month to live. My mother, Nadia,
drove to a bakery and bought him a flourless chocolate cake, his
favorite sweet—no filler or frills, just an oversized candy bar. He
ate it sitting up in his hospital bed, full of urgency, while we—
my grandmother, my mother, and I—sobbed beside him. This
is how we were—melodramatic like the old Egyptian movies
we watched. I had been doing homework in the waiting room,
and after finishing his cake, Oscar told me to write down in my
notebooks the stories he had told me countless times before. He
had already written them in the three Price Club notebooks,
tucked away in a closet of our home in Los Angeles, that he'd
implored me to read. At the time, I had no interest in dwelling
in his past. Only after I lost him did anything we had been seem
to matter to me. If I wouldn't read them, he must have thought
in his hospital bed, faced with his own expiration date, he would
dictate them to me. He was clever.

In one story he told at the start of his last month, he was a
preteen hoodlum roaming the streets of Alexandria, Egypt, with
a band of friends, little cherubic faces with slicked-back hair and
mischievous eyes, a mixture of Muslim, Christian, and Jewish
Egyptians, Levantines, Maltese, Armenian, and Greek children.
In other words, a population sample of middle- and upper-class
Alexandria of the time. On one occasion, they decided to steal
cactus fruits from the garden of a wealthy man who was rotund
and sported a handlebar mustache—a Monopoly dandy. They
hopped over the man's fence in Ramleh, the seaside neighborhood where my grandfather's family lived, but as they began to
pick the fruit, the dandy appeared shouting, flanked by a gigantic,
snarling dog. In a panic, Oscar and his friends rushed through the
cactuses and hopped back over the fence. On the other side, they
found that their hands and clothing were covered in thorns. The
moral, Oscar said, was not to steal. Oscar's stories always had a
moral, its weight sometimes not commensurate with the length
and nuance of the story.

For instance, in the fables Oscar told, there was a recurring
character—Joha, or Goha in Egyptian Arabic. One story went
that Goha was sitting beside a river and a man on the opposite side shouted to him: How do I get to the other side? Goha
shouted, You already are on the other side, idiot! The end. It
would be easy to dismiss this story as totally inane. It takes great
patience and modesty to see the wisdom in my grandfather's
simple, unpretentious tales—a kind of Egyptian comedy I'm
only beginning to understand as I grow older. My appreciation
of these half-serious philosophies—like my lactose intolerance
and aversion to cilantro—grows within me as I age.

Sometime after Oscar died, I lost the notes I had taken from his dictation, but I did find the Price Club autobiographies among other artifacts of Oscar's life.

The first notebook is bound in a floral print cloth, the second in a kind of paisley with saturated colors typical of the 1980s, and the third has an art deco design. I'd always assumed the notebooks contained the story of a life that fell easily into three parts: in the floral print volume would be his life in Egypt up to his early thirties when his family left the country in haste; the paisley volume would follow his life in Israel, then in France; and the art deco volume would follow his journey to Los Angeles. Oscar wrote hurriedly in these books, in a frenetic, sloppy handwriting. There was an urgency he seemed to feel that I feel now too as I try here to tell his life. For Oscar, the haste was because as an ailing old man, he only had so much time to paint for me his life in an Arab world that no longer exists. For me, it's that the broad-stroked dualism of the Jew and Arab continues to terrorize and to kill and to disfigure.

It took time, deciphering my grandfather's hieroglyphics—which I say not just because he was Egyptian but because he often drew crude sketches in the marginalia that represented things like a tarboosh, which he assumed we'd eventually forget. As I read, I realized the books didn't contain the neat three-part stories I'd imagined. Rather, every time the writing began to turn to his time in Tel Aviv, to Paris, to the United States, his thoughts reverted to Egypt. And then, with the story of Oscar in Paris, trying to find *molokheya*, a traditional Egyptian garlic-infused stew made from jute mallow leaves, the account abruptly ends—before he met Daida, before having children, before he even dreamed of setting foot in America.

Oscar's life had ended in Egypt, it would seem from the notebooks. His life continued in an Egypt of the mind. He always
promised that we'd return together, if only for a visit. As a child,
Oscar seemed to me so much more remarkably foreign in Los
Angeles than most other immigrants, including his wife, Daida.
There were things that seemed to perplex him abroad—how
Daida went to night school and eventually arrived at a job much
higher in rank than his own, how his teenage daughters had pre-
marital relationships and took drugs in the 1970s, and how the
intense capitalism of American society left some in the streets to
die, as he often warned me.

Oscar's countless returns to Egypt in his journals often begin
with him sitting on a train, chatting with someone or looking
out the window or standing between cars enjoying the golden
countryside or the desert. Children would run from their homes
down to the tracks to wave and lift a single finger to the heav-
ens, a sign to the passengers that there is but one God: "La illaha
ilAllah!" (There is but one God), as Muslims say—in their case,
coupled with "Wa Mohammed Rasoul Allah" (And Mohammed is God's prophet). Jewish Arabs once sang "La illaha ilAllah" in our *taalil*, our celebratory Arabic-language songs for bar
mitzvahs, weddings, and other joyous occasions. It was a sentiment where the Arab faiths intersected.

Oscar never kept his promise to return with me to Egypt, but
I see the young Oscar on a train now, as I write: elegant, clad
in a suit, holding his briefcase full of pharmaceutical catalogues,
doffing his tarboosh to his fellow passengers.

Oscar's journals are a dreamlike flurry of senses—sights, sounds,
flavors. His first memory, he writes, was when he was four years

old, in the early 1920s. He was playing with a cousin in his childhood apartment in Alexandria while his mother, Rosa, made fries, their perfume filling the apartment. Little Oscar waited for her to leave the kitchen, and then, crawling on all fours, he swiped a couple of bites. Rosa returned to find him stuffing them into his mouth. "My mother admonished me: Little thief," he wrote, adding the Arabic word she used, now so smudged that it is illegible. "In Arabic, we say harami for robber—[the now absent word] being the version to talk to a baby, which I was."

The word that began Oscar's life was likely from an Arabic dialect unique to the Jewish community. Oscar never taught me that language in our Arabic lessons—he insisted that standard Egyptian Arabic was superior, even to the Moroccan dialect he also spoke. But occasionally he'd tell me the meaning of a Jewish Arabic word he used with Daida. *Rassra*, for example, comes from the mainstream Arabic word for "head," *rass*, and means a depression or a circumstance that causes a headache. *R'kiik*— from *r'kiika*, to describe a woman or female thing—means "imbecile" or "lame," in the colloquial American sense. I have heard Jewish Iraqis, of my grandparents' generation, use these words. Some of our Judeo-Arabic was geographically specific; some of it spanned the entire Arab world.

There are disembodied sounds in the accounts of Oscar's youth. As a child, lying in bed in the early morning, Oscar heard farmhands who had traveled to the big city to sell their produce singing in the streets. "The cucumbers," one of the farmhands crooned, "El-khiyaaaar," in Arabic . . . "The cucumbers are going away!" The cucumbers were going out of season, and the Hayoun home would ring with laughter at the image of the departing cucumbers, marching off into the horizon.

Oscar's earliest memories were not unhappy. His family went on frequent vacations to visit relatives in Cairo, a few hours away. There is a photo in our home of my grandfather as a baby, seated on his mother's lap on a camel in front of the Sphinx in Giza. His father, Yaqoub, the proud protector of the family, stands before them, holding the rope attached to the camel's harness. For Oscar, Cairo was a splendid place, a great mass of humanity huddled against itself, but it was ultimately culturally inferior to cosmopolitan Alexandria.

In Oscar's childhood in Alexandria, there were magic and puppet shows. Once, a magician invited little Oscar to participate on stage. The magician gave him a cup of juice. After Oscar drank it, the magician exclaimed that it had been the wrong glass, the juice had been poison. The neighborhood children gasped, their eyes opened wide, mouths agape, and Oscar was frantic. But then, pressing a magical contraption to Oscar's abdomen, the magician appeared to extract the liquid through his bellybutton and through his shirt. The magician proclaimed that he had expelled the toxic liquid and that little Oscar would live. The crowd cheered, delighted, but in his recollection decades later, it appears old Oscar was still very much upset. Such was Oscar's personality. Not much fazed him, but any threat to his life or dignity provoked undying resentment and indignation. When relatives he disliked visited our home for the Jewish holidays, he remained passive and silent as they bickered or made fools of themselves. He was a quiet man. Such were the real men of his generation—theirs was an economy of words and emotional expression.

As a child, Oscar, his parents, and his two elder sisters lived on the fifth floor of an apartment building known to the family as the "tall house" on El-Ehraz Street, in the upper-middle-class neighborhood of Alexandria named for an Ottoman military commander. The street appears to have since fallen off the maps in the postcolonial renaming of things.

Oscar's father, Yaqoub, was the son of Moroccan émigrés. In photos, Yaqoub looks like an Arab Groucho Marx, unsmiling, not because that was the custom for photos in the early twentieth century, but because he was a sullen and stern man. Oscar's mother, Rosa, was a frail, lighter-skinned beauty from a well-to-do Egyptian family—the Levys. She had large, mournful almond-shaped eyes that recall Byzantine mosaics and an abundance of long, thick, dark hair. Women of this generation wore eyeliner—only eyeliner was respectable then, Daida explains—to emphasize the largeness and intensity of the eyes. In her portrait in my home in Los Angeles, Rosa's eyes follow you, as if to say, "Little thief."

Oscar wrote almost nothing about his maternal grandparents in his journals. In our culture, the father's line is the one that counts; Oscar's identification with Morocco over Egypt was a symptom of this. Another symptom is that I know very little of his mother's family or of his paternal grandmother. As we've discussed, Rosa's mother, Messaouda, was recalled to me mostly in comparison to Maryam, his father's mother; Messaouda was lighter-skinned and more beautiful, he would say.

Rosa married in her early twenties, noticeably late for an attractive woman from a good family. The reasons are unclear, since such things were never discussed in polite society. But Rosa had always been of delicate health. If a woman was considered to be too old, poor, sickly, or homely, her marital prospects diminished. She might be matched, for instance, with a divorced man, possibly with children from his previous marriage. Instead, Rosa was married to the son of a foreigner—which was likely suboptimal in her family's reckoning of things—but who was not unhandsome or uneducated, and who was upwardly mobile: a relatively dark-complexioned man of average height named Yaqoub.

Yaqoub was for much of his life an accountant at a shipping company where he had many Muslim coworkers. He fasted in public during Ramadan, out of respect for his work friends, Oscar said. Didn't he go to the bathroom for a snack in private? I asked my grandfather, breathless at the prospect of a month of fasting in addition to Yom Kippur. Maybe, Oscar responded. Even today, many Christian Arabs typically don't eat in the presence of Muslim friends during the days of fast; that would be undignified. Yaqoub was a severe and pious man, one who, like so many religious people, forsook all worldly pleasures to build his way to a paradise of consolations. It seemed he loved to suffer, such that Yom Kippur and Taanit Ester (the Fast of Esther) and other Jewish fast days would not suffice. No one forced Yaqoub to fast during Ramadan. It was something Yaqoub did, customarily, in order to live in tandem with colleagues who did observe, perhaps out of love for them.

Yaqoub had a voice like honey, Oscar recalled. He often worked as a stand-in cantor at several synagogues in the Alexandrian area and would drink raw eggs to make his voice sound smoother. It was customary for the synagogues' congregants to give Yaqoub a gift—often fine cloth from one of the congregants' shops. Whatever gifts Yaqoub received, he would give them to his children, friends, and relatives. The cloth from his Shabbat singing was used to make suits for Oscar. If Yaqoub was carving a roasted chicken, he would take the worst piece, full of cartilage and ligaments, for himself, "because this is how he liked to live—as a martyr," Oscar wrote. Yaqoub's self-denial became customary. On one occasion, much later, when Oscar was an adult, the family went out together and purchased *fatayer* pies stuffed with spinach, a treat from Alexandria's large Levantine Arab communities. Everyone in the family got their own, and Oscar purchased a single pie for his father to share with an infant nephew, knowing that the infant could only eat half and that his father would never accept the decadence of his own spinach pie.

Being a Moroccan and of a certain generation, Yaqoub was very superstitious. He always met a compliment not with thanks—it would have been immodest to agree with a compliment—but with a distraction. For instance, if someone complimented Yaqoub's sweater, Yaqoub would say, "Oh, it's actually very old!" This was to avoid the Evil Eye, the cultural concept of misfortune born of people's envy. Many people in Morocco today, fearing they've been visited by the Eye, consult a *shawafa*—an occult worker professing to work within Islam or Judaism, although many religious authorities condemn them as blasphemous. The Eye is how people explain hard lives. In our home, belief in the Eye persists even now. On our walls and tucked in drawers and breast pockets are countless Hands of

Fatima, as they are known to Muslims, or Khamsas ("fives" in Arabic), as they are more commonly known to Jews. The charm is in the shape of two hands pressed together and is believed to help block the Eye. The symbol is not just of spiritual but also of great cultural significance, since it is believed by many to pre-date monotheism in North Africa, and has become part of the syncretic faith practiced there. Many Muslims put holy words on their Hands of Fatima, as Jews put their own holy words on their Khamsas.

The tall house on El-Ehraz was governed by Yaqoub's self-deprivation and the fear that without our religion and our magic charms, we would suffer boundless sorrow. Oscar spent his life rebelling against these dour things. He wanted to live well, which explains some youthful rebellion—a lot of fast times in fast cars.

Before Oscar was old enough to be segregated from women, he accompanied his mother and his elder sisters, Iris and Vivi-ane, to the hammam (the public bath). Rosa visited the baths with frequency, owing to our family's belief in their curative powers. She suffered greatly from pellagra, a disease induced by vitamin deficiency that ravages everything from your skin to your sanity. It was rampant in Egypt around the time of my grandfather's early youth, across faiths and classes.[1] And as Rosa sometimes reminded her children—particularly in the hot summer months, when she tended to lash out at her husband—she was dying.

Even before his mother's death, Oscar was a frenetic and misbehaved child. Before Oscar, Rosa had given birth to two sons—preferable to daughters in our family, as in much of the world at the time—both of whom died. One brother, Sami, suffered from croup as a baby; a family doctor slit his throat to open an airway and almost instantly killed him. By the time Oscar was born, his family had poured all their hopes into him—he would want for nothing. He was constantly in the street, an entitled hooligan, unchecked by authority.

"I was playing most of the days in the street," he recalls. "In fact the day my mom died, I was playing in the street, building something in the dirt." Rosa was little over thirty-five years old when she succumbed to pellagra. Latter-day pictures show that the almandine eyes had become gaunt—wider than before, with the terrors passing through her mind. Oscar was living with his eldest sister, Iris, at their maternal grandmother Messaouda's house while their father and Viviane watched Rosa die. My great-grandmother Rosa remains buried in Alexandria's city center, in the neighborhood of El-Shatby, in Egyptian soil. Among the many reasons why Egypt remains my nation is the fact that she and her ancestors are there.

Everyone in the apartment on El-Ehraz Street changed after Rosa's death. Yaqoub, who would never remarry, deprived himself with an even greater ascetic fervor, convinced that there is only a finite amount of happiness in the world and that his religious and superstitious suffering would reserve what good fortune he had for turbulent times.

Immediately after Rosa's death, Yaqoub brought his children to Cairo in an attempt to distance them from the specter of their mother's madness and death. First they rented a home in the traditional Jewish Quarter of Old Cairo. Yaqoub needed to be able to walk to a synagogue every Friday night and Saturday to stand for the Kaddish, the Jewish prayer of mourning. The streets of the neighborhood surrounding Cairo's Jewish Alley, like many others in Old Cairo, are very narrow, and Oscar would roam through them with his sisters. Eventually, they left the Jewish Quarter to stay with cousins in another neighborhood of the capital.

The Hayouns returned to Alexandria, moving into a house Yaqoub had built in Ramleh, a neighborhood livened with cafés and other entertainments in Ezzahra (Flowers) Street. He had left his job of forty years, and his boss gave him, as a farewell, a sum of money large enough to finish the construction of a home on the Mediterranean, where he had anticipated he would finish a life of agony.

Yaqoub built, in the backyard of that seaside home, an apartment for his parents, Issrail and Maryam, who at the time were living apart "because they could not get along," Oscar wrote. The tiny apartment was intended to bring them back together so that Yaqoub could care more easily for them in their old age. Over the years, Yaqoub would add more floors to the home in order to house more relatives. In the Arab tradition, multiple generations and branches of a single family tree would live under the same roof. On the roof, he built a sort of cabin that, like other Alexandrines, they would rent out to wealthy Cairene families escaping the hot summer months.

This was the home in which my grandfather would come of age. It was the home that would bear witness to the rapid changes of a tumultuous twentieth century.

The Jewish community of Oscar's youth was one that practiced its faith openly—unlike in the various periods of history
in which Jewish Arabs have had to profess outwardly a belief
in Islam to survive in their homelands. "No one was afraid to
declare their Jewishness in this time," Oscar wrote of his childhood. "It was a wonderful time. In fact, if a family donated
a new Torah to a synagogue, the temple . . . would carry the
Torah from the home of that family to the temple, dancing and
singing joyful songs." In his Price Club notebooks, Oscar con-
trasted this to his later days in Egypt, when Zionism had turned
the country against the Jewish Egyptians. In those times, Oscar
would pass himself off as Muslim or Christian.

Religion was one way Yaqoub ensured that his son Oscar
didn't descend into barbarism or insanity in the absence of
a mother. Each Saturday, Oscar was expected to get himself
to Shabbat services or get a *treha*—a "correction," in Arabic,
often with a slipper or belt—and Oscar would often implore
his sisters to intercede. He would, however, end up employ-
ing a similar threat against me. "I'm going to give you a *treha*"
was the way Oscar would tell me that I was in for a spanking,
until in the carpool line of my elementary school one year a
friend's Caucasian American father told him to take it easy on
me. It was one of many instances in which I observed white
men speaking down to my grandfather, but it was also the end
of the *treha*.

From their home in Ramleh, the young Oscar walked about
four miles to Moharrem Bey, where he went to the Temple
Castro, which administered to Sephardic and indigenous Jews,

while Ashkenazi (European) émigrés sequestered themselves in separate institutions.[2] Castro and other such synagogues were "named for rich men who had donated to the building of the synagogues," Oscar wrote. Egyptian society—Jewish and otherwise—at the time was heavily stratified by wealth and provenance, and the relatively affluent Sephardic Jewish Egyptian community dominated. Stanford University professor Joel Beinin, a noted scholar on the history of the Jewish Egyptians, writes, "Alexandrines were typically more cosmopolitan than Cairenes. However, there were also thousands of indigenous, poor, Arabic-speaking Jews in Alexandria whose existence has generally been ignored because the cosmopolitan and commercial elements of the community were so prominent. Even in Cairo, except in [the Jewish Quarter], where the language of the school and the home was Arabic, it was rare to find monolingual Jews. Among cosmopolitan and Europeanized middle- and upper-class Jews, intermarriages with Christians and Muslims were not uncommon."

The Hayouns were not poor and they certainly had longer-running ties to Egypt and to the region than many Sephardic, Turkish, and Ashkenazi Jews living in Egypt at the time, but they were part of a class that found itself dominated by wealthy Ottoman Sephardic Jews.

Oscar befriended two boys from his neighborhood, Salim, a Christian Syrian, and another also named Oscar, a Christian Maltese. The boys would insult each other's faiths with relish. Using a stick, Salim and Maltese Oscar would draw a Star of David in the dirt and stomp or spit on it, and my Oscar would draw a cross in the ground and stomp on it. "Other than that, we were good friends," Oscar wrote.

The three attended the newly opened French-language Catholic boys' school, Collège Saint Marc, the alma mater of notables including legendary filmmaker Youssef Chahine and film producer Dodi Al-Fayed, who died in a Paris car crash with Princess Diana.[3]

The director of the school, Frère Pierre Cyprien, was a severe man. Once, passing a classroom, he believed he saw Oscar writing on a school desk. The brother didn't see that Oscar was in fact writing on a piece of paper and called him out into the hall, where he slapped his face. Oscar didn't bother to defend himself; it wouldn't have helped. Frère Cyprien was a man of many moods, a character you might expect to see in a Luis Buñuel film. One Saturday—children went to school on Saturdays—Oscar and another pupil found Frère Cyprien in the schoolyard. There were two birds in a nearby tree, and the director asked the pupils with excitement whether they wanted a bird. Yaqoub had always instructed Oscar not to accept gifts out of modesty, so he politely declined, but his friend said yes, so Frère Cyprien ran into his office, retrieved a shotgun, shot one of the birds, plumed it, and gave it to the pupil later that day.

Oscar was not always blameless. He and his friends often earned their *treha*. In Catechism classes, the students learned the Lord's Prayer in French. The final utterance, "Ainsi soit-il" (May it be so), a sort of Amen, they habitually replaced with the similar-sounding Arabic "qasis tawil" (tall priest). The substitution provoked much laughter and, of course, a *treha*. Oscar's Classical Arabic teacher was a Muslim and unfamiliar with the

Catholic prayers, so a boy who Oscar described as the class clown frequently offered to lead the class in prayer before their lesson but would replace the names of saints with ridiculous European-sounding names.

Soon Oscar grew into a lithe man, all of five feet seven, with slicked-back black hair, his mother's almandine eyes, angular features, and slightly hollow cheeks. His blazer was always a bit baggy, but he was otherwise fairly dapper. He was handsome and often looking for a good time, and he found it. In no two entries in the Price Club notebooks is there mention of the same woman. There are Arabic names, Hebrew names, French names. One of the women was a widow in her early twenties with a child. Another was a divorcée who, owing to Egyptian views of formerly married women, he had no intention of marrying (in what feels like a karmic reprisal, I was born to a single mother). Oscar dated a Christian Syrian, whose picture my great-aunt Viviane showed my grandmother in the spirit of resentment that marked their relationship. Marriage was, he told me often, not really the object, but to marry a Muslim woman he would have needed to convert, as other Jewish Egyptian men had at the time. That would have been unacceptable, not only because of Oscar's strict and devout father, but because Oscar himself was very much a believer. Separately, Oscar and his friends frequented sex workers, which was not uncommon for men of their age in Egypt and other societies governed by people of ostensible faith. When I was fourteen, Oscar came into my room and implored me to go out and live. "At your age, I'd already slept with four prostitutes!" he exclaimed. I would remain a virgin for another seven years.

Nonetheless, Oscar grew up in a society that refrained from overt discussions of sex. Watching the 1944 film *Rissassat fil Qalb* (A Bullet in the Heart) in Los Angeles when I was young, Oscar recalled how in Egypt, when the film was released, the audience was scandalized when the young, dapper Mohammed Abdel Wahab sang a song while shirtless in a bathtub. Oscar's womanizing and his society's prudishness may seem like a disconnect, but you likely don't have far to look to find your own society's puritanical hypocrisy.

Oscar was looking for fun—for friends, for sex, for anything more festive than his father's martyrdom. I remember when I was a child Oscar told me, out of the blue, never to try "hashish." A pregnant pause followed, with no explanation, and then he walked away. He enjoyed the Luna Park near Cairo, one of the amusement park franchise identifiable by its disturbing emblem of a glaring 1920s dandy. Throughout his youth, he embarked on countless misadventures only to regret them almost immediately. For instance, a friend told Oscar about a young man in their neighborhood, Goubran, the child of a wealthy Muslim family, who had an Oldsmobile—an "Olds," as Oscar called it in the Price Club notebooks. Goubran had invited a mutual friend to ride on the hood of his car while he drove at a slow speed. Of course, he ended up speeding through the villa-studded streets of Alexandria's quiet Smouha neighborhood at night, the friend screaming for his life. The story excited my grandfather, who quickly managed to get himself on the hood of the same car, screaming at the top of his lungs and holding on for dear life.

Oscar wasn't an especially prudent young man.

———

Oscar's grandfather Issrail, who lived with his estranged wife, Maryam, in the small apartment behind the house on Ezzahra Street, arrived in Egypt from Morocco at a time when Syrians, Italians, Armenians, and others were emigrating there to be part of a thriving international commercial scene. Issrail was a stern man with an impressive, weatherworn face, who wore a tarboosh and flowing robes, known today among Egyptians as the galabeyah. His portrait, with its quiet, knowing eyes, sits in my home—one of only a few images that illustrate how our family used to dress before colonialism. Unkempt is how Oscar would describe his grandmother Maryam in her old age. A world existed in their apartment that was geographically and culturally separate from Oscar and his sisters. Neither Issrail nor Maryam spoke French, English, or Italian, the languages of the Europeans who arrived in Egypt around the turn of the twentieth century. They spoke Arabic (and Oscar addressed them only in Arabic—not the mix of Arabic and French that had by then become customary in his family), and so the elders were confined to a shadow society of people who could only interact with other Arabic speakers, a generation that recalled an Arab world before the European incursion, whose lives—as evidenced by their dress—continued as if the Europeans had never arrived.

Not long after the house's construction, Issrail fell from a step leading to the apartment and broke his hip. "Blasted step!" Oscar wrote, affecting a characteristic Britishism. When she saw what had happened, Maryam, whom Oscar, his father, and sisters hardly ever saw, took a ladder and tapped frantically on a

window of the main house, shocking everyone. It was not just
the tapping that startled them; they seldom heard from her at all,
let alone in this way.

After his fall, Issrail was bedridden. Yaqoub would buy him
tobacco and rolling papers, and Issrail would sit in bed all day,
chain-smoking. After Saturday night Havdalah prayers marked
the end of Shabbat, Oscar would walk the scenic path back to
Ezzahra from Moharrem Bey, passing stately villas, a Greek
cemetery, and a series of cafés that became dance bars at night.
Occasionally, Oscar would go to the back house to tell Issrail
that he had prayed for his health and they would converse for a
few moments. Issrail had trouble pronouncing his own grandson's strange European name, so he called him Kokar, which
was how Oscar sounded to him. It is a tradition in our family
and those of us who go by a European name have an alternative Arabic name that we use among ourselves, and Oscar was
sometimes called Aws, an Arabic name meaning "gift" and an
abbreviation of the Arabic spelling of Oscar, Awskar.

Oscar never asked his grandfather about Morocco or our
ancestors there. In his youth, Oscar was too preoccupied with
romance to take interest in his grandparents. For some time, he
had fallen for a very beautiful girl from a conservative Jewish
family, whom he met for strolls in a public park on Sundays; she
would write "yes" or "no" on a given page of the telephone book
at the local post office to let him know if she would meet him.

Meanwhile, Maryam was ailing. Once, as a preteen, Oscar
returned from Saturday morning prayers to find Maryam pacing
frantically in front of the main house. "What's wrong?" Oscar

asked her. "Your father-in-law is dead," she said. Unmarried, Oscar had no father-in-law. She must have meant Issrail. Oscar was afraid to go into the apartment alone. He asked a young man on the street—a Muslim, he recalled in his journal—to go into the apartment together with him to check if his grandfather had died. When they entered, they found Issrail alive and well, smoking his rollies in bed and confused by the commotion. I'll never know what led to the deterioration of Maryam's mind late in her life. Perhaps it was something in her diet. Perhaps it was dementia. Perhaps it was the misery that would have afflicted many women at a time when it was more universally accepted that they existed solely as accessories to their husbands.

In her old age, Maryam liberated herself from the tiny apartment with a frequency that dismayed our family. She would wander the backyard like an errant spirit and then occasionally break out into the neighborhood, where Oscar and his sisters had to run to find her.

When Issrail died, years after Maryam, Yaqoub asked Oscar what he thought about razing the apartment where they had lived. In the same way that Yaqoub had taken his children to Cairo after the death of their mother, there was superstition at play. They needed to rid themselves of the aura of death and dementia. Oscar agreed. Save the photo of Issrail—and not a single one of Maryam—Yaqoub and Oscar saw to it that nothing of their precolonial world survived Issrail and his wife. Everything was discarded. Even if I were to return to Egypt today to meet whoever resides in the house on what had been Ezzahra—and to embrace them, as I've long imagined I would, and to ask them what had transpired within those walls since my family left—there'd be nothing of that world hidden in the backyard.

In his youth, it was Oscar's dream to move to Beirut to study medicine. "I could have gone to Beirut and been a doctor," he'd say sometimes, sighing and looking into the distance from his recliner in Los Angeles. Oscar considered Lebanon to be a bastion of sophistication—the Paris of the East, as it has been dubbed. A great many of my grandfather's friends were Levantine Arabs of different faiths, and they had told him of their homelands' beauty. Among the records my grandfather carried from Egypt was one by the bleached-blond Christian Lebanese singer Sabah, who sang pan-Arabist ballads like the legendary "El-Watan El-Akbar," as well as the records of Syrian Egypt sister-brother duo Asmahan and Farid al-Atrash. Correspondence between family members written after their departure from Egypt tended toward Levantine Arabic, with moments of Egyptian and Moroccan colloquialism and occasional Judeo-Arabic words.

On Sundays, before meeting with his paramour from the conservative Jewish family in the park, Oscar would read medical books at a local library. He was not a bad student. Years in the Catholic school system had set him straight, if only in the classroom. At around sixteen, Oscar told Yaqoub of his Lebanese dreams. Yaqoub didn't disapprove. He asked his son if he was certain of his success. Yaqoub had saved money—enough to build the house on Ezzahra, which he would rent out to supplement his retirement savings—but they were not a wildly wealthy family. There was only so much money available for

his children's futures. In the Jewish community—unlike in the
Muslim community, where it was the reverse—the bride paid
the husband a dowry. For Oscar to pursue his dreams abroad, he
would need to make enough money to pay for the dowries of
his two unmarried sisters. If not, he would effectively ruin not
only his sisters' lives, but that of his father, who would have to
provide for his daughters for the rest of his days.

Uncertain of himself and buckling under the weight of his
family's future, Oscar decided to forgo his plans. At the time,
he thought he would find work in Egypt and save enough money to pay his own way in Beirut. But he graduated from the
Lycée Français—the secular French high school—at the height
of the Great Depression in 1934. Competition was fierce for
the few jobs out there, and he was without a college education. "The worst time of the world. Depressing," he wrote. "I
couldn't even find a non-paying job," which were also highly
sought after at the time for want of something to do with one's
time. At one point, Oscar found a job that promised him a
wage, but three months in he had not seen a single check and
finally he quit. Having nothing to do was worse than having
no money, and he hated the feeling that he was leeching off his
retired father, who was counting pennies to feed his three fully
grown children.

In Oscar's Alexandria, a man's identity was inextricably
linked to what he did for a living. "Being a worker in a factory, carpenter shop, or any kind of [work done with the hands]
was considered undignified, contrary to office work [which
was] considered suitable. If a boy is not good at school, he had
to go to a special school to learn a trade: plumber, carpenter,

bricklayer, etc. What a shame for him! Stupid idea because in the U.S. those trades are sometimes better paying jobs!" Oscar wrote. Imagine, in such a society, what it meant to enter the workforce, look around, and find nothing at all.

Eventually, Oscar found an unpaid secretarial job taking shorthand, typing, and hand-delivering letters at a shipping company owned by a Jewish Egyptian who warned Oscar from the start that he had a habit of berating his staff. Even workers several decades older than Oscar were called *hmar* (donkey), an insult still popular in the Arab world today. Oscar's superiors relished their superiority. "The boss was a fat pig, his son more or less better, and the manager was of the meanest kind," Oscar wrote. The first time his boss fired Oscar, he went to clear his things out of his desk, but his coworkers advised him to return the next day, telling him that his boss would have long forgotten.

The Egyptian jokes Oscar told me as a child were a bit mean-spirited, like this Egyptian boss. Many were at the expense of the poor, I thought. They gawked at what they saw as the stupidity of the uneducated. And yet my grandfather continued to tell them—a world away and decades later in the United States. When we got internet at home, Oscar searched for Egyptian jokes and sat beside the computer, recording them. I found the cassette as I wrote this book, among a pile of others, one entitled "Elvis and Farid al-Atrash" and another written in Arabic, "Sabah's Most Beautiful Songs." In a boisterous, unmistakably Egyptian patois, the comedian talks about a traveling salesman from the countryside who bought perfume for his wife. She loved the smell so much that she put it in the *molokheya* stew. That's the punchline, and with it, the crowd goes wild with laughter and applause, and I'm left scratching my head. To his first boss, Oscar had been on par with the *molokheya* lady—a ridiculous dope, the butt of an Egyptian joke.

The third or fourth time Oscar was fired, his father, Yaqoub, told him to "take the boss's word for it," Oscar wrote. The job was unpaid, after all. Two days later, by some great stroke of luck, a friend introduced him to the owner of a pharmaceutical company that supplied pharmacists across the country. "This was the last job I would ever hold in Egypt," he wrote, and it would send him across the country. It would also last him a decade—the tumultuous 1940s that robbed us and others of our nations.

Days after Oscar finally found a job in late August 1939, war was declared. The Egyptian government called for Egyptians to volunteer for local neighborhood air raid brigades. Oscar and his childhood friend Salim decided to volunteer.

"I went to a night course on poison gas and became an air warden. The government issued us a metal helmet, a gas mask, a special coat, and a flashlight. We were to wear a special armband during air raids and see to it that nobody stayed in the streets except authorized personnel," he wrote. Their duties involved killing stray cats, whose eyes reflected a light that could catch the attention of the Italian and German bombardiers overhead. There were also perks. "All the air wardens had the right to go once every month FREE to Cairo or any other city away from Alexandria," Oscar wrote. "I took advantage of that privilege often."

At the time, friendships were forged exclusively with other

Arabs of all faiths who had volunteered for the government's war defense efforts. "Every night, after our round to make certain no lights were visible from peoples' windows we used to go four or five hours to a cafe for tea and often for a piece of honey cake called bassboussa or harissa. It was splendid to spend hours talking into the night. I returned home at 11 or 12 and I'd sleep until late."

Ironically, perhaps, it was a time of siege, with several overlapping invasions threatening Egyptian lives and liberty, that impressed upon Oscar memories of partaking in the Egyptian agora that was and still is the late-night coffee shop.

As I begin to write about Daida's youth, on November 8, 2017, I sit in a waiting room of Kaiser Permanente in Los Angeles, waiting for her to have gallbladder surgery. Her heart rate had soared as she headed into the surgery, but finally it regulated enough for the procedure.

Daida's father, Sami, used to tell her that no one really cries for the dying; they cry for their loss. How selfish to let the dying see you cry. It's undignified, for a man especially, to cry. I put my shaking hand in my pocket and tried to regulate my breath. After the anesthesiologist confirmed with her in the prep room that she didn't want to be resuscitated, I had a moment to speak to her before her operation. In a daze, she told me not I love you, not so long; those things were implied. Instead, she told me to keep writing this book. "I know what it will do," she said. Her last word to me—the last to my knowledge that she ever spoke—was *O'mri*, an Arabic term of endearment meaning "my age" or in effect, "my love."

In the months up to that moment, my grandmother had written her life hurriedly in a set of notebooks purchased on clearance from Target: a red notebook about Tunisia, where she was born; a yellow notebook about France and visits to her in-laws in Occupied Palestine, which she was halfway through. A third one, on the United States, had been forthcoming.

As Daida neared death, she embraced it. She had told me that she had never anticipated certain indignities that come with age. For hours, not conscious enough to speak, she overpowered the doctors and nurses struggling to strap an oxygen mask onto her face in a futile attempt to keep her alive. When finally they restrained her arms, that didn't stop her from endeavoring to reach up and rip that unnatural apparatus off her face and to die as she lived—exceptionally and intentionally. May she rest in strength.

Waiting for her to die, I wandered across the street from the hospital to a house with a docile guard dog. In the front yard grew a small jasmine shrub that spilled through the wrought-iron gate and out onto the sidewalk. Jasmine is, of course, Tunisia's flower and the namesake of the 2011 Jasmine Revolution that Daida and I both watched with hearts aflame. The flowers' perfume hit me suddenly. In classical mythology, spilled blood can give rise to flowers. Where a Tunisian died in far-flung Los Angeles, jasmine sprang from the dirt.

As I write this next line, the next day, she is gone. So suddenly it seems I could reach my hand into yesterday and pull her into the present. I can still hear the echoes of her sponge-cake-light voice singing folk songs in the next room. I've lost the woman who raised me. On the day of her funeral, I ransacked our home,

breathless, for memories of Daida. I found an earlier, more comprehensive autobiography than the one she had left, a large blue
bound journal. In it she writes, with a younger, steadier hand,
of her home: "The images formed in my mind are still with me,
the sounds of music, of traffic, of children's games, the laughter,
the crying, the screaming, were for me unique because of the
diversity of people. It was North Africa—Tunisia. The Green
Land."

Tunisia has been known as many things. After 2011, it has
become the Mother of Revolutions. It has, to European and
European American pundits, become the only so-called democracy in the Arab world, the only country with a semblance of
accountability to its people. But in my grandmother's time and
across the Arab world since then, Tunisia was, is, will remain
Tunis el-khadera (Tunisia the Green) for its verdant valleys, a
place my grandmother saw when she closed her eyes that last
time, a place to which my soul will return someday when we
reunite. And thus, at the end of her magnificent life, we begin it.

See Daida as a young girl. She was five two, the shape of a little
African fertility doll, small with rounded arms and hips. Black
curls, large eyes, strong nose. The darkness of her lashes and
brows amplified the force of her gaze. Once, Oscar told me, in
a walk together in our neighborhood in Los Angeles where we
picked our neighbors' fruit (he said they had an arrangement,
but likely they didn't), that Tunisians have beautiful eyes, and
that I have the eyes of my grandmother. I see things now with
her eyes.

Daida smiled as a young girl in pictures, head often turned up in defiance. That's remarkable because in all the old photographs we have from North Africa, no one smiles—especially not women. It was considered undignified, Oscar once explained; better to look sullen than be immortalized as a grinning idiot. But in her photos, Daida is often the only one in our family who looks like she's about to laugh. In her final days, she laughed sometimes with pleasure, but most of the time hers was a fake laugh, sometimes out of a need to convince herself she was happy, often out of disdain. She was immeasurably thoughtful and self-controlled. In these photos from Tunis, I believe she laughed as a sort of fuck-you to a society that advised against laughter. Laughter is more useful than crying, she often said.

Daida's father, Sami, was from the Boukhobza family in the coastal town of Mahdia. Traditionally, the Boukhobzas worked in olive oil production. Her mother, Kamouna, from the illustrious—and in Qaid Nassim's case, infamous—Shemamas, was one of five surviving children. The others, her mother said, had died from illnesses her mother attributed to evil spirits in their home. Kamouna had survived, the story goes, because a wise woman had advised her mother to never speak Kamouna's name for a year when she was still an infant—to ignore her and hide her under a bed when she wasn't being fed or washed, to throw off the jinn, the wicked spirits. Also, whenever anyone—especially a potentially jealous person, since envy rouses the dreaded Eye—inquired after Kamouna, it was important to casually mention eggs, a symbol of abundance in Tunisian kitchens.

How's your baby?

Not bad. I had an omelet today.

Sami, whose family had traditionally worked in olive oil production in Mahdia, found work with Kamouna's father, Yaqoub,
nicknamed Ba Kiki, who owned a small olive oil factory in Tunis.
After the factory went under, Sami found work at a French-
owned winery near Tunis, affording the family a decent income
and allowing them to move to a more well-to-do neighborhood
of wealthy Muslim and Jewish Tunisians and Europeans. Daida's
was the only indigenous Tunisian family in the building on rue
Beulé, renamed nahaj Libya (Libya Street) after independence.
If any other Tunisians were there, "they were used as a hired
hand to do menial jobs," Daida wrote, explaining, "Tunis was
a French protectorate, and Tunisian citizens were looked at as a
minority in their own country." There were many poor Jewish
Tunisians who, like their Muslim counterparts, were not only
unable to live but were also generally unwelcome in Daida's
part of town. At the time, the 100,000 Jewish people in Tunisia,
indigenous and otherwise, came from vastly different socioeconomic backgrounds. The Boukhobza family, who had access to
this well-to-do bubble, were relatively comfortable, while their
countrymen were second-class citizens in their own homeland.

In Tunis, it was considered embarrassing to act Tunisian or,
to use the term they would, "Oriental," in one's everyday life.
Daida wore traditional Tunisian clothes on special occasions—
bar mitzvahs and the birthdays of my grandmother's eldest
brother Youssef, her mother's preferred child, owing to Tunisian custom. In her father's hometown of Mahdia, the family
only spoke Arabic, since their relatives spoke no other language.
Sami's eight brothers and sisters—there were several more who
died as infants or children—rarely made the trip to Tunis. On

occasion, an uncle would arrive, dressed in a traditional Tunisian vest, shirt, and puffed pants, with a basket of olives to let them know that the family in Mahdia needed money for a bar mitzvah, wedding, or funeral. On one of Daida's frequent vacations to Mahdia, Sami purchased a hen for Daida that she named Khadouja for a family friend she recalled who made the best *tabouna* (Tunisian oven-baked bread). One day, Daida and her brothers returned from frolicking around Mahdia's famous seaside rocks and grottos, and the family served a chicken dinner. It was Khadouja the hen, Daida learned mid-bite. This was a story she told in our home whenever we raised the subject of vegetarianism, what she recognized as a noble aspiration not compatible with our culture.

Daida was especially fond of the Muslim holy month of Ramadan. In recounting to me what was Arab about her upbringing (and what was distinctly non-Arab), the first thing she cited was the evening Ramadan break fast—*ftour*. Each day ended with merriment in cafés and mosque communities, and the festivities, and the month ended with even more celebration on Eid al-Fitr. For little Daida, for whom Ramadan was not a religious but a cultural observance shared with Muslim friends, Ramadan was an island in time when Tunisia was permitted to be Tunisian, when she and her family left their neighborhood and went to a nearby mosque and an adjacent souq and the homes of Muslim friends for a carnival of sweets and toys reserved for the season. On some occasions, in those moments after breaking fast, when families poured into the Tunisian quarters of the city (in Daida's family's case, to eat as though they had fasted), she stopped wearing the Western dresses her mother had made her and donned traditional Tunisian kaftans. Daida's family—men and women—also wore Tunisian clothes for Jewish holidays like Rosh Hashanah and Passover. On Yom Kippur, the men in our family wore a white *jebba* (a traditional silken cloak) and prayed, often in the homes of community members, always ethnic Tunisians like ourselves, for absolution from their sins and another year of life and blessings.

The Muslim Eids were, on occasion, a trip to Mahdia, where the Boukhobza family lived in a house on a cliff right on the coastline. At night, Daida could hear the sound of the Mediterranean crashing against the side of the house, and, unconcerned that she might be swallowed by the sea, she slept. The house had multiple stories—Sami's parents lived on one floor, and his two brothers and their families lived on separate floors. Nearby, there was a Muslim Tunisian–owned olive oil factory, where some members of the family worked.

The Boukhobza family was tied very intimately to a wealthy Muslim Tunisian family, the Ben Rhomdanes, who were very influential in the Tunisian government. They were of partial Ottoman Turkish ancestry, Daida said, and their family were characteristically light-skinned, at least relative to her own family. In my travels back to North Africa, I have found that a certain class of light-skinned North Africans frequently lays claim to Ottoman ancestry.

Some of the Ben Rhomdane sons, whom Daida found to be attractive as they rode about their estate on horseback, married French ladies, which in Muslim and Jewish Tunisian families of the time was considered unusual. But where Oscar had affairs with Christian Arab women and would only marry a Jewish

Egyptian—preferably from Alexandria—Daida's family was never very adamant about anything, including religion. They were too jovial for that. Daida would not have turned down one of the Ben Rhomdane sons if asked, she said, recalling then that her father would have disapproved. But then again, she added, Daida's children would have been Jewish in the eyes of the Boukhobzas and Muslim in the eyes of the Ben Rhomdanes, since Islam is passed paternally and rabbinic Judaism is passed maternally.

Perhaps the Boukhobzas had worked, at some point, for the Ben Rhomdanes. Perhaps one family had done the other a favor. But the tie between the two families spanned generations—as though we had both come from the same family, but ended up pursuing different spiritual paths. Sami's father, Youssef, had been very close friends with a Ben Rhomdane family patriarch, whose name Daida no longer recalled.

Daida's father had a horse beloved by all the family, with a light coat and golden mane, named Tchi-tcho. One of the sons of the Ben Rhomdane family encountered Sami riding the horse in town and asked to purchase it. On account of the strange union between our families and a cultural inability to decline such a request, Sami agreed "despite his children's tears," Daida wrote.

During Ramadan at the Ben Rhomdane estate, the women of the Boukhobza family could be heard singing from afar, in the estate's vast fields. Folk songs, sung with light voices, their harmonies a bit shrill, with some gutturals particular to the Tunisian dialect. The women were helping to make sweets for Ramadan and Eid. Preparing food for Muslim festivities was an expression of our culture for which in little Mahdia we became famous. *Boukhobza* means "the son of a bread baker" in Arabic, and the women of our family were renowned for their innovative baking, taking old classics and making them fresh. They made classics like *makroud*, the ubiquitous North African semolina date cookies. But they were also adept at marzipan and all manners of dough, flavored with the blossoms of the orange trees in Tunisia that yield a fruit of a particular depth of flavor found nowhere else in the world. For the predawn Ramadan meal, *suhour*, they made sweet couscous dumplings with nuts and dried fruit, and often sweet breakfast cereal-puddings like *assida* and *bsissa*, which are intended to give fasters energy for the day. One of these Boukhobza women, an aunt, made marzipan delicacies resembling traditionally savory dishes. Their feats went beyond baking. Kamouna was known for a signature dish that involved stuffing fish with eggs, tomatoes, rice, and other foods believed to have spiritual properties, and then delicately slicing it like a sausage. Daida described the result as a kind of a savory stained-glass window. These women helped develop a cuisine that belongs to all of Tunisia today.

Often, Daida's family traveled to Mahdia for a Ben Rhomdane family wedding or a henna party, an Arabic bachelorette party where henna is applied to the hands for luck. The men have their separate party, which Daida never saw. The bride was sometimes a foreign woman whom the family would dress in traditional Tunisian regalia to my grandmother's and the other Tunisian participants' amusement. Dripping in their finest kaftans and jewelry, the guests would ululate to scare away evil spirits. Jewish relatives and friends also had henna parties, if not as lavish as those of the Ben Rhomdanes. At the Ben Rhomdane events, among the laughing and lewd jokes and singing and overeating, no one would turn to Daida and say, "But you are Jewish and I am Muslim." It would have been considered vulgar, Daida explained, to observe differences between two guests. Daida was aware that there were elements of Islam underlying these parties and that her ancestors had struggled at some moments in North African history to maintain their faith. In moments of prayer and during Islamic rites, she was a silent observer. But insofar as Islam is a faith first introduced to the world by Arabs, Ramadan, Eid, and Muslim weddings belonged to and included Daida.

Our different experiences of Islam unified us. So too did beliefs shared among many peoples in North Africa before the introduction of monotheism, for instance, the so-called Hand of Fatima, or Khamsa. In my youth, Daida believed that pressing a circle of henna into my hand would help ward off the Evil Eye. As a child, she had worn the Khamsa hand with a blue pearl in the middle. I was born with my own Khamsa. There were all sorts of magic workers—Muslim and Jewish—in my grandmother's North Africa that might have bordered, in some people's eyes, on blasphemy. It was not uncommon for a Muslim or a Jew to consult a spiritual healer of the other faith. These occultists lived quietly on the margins of society. Their practices were condemned, mostly by men, but they were embraced by many women who, lacking power, had invented their own from nothing.

Daida's mother, Kamouna, was more devoutly Jewish than her husband, Sami. She kept a kosher home; she made pilgrimage to the island of Djerba and the ancient, sacred focal point of Tunisian Judaism, El-Ghriba Synagogue. But Kamouna would also hire Muslim dervishes to come to their home to perform rituals, twirling in their living room, to expunge wicked spirits from their lives. In one instance, Kamouna twirled with the dervishes to expel a spirit she believed was causing her illness and suffering. At the end of the ceremony, Kamouna collapsed on the floor, taken by convulsions, praising God—the single God shared by her and the dervishes—for delivering her from the curse. These beliefs were imbued with Islam, and yet it didn't seem to run counter to Kamouna's deeply felt Judaism. In other words, we were very staunch about maintaining our Jewishness, but we often recognized that there was within us much that was from and of Islam—and that we were all serving or begging for succor from the same one God.

There are forms of misogyny that the West often pins on Islam that in reality have not much at all to do with Islam, or at least are not specific to that particular faith. Islam's holy books say as many perplexing things about women and others as the holy books of Judaism and Christianity. There were elements of Tunisian Arab culture that, in Daida's youth, were cause for rebellion, and yet somehow, without the salvation of a single Western feminist, Daida rebelled and won. She won growing up in Tunisia and later, faced with Oscar's deeply ingrained conservatism on gender, in the West.

Autobiographical accounts came out of the woodwork after Daida died. In an early autobiographical account in a notebook I had not known existed, she writes of the complexities of growing up a girl in a traditional Tunisian home. "In my family, I was the only female besides my mother. Of course, it did have its privileges, but at the same time, and often, it worked against me. I was my father's preferred child, and that felt very good. As for my mother, I was her thing—an object to do with it whatever she felt like doing. Some days she was nice, but more often she was demanding and treated me worse than a personal maid. Changing and making the beds, washing the floors, the laundry by hand for the entire family. My mother took it for granted. In many ways, it helped me become a woman of strong character. I was able to use my hands to accomplish anything I wished to do."

Daida attended L'École de la rue Hoche (named for a French general), a gender-segregated French-language school a short walk from her home in the Lafayette neighborhood of Tunis. She learned subjects like math, French history, and sewing. Compared with her mother, Kamouna, and her female relatives in Mahdia, who had no schooling at all, the schooling Daida received was progressive and unprecedented in the family. But when Daida was eight or nine years old, her family decided it was time to take her out of school to prepare her for marriage. As in many Muslim Tunisian families, marriage is seen as the best way to avoid any mark on the family's honor, and the unspoken reality was that she was about to begin menstruating. Daida often spoke of the severity with which her family hoped to safeguard her virginity as though it were a family treasure and a reflection of their social standing. She was never to be in the presence of male nonrelatives without her father or brother present. This fixation with virginity manifests itself in different ways across Arab countries and indeed neighborhoods and families. In some quarters, as in parts of Egypt until recently, it can take the form of female genital mutilation; for Daida, it was the prospect of becoming a child bride and being forced to forgo continuing her education.

The lot of the Jewish Tunisian women of my grandmother's generation was in some ways a reflection of international norms at the time. There was the perennial Madonna-whore complex. *Qahbah* (hooker) was an insult, which would almost immediately make Daida burst out into laughter when she heard it. It was so funny to her, I believe, because it was unfathomable that any woman in her orbit would ever merit such a title, much as we joked that some women in our family were especially lusty (with their husbands) and much as our men frequented sex workers. Daida, who had only had sex with Oscar, was a *bint el-nass* (literally, "daughter of the people" in Arabic—a good girl, as people say in English). She was a virgin until she was married, and a good daughter, wife, and mother.

Often, Sami would return home from work on horseback with a gift for Daida. Typically, it was a small bouquet of jasmine, or if he had been drinking tea with his farming friends, fat dates, oranges, and olives for her to enjoy. On the day she was taken out of school, Daida felt that even her father had abandoned her. "I never cried so much," she wrote. "I knew then how unfair their decision was, as I loved going to school. I was really very good at it, especially in math." Her school remains to this day. After Tunisia gained independence from France, rue Hoche became nahaj El Hind (India Way). It's an especially sunny street, and the school is a white building with turquoise trim in the style of many Tunisian buildings. Children merrily run and skip in and around the premises. It's idyllic. So close to where Daida lived and likely passed to buy groceries, it must have been a reminder of how she had been deprived of her education.

As a young child, the second-to-youngest of four, Daida had been a servant to her mother. She did the family's laundry, ironing, cooking, and cleaning. It was customary that a daughter, especially a younger daughter, liberates the mother of household chores, and in the process educates herself in the duties of wife and motherhood. Kamouna was not a lazy woman. She labored over her family's many illnesses, prepared holiday feasts, and sewed to bring in extra income. She also, understandably, loved to visit her friends to play cards, gossip, drink *boukha* (a high-proof Tunisian liqueur made from figs), and smoke shisha.

Daida's mother and aunts held a party to introduce her and other female relatives around her age to male cousins. Daida's match was a few years older and very hairy, she recalled. She refused the engagement with such ferocity that her parents relented. Years later, at the age of fourteen, after refusing several subsequent matches, and to her family's bewilderment, Daida enrolled in a typing class with the intention of bringing the family extra income. When she returned home from class one day, her brother Youssef told her that their parents had decided finally to marry her off. Later, at dinner, they told her to skip class the next day but did not explain why.

That evening, Daida planned her great escape. Her aunt Laly lived in an apartment next door. Laly would leave her bedroom window open every day before she went shopping, and so in the morning Daida quietly climbed from the family apartment's veranda onto her aunt's veranda, entered her bedroom through the open window, and left the building for her typing class.

When Daida returned home, her family was "furious with me, but I did not care," she wrote.

Daida's upbringing was made difficult by her family's view of women's roles. It was character building, she would say, since she found no solace in crying. But her childhood was not unhappy. Daida's family and a society were full of contradictions. A good daughter from a good family—a *bint el-nass*—didn't interact with men outside of her family until she was matched with a suitable husband. But Daida's family were far from prudish; they possessed a levity and sexual openness that many in the West would have balked at in the first half of the twentieth century.

In 1930, the year after my grandmother's birth, a legendary Jewish Tunisian singer, Habiba Messika, was burned to death by one of her legendarily numerous lovers, among them Egypt's prince Fouad I himself. She was raised in poverty by her aunt, another musical performer, Leila Sfez, and without a male guardian, she gained a reputation as a libertine. In Daida's old age, I found a Messika song on YouTube—"Habibi el-Awil" (My First Love)—and played it for her. It had famously livened up the room when she was a child in Tunis, the family crowded around the phonograph. The lyrics go:

> حبيبي الاول, والله ما ننسى . . . ومحبة في قلبي . . . والله عمري ما
> ننسى — *My first lover, I shall truly never forget . . .*
> *and his love in my heart, really I will never forget.*
> حبيبي الثاني, والله ما ننسى . . . ومحبة في قلبي . . . والله عمري ما
> ننسى — *My second lover, I shall truly never forget . . .*
> *and his love in my heart, really I will never forget.*

And so on.[4]

Habiba Messika performed internationally, including for Egyptian royalty, and she was a symbol of openness in Tunisia and the Arab world that existed around the turn of the century, one that, despite their conservatism, Daida's family respected and admired. Messika was allowed to exist in the Boukhobzas' universe, even if their own daughters had to remain virgins. Today, Messika is buried in an auspicious section of the Jewish cemetery near sainted rabbis of the Tunisian Jewish tradition. She is proof that only where they attained a certain level of wealth and fame were women allowed to be libertines.

Beyond questions of sexual propriety, the Boukhobza family enjoyed life. They threw wild parties. Days of chores were punctuated by family trips and fêtes—not just for the Jewish and Muslim high holidays, but because people in our family loved to eat and drink and be seen as generous. In summer, the extended family, with in-laws and cousins, would rent small cabins on the beach in the coastal town of Nabeul. "Every night our entire street had become a place of entertainment," Daida wrote. "We drank lemonade and almond syrup. We ate all kinds of honey cakes, and sometimes two uncles called Shoani and Yaqoub, one very fat and one very thin like Laurel and Hardy, would dress as belly dancers."

The musicians at an adjacent casino would join after finishing their set at midnight. "They would play Arabic music until the early hours of the morning. One of Yaqoub's pranks happened around 2am. In his birthday suit, Yaqoub ran from house to house, banging on the doors, and as the door opened, he showed his derriere with a lighted candle. After shocking everyone in the family, he would return to each cabin with a tray of honey cakes as a consolation for having mooned his relatives." A great many of these stories involved similar pranks and what was then called cross-dressing.

Kamouna's sister Emna, who became Emma as she grew up and the French protectorate took a deeper and deeper hold of the country, and her daughter Aziza, who became Suzette, would famously moon the family in their late-night Arabic dancing. When I met Emna briefly in Paris, I was a child and she was in her eighties. We brought her, among the requisite gifts, a gauzy, silken night robe from the United States. "I will wear only this when I dance!" she declared, shaking a hip in the Arabic style, letting out a cackle that frightened me at the time but that fills me with joy now that I know who she was. And who we were.

3

La Rupture / The Rupture

There were two Egypts, two Tunisias. So far we have observed the Arab Egypt and Tunisia, mostly separate from the colonial Egypt and Tunisia, insofar as it's possible to ignore conquests that so thoroughly penetrated indigenous societies. Daida's and Oscar's bodies and minds were colonized. By the time they were born, the colonizers had already established their institutions to carefully engineer their transition away from Arabness. If Oscar and Daida stand out in our family line, it is because they were the last generation to witness Jewish Arabness before exile.

Colonial-era policy in the Arab world aimed to divorce Jewish Arabs not just from other Arabs, but from other Jewish Arabs. The colonizers envisioned family trees in which Jewish Arabs became progressively less Arab with each generation, and imposed policies to that effect. The colonized, filled with self-loathing, in turn attempted to distance themselves culturally from the greater mass of indigenous people, who in the new world order were seen as backward and whose identity became shameful. The imperialists separated Jews and Christians from Muslims and the rich from the poor. They drove wedges into our very households, such that parents began to look—in their dress, manners, and language—very different from their children. These separations—across countries, cities, and households—weakened the state and facilitated the systematic rape of our lands and our people.

Forgetting was made desirable to Daida and Oscar. They often wanted, in the pitiful way that Frantz Fanon in *Black Skin, White Masks* describes, to resemble the colonizer. Sometimes they eliminated those elements of their pasts that their new rulers indicated were distasteful. Oscar and Daida wore Western clothes—theirs was the first generation that considered it embarrassing to wear traditional, non-Western clothes in public. They spoke French often and with disdain for fellow Arabs who could not, and they prided themselves on, as Daida often said of herself, knowing how to deal with the French. Daida was never welcome as a full participant in French circles, especially not in Tunis. She had no French friends. But she was never entirely banned from their society as most Muslim Arabs and many Jewish Arabs—particularly poorer Jewish Arabs—were. For her, this was a source of pride. Not to be violently cast out of the powerbrokers' world, built on the ash heap of our civilization, was a virtue because France had established it was a virtue, decades before Daida was born. Under French dominion, it didn't matter to Daida that she was a second-class citizen in her own ancestral homeland. She never even thought to question it.

This perplexed her greatly in her old age, when she realized it was just one psychological component of a multifaceted colonial project. She described a kind of Stockholm Syndrome that allows a criminal act—the devastation of a nation—to transpire unnoticed. Oscar, for his part, venerated the British who conquered Egypt. He came to admire them so much that on one occasion it nearly cost him his life.

The colonization of Oscar Hayoun and Daida Boukhobza was never complete, though. As we have seen, there were a great many things about my family that were tied fundamentally to Arabness. It seemed unthinkable to Oscar's family, before World War II, to leave the Arab world. When Oscar's grandfather Issrail left Morocco, it was not for nearby Spain or France or even Palestine, the land of Jewish holy sites, but for faraway Egypt; if Oscar left Egypt, it would have been to study medicine not in Paris or London, but in Beirut. Daida often expressed that until her departure, she expected that she would live and die in Tunis. To her mind, even the several-hour drive to Mahdia seemed far, and to traverse the border into neighboring Algeria or Libya was an adventurous undertaking.

For Oscar and for Daida and indeed for many Arabs, the peculiar mix of East and West that existed in their generation—as captured in its films and fashions—was alluring. But colonialism is frequently deceptive, and what drew them to that generation's westernization was also malignant. They were among hordes who were similarly convinced to aspire to westernization. Few Muslim, Jewish, and Christian Arabs of means who weren't decolonial socialist activists bothered to question whether the Western part of that malignant mix should be there at all.

Much as Daida and Oscar, as well as many other middle- and upper-class Arabs of all religious backgrounds, appeared to deliberately forget their Arabness, it was not entirely a choice. The Jewish Arabs who refused to forget, those who clung to their nation and the recollection of a world in which their ethnicity was not detestable, faced prison and exile. The stories of the Jewish Arabs who dared to recall a time when we were Arabs, who faced harsh reprisals from the authorities, are seldom told. In some cases, their passion for their nations burned so bright that, if only occasionally, they are mentioned in contemporary Arab retellings of our liberation from European dominion; others are dead and forgotten.

Memory can subvert colonial authority, it can frighten the colonizers because it allows us to reconfigure this miserable world we live in now, depose the white supremacist, topple his statue in the public square, and approach the European sector with open eyes, ready to disassemble empire.

Several worlds turned in tandem in Oscar's Alexandria, colliding most meaningfully in the marketplace, which brought together the Swiss and the Armenian as well as the indigenous Egyptian tycoon and coolie. Romanticized accounts of Alexandria brag that the average Alexandrine became a polyglot by virtue of living among such diversity. In reality, Alexandrine communities spoke different mother tongues, ate different foods, and had different manners, and the boundaries of their little worlds were demarcated by color and class lines and were enforced by language. A poor Egyptian Alexandrine without the means to afford an education wasn't likely, for instance, to speak more than a few phrases of French or English, much less Greek and Italian. The marvelous multilingual multiculturalism of the time described by André Aciman and company was a great and rare privilege and helped to ensure that poor Egyptians remained sequestered from society's decision-makers. In this city of divisions disguised as diversity, the British—the colonial arbiters of this society—were also the most inaccessible. More than the Greeks and the Italians, the British walled off their social circles and refrained from any substantial social interaction with the Egyptians, rich or poor, Christian or otherwise.

The near veneration of the French language in Egypt, both then and now, is a curious thing, not least because Oscar's Egypt was occupied by the British. The French had superimposed themselves onto British Egypt through the education system, undermining British influence by having instructed the elevated classes in the centrality of France. The struggle between France and Britain played out in Oscar's French classrooms in Egypt. The British dominion over Egyptian government and the French dominion over Egyptian society continued even as Oscar sat in those Egyptian cafés, eating his *bassboussa*, not thinking very many decolonial thoughts.

The street signs in that Egypt were emblematic of Europe's influence. Take, for instance, the street where Oscar grew up, rue Zahra. *Rue* is the French word for "street," *zahra* the transliterated Arabic word for "flower." The street signs in more opulent areas were in French to allow Europeans to navigate them easily and effectively encouraged lower-class Egyptians and other non-Europeanized peoples to stay away. Official Egyptian government documents—not to be confused with the decrees of their British overlords—were in French so that Europeans could read them and the hordes of poor Muslim, Christian, and Jewish Egyptians without a means of obtaining a formal education in French could not. The Alexandrines of that time were subject to different legal jurisdictions, and in mixed trials between natives and European expatriates, the language of the proceedings was not Arabic but French.[1] The language used in those courts made clear that what justice system did exist in that Egypt did not favor Egyptians.

Education is universally accepted as a public good; to deny that automatically aligns the critic with a kind of barbarism. That is how, in colonial North Africa and the Middle East, the colonizers successfully entered the region and produced generations of colonized minds. The educated middle and upper class—for it was those classes that could afford tuition—became advocates for Western intervention and helped pave the way for European conquest.

In the early nineteenth century, Mohammed Ali Pasha, the Ottoman ruler of Egypt, welcomed European—mainly French—technocrats to the nation in a bid to modernize Egyptian medicine, military, and bureaucratic infrastructure.[2] Just after France formally occupied Algeria in 1830, as it began to insert itself into the affairs of neighboring Tunisia and Morocco, France's standing in Egypt's Ottoman halls of power began to swell. In 1844, more than a half century before France enacted a law on French-style secularism, or *laïcité*, at a time when the Church and State worked more explicitly in tandem, Mohammed Ali welcomed French Catholic clergy to open schools in

Egypt for Egyptian children, at the request of a growing community of French elite in Egypt.[3] Later, the French opened secular, state-sponsored institutions.

By the time the British arrived in Egypt in 1882, French
schooling had already firmly established itself as an institution of
Egypt's wealthy and powerful. "The French language, language
of the economic and technical modernization of the country
in the nineteenth century, became little by little the language
of modernity and progress for the upper classes," writes Doha
Chiha, French professor at Alexandria University.[4] The British installed their own academic institutions, such as Victoria
College in Alexandria—institutions that the upper-crust British expatriates, as the French, would not themselves attend if
they could afford to send their children to boarding school in
England. But France maintained its educational dominance in
Egypt, and its influence endures to this day. Oscar's old schools
are still up and running and cater to the children of Egypt's posh
and privileged.

As Catholic and secular French schools began to attract the
Egyptian elite, so too did their Jewish counterparts. The pupils
were taught by their instructors—at first mainly Jewish French
males, before the preparation of indigenous instructors—that
their parents and ancestors were Oriental Israelites, members of
the once-glorious Biblical nation of Israel, made primitive by
their proximity to the backward Muslim Arabs. The student
went home and recognized in their parents, in the couscous they
ate with their hands, in the saturated woven colors of the Arabic
majlis sofa where they sat cross-legged, in the overpowering smell
of the *bakhour* and its esoteric purposes, a betrayal of aspirations

toward European-ness, toward modernity, progress, liberalism, cleanliness. Imagine the tone that child begins to take with their parents for not having the gentile European manners taught in these schools, for being ill-equipped to divorce themselves from their freshly denigrated Arabness. Imagine the parents who, eager to put their child close to the emerging power, encourage them to debase and disavow their families and themselves.

Oscar attended primary school at the Jewish French École Harouche in Moharrem Bey. It was the first of three schools he would attend that ran the gamut of French institutions open to young Egyptians of means in that time: a Jewish French school, a Catholic French school, and a secular French school. All were sponsored in part or in full by the French government.[5]

Isaac Harouche, who founded the school in 1915, had been an instructor at schools in Alexandria that were operated by the international L'Alliance Israélite Universelle (the Universal Israelite Alliance), which had its headquarters in Paris. A French statesman, Adolphe Crémieux, who would twice serve as France's justice minister, launched the organization in 1860 together with other wealthy Jewish French with an explicit "mission civilisatrice."[6] This "civilizing mission" sought to promote French language and culture in Jewish communities in the Middle East and North Africa and lift them out of what they considered to be Oriental barbarism. It also aimed to introduce them to the concept of Jewish nationalism that would eventually nourish the Zionist project.

At this school, the little Oscar learned standard Arabic and the Hebrew alphabet. But the centerpiece of the curriculum was

French. French was the language of the remainder of his education and it became more universally understood, even among
the lower-income Egyptians struggling to keep up with a community that prided itself on success in business.

There is a photo of Oscar at the École Harouche, his little
dark knees pressed together and poking out of his white uniform
shorts, a small, round, unsmiling face, hair combed down to the
skull, almandine eyes staring right at the camera. The photo is
on a small, jagged sliver of thick cardstock. It had been a class
photo, but Oscar had cut himself out. It was a peculiar decision
for him, as he considered pride and vanity to be embarrassing. At
some point in life, Oscar discarded the school and kept himself.

Among the other artifacts of Oscar's education, things so
important that they survived multiple emigrations, was a well-
loved copy of *Les Misérables*, purchased in Egypt and printed by
a publishing house in France. Oscar read this book as a child,
either at Collège Saint Marc, a French Catholic school in Alexandria, or the Lycée Français, the secular French high school he
attended later. I have it now, in Los Angeles, its pages crumbling
as I turn them. On the brittle, yellowed title page, now divorced
from the binding, written in a seemingly unsteady hand with
sapphire ink, is "Oscar Hayoun, rue Zahra," so it would never be lost or, if so, returned to that house in Alexandria. The
Hebrew teacher's historiography and other books—including
Jewish prayer books—are conspicuously without these safe-
guards against loss. *Les Misérables* was something Oscar elevated
above the other tokens of his life in Egypt.

Les Misérables is a book about the individual lives that sparked
the French Revolution—a revolution that did little to affect the

personal liberties of Jewish Arabs until the descendants of the French revolutionaries came to our shores to occupy us. And yet the reader is meant to read what transpires as universally relatable. French education in Egypt, as in Daida's Tunis and elsewhere, taught French history not in addition to but instead of local or Arab world history. Indigenous historical recollections could easily be weaponized into movements to drive out the colonial power, so in the colonial educational system, they often ceased to exist.

In the first colonized generations, there had been strong opposition among Jewish Arab parents to the Alliance Israélite and French education, which its pupils often interpreted as ignorance of the irrefutable good of Western learning. In another Jewish North African family saga, *Les filles de Mardochée* (Mordechai's Daughters), Jewish Tunisian writer Annie Goldmann, born Taieb, writes about the generational divide caused by the Alliance. Goldmann is the granddaughter of Mardochée Smadja, a Jewish Tunisian statesman who was the son of a souq merchant and the grandson of a Tunisian rabbi. When the French arrived, Smadja went to an Alliance school to learn French, despite his father, who was "vehemently opposed to everything coming from Europe." Mardochée continued his studies in secret from his family, who only spoke an Arabic dialect and recited—likely without understanding—Hebrew.[7] The community leaders and parents of that generation opposed their children receiving an education that placed France, and not traditional Tunisian Judaism, at its center. They opposed young girls leaving home without supervision and the way Alliance students began to wear European dress and affect European manners.[8] Taieb's

account refutes the notion that Jewish Arabs—particularly in
North Africa—readily welcomed the French and British and
their imposition of a Eurocentric education that they marketed
as enlightened in the universal sense. They in fact opposed their
conquerors, although there is no recorded account of a full-scale
Jewish Tunisian rebellion—no burning down of newly con-
structed classrooms in the way that non-Jewish Arabs frequently
attacked colonial outposts to regain control of their homelands.

There were occasional differences in the degree to which
Alliance institutions de-Arabized and secularized their pupils.
Expediency reigned. France's political agenda in different cor-
ners of the Arab world dictated the degree to which pupils were
taught to be more or less Arab. Around the turn of the century, in Egypt, Alliance educational memoranda reveal a sudden push to re-Arabize, through language and other curricula,
the Jewish Arabs that they themselves had previously worked
to de-Arabize.[9] The British had just formalized their dominion
over Egypt, which was of great strategic importance as it lay at
the nexus of Asia, Africa, and the Mediterranean, by declaring
it a protectorate in 1914. Against that backdrop, the French Alliance attempted to arouse Egyptian nationalism among the educated Jewish Egyptians of its schools that pushed for the ouster
of the British, effectively undermining their rule.

In Tunisia, where the Alliance promoted the de-Arabization
of the Jewish community, Daida clung to French. The Alliance's
efforts were reflected in our home, decades later. In our exile
in Los Angeles, Oscar was the one who wrote and read fluent
Arabic, in addition to colloquial Egyptian Arabic and Jewish
Moroccan Arabic. Daida only spoke colloquial Tunisian Arabic

and understood some Egyptian Arabic from the movies she had seen. Oscar identified more consistently with the cultural legacy of the Arab world than Daida, who, for instance, was mortified that Oscar and I would eat certain Arabic foods without utensils. "Like savages," she would say, shaking her head.

The Jewish French education system was a central function of a broader European colonial project to penetrate Jewish Arab societies and, through them, the Arab world. Much of that project and its effects on our family was dictated in an 1842 French government policy paper entitled the "Rapport sur l'état moral et politique des Israélites de l'Algérie et des moyens de l'améliorer" (Report on the Moral and Political State of the Israelites of Algeria and the Means of Improving It). As the title suggests, the document is a survey of the Jewish community in Algeria, but its sights were much broader. The report illustrated how the French viewed the Jewish Arabs in its North African territories and farther east, where it was competing with Britain for the conquest of Arab lands. It also expresses how Paris hoped to use the Jewish Arab to further its colonial footprint across the region.

About a decade after France formally colonized Algeria in 1830, Paris sent Jewish French statesmen Joseph Cohen and Jacques-Isaac Altaras on a fact-finding mission to observe the Jewish population of its new territory and make policy recommendations. Their voyage marks the first official encounter between Eastern and Western Jewry and would inform both French policy on Jewish indigenes in the Arab world and Middle East and the establishment of Crémieux's Alliance Israélite and its schools, writes Aron Rodrigue, a Turkish-born Stanford history professor in *French Jews, Turkish Jews*.[10] The mission yielded the 1842 report, in which one catches a glimpse of what life had been for the Jewish Arabs around the time the French arrived. The report offers a rare window into that society, since contemporary accounts of Jewish Arabs whitewash the chaos and poverty inflicted on the subjugated.

Throughout the report, Altaras and Cohen argue that France should use the Jewish Algerian community as native informants: "The Israelite element appears destined in these diverse reports to serve as a point of contact between the French and the former conquerors of this land, but if we penetrate more intimately the secret of their existence, we find among them an admirable aptitude to assimilate into the principles of the civilization where they exist, an intelligence, that, excited by persecution and by the difficulties of maintaining themselves under the iron yoke of the Arabs, developed itself marvelously."[11] That the Jewish Algerians so closely resemble other Algerians is a sign, in Altaras's and Cohen's estimation, not that Jewish Algerians are as Algerian as their Muslim compatriots, but rather that, with their "Oriental physiognomies" and habits, they possess a keen talent for assimilation.

It is crucial to note that Jewish French had only been granted full citizenship rights in France and permitted to serve in government a few decades before Altaras and Cohen composed the report. Their official belonging—at least from a legal standpoint—to France was still on shaky ground.[12] Altaras and Cohen suggest that Jewish French would prove indispensable to the larger French imperialist effort as emissaries to a key indigenous community in Algeria. The Jewish Algerians, in turn, would prove indispensable in helping France to colonize their Muslim compatriots. Throughout the report resounds the usual colonial promise, a win-win for the colonized when, in fact, the colonized gain very little in exchange for their liberty.

At one point, Altaras and Cohen raise some of the same questions on the Jewish Arab's origins that I raise in this book: "Where do these original [Jewish] populations come from then? Are they the remnants of the grand Oriental migrations of which the Roman historians spoke? Are they the descendants of the Judaized Berbers that occupied the minds of the ancient Arab historians? These questions of archaeology are useless to answer now; but it seems their habits, identical with the Berber population, indicate similar historical fortunes and that without a doubt these Israelites constantly inhabited this land with the indigenous populations."[13] The Jewish Algerian resembles the non-Jewish Algerian, who it is implied is the more indigenous. Only the Jewish French are given the luxury of feeling true bonds to their homeland and non-Jewish compatriots, the report implies in its frequent references to France as "our nation" and to Paris's interest as "our interests." Altaras and Cohen aren't interested in the Jewish Algerians' origins; what came before is insignificant to the colonial project. The key here is that they look like other indigenous people and are therefore well positioned to act as native informants.

Why the Jews and not some other marginalized Algerian community? Because there are Jews living across the Arab world, they write—communities of people who have faced discrimination for belonging to a religious minority and who are relatively easy to divide from the remainder of the population. The report on the Jewish Algerians is not actually about the Jewish Algerians; it's a report on how Jewish communities might be "useful to the legitimate interests of our colony" and in other yet-to-be-colonized nations in the region: "Let us add that these relations don't stop at our African possessions. Morocco, where public affairs are essentially in Israelite hands, the Regency of Tunisia where their commercial activity is so prominent, Egypt where they are very numerous, form together with Algeria, as a modern writer has put it, a vast association of Israelites, the sons of which are all eager to take part in the interior commerce of Africa."[14]

In their review of the Jewish Algerians they visited, Altaras and Cohen conclude that they are largely a people deeply in need of what they describe repeatedly as moral improvement. The envoys weren't especially fond of Algerian children, it seems. What they describe are a mix of Jewish and Muslim Algerian hoodlums, indistinguishable from each other, for they have at that age not yet taken on the recognizable dress of their faith communities' elders, running around in gangs. "These children belong in large part to the Jewish population, and if we don't tend to this matter, they will form a class that sooner or later could become dangerous," they write.[15] Frantz Fanon explains the colonial fear of this sort of indigenous child in *The Wretched of the Earth*. Fanon writes that colonizers habitually portray indigenous children "who seem not to belong to anyone" as a "headless, tailless cohort" that is threatening in their uncontrollable behavior and disregard for European hygiene and politesse.[16] The Jewish French report suggested that Jewish Algerian

elders will die with their nostalgia for their precolonial homeland, but the children who are not bent to the colonial will pose
a great danger to the occupation.

As for Jewish Algerian women described in the report, there
were only two kinds: servants and whores. Some women of the
capital, Algiers, found success by becoming maids for the incom-
ing French, they say. In Algiers, there were 500 Jewish Algerian women who had become domestic workers for the 10,733
French residents, and in their proximity to the French, they have
"taken on all the allures of our population," the authors wrote.[17]
And if they have successfully found their place in the new colonial society, it's thanks to the fact that even before France occupied Algeria, Algiers had been overrun by the French. This is
the least derisive part of the entire report: the French-speaking
Jewish Algerians make splendid maids.

The report referenced a popular French stereotype of Jewish
Algerian women: des filles publiques, public girls, or sex workers,
whose industry was undoubtedly inspired by the French presence. But Altaras and Cohen were eager to dismiss the suggestions of other non-Jewish French travel writers that Jewish
Algerians were biologically predisposed to "impurity."[18] Jewish Algerian women faced "a thousand reasons" to descend into
debauchery, they argued, explaining that at the onset of France's
occupation poverty and famine abounded, particularly as anti-
French violence halted production in Algeria's agricultural sectors and French soldiers entered Algerian cities—an accurate
assessment of the devastating impact of the French incursion.[19]

The authors determined, in the part of their report that pre-

figured the Alliance Israélite's education institutions, that the
best possible way to uplift the Jewish Algerian community—to
allow it to achieve its projected purpose as the henchman of
the colonial regime—is through education: "Insofar as uplift-
ing important populations to the height of modern civilization,
and destroying their prejudices, to conquer their sympathies and
to develop among them intelligence and morality, we understand that public instruction must play the foremost role in
social reform."[20] That education should make Jewish Algerians
resemble the French, where possible. It was important for the
Europeans in Algeria to absorb the Jewish element by allowing
them to live among the Europeans and to adopt European dress
so that the Muslims could see how an Algerian could be civilized, they said.[21] This must be done over a series of generations.
"Even in mature years, man doesn't easily change his habits;
societies are as such [that they don't change their habits easily].
A brusque rupture with the past, the sudden transformation of
their law, their ideas, their economic organization, will provoke
in their breasts a morbid chaos," they wrote. "The necessary
conditions of all social reform are therefore the study of manners
and of men, the gradual development of doctrine—in a word,
an initiation."[22]

In sum, I and the Jewish Arabs of my generation were intended by Altaras and Cohen to resemble our Western colonizers.
And by all signs, I and many of us do. France counted on us
struggling to get a Western education, modeling ourselves after
Westerners, speaking French. Daida and Oscar were intended to
be part of a transitional generation, emerging from an Arabness

that Altaras and Cohen associated with the primitive. My only hope lies in my refusal to forget what came before.

France and the rest of imperialist Europe often capitalized on anti-Jewish violence and discrimination in the Arab world to assert their authority over indigenous Arab administrations under the guise of salvation. For instance, Nassim Shemama, the infamous qaid who was Daida's indirect ancestor, employed a Jewish Tunisian carriage driver named Batto Sfez. In 1856, a Tunisian court convicted Sfez of insulting Islam in an argument with a Muslim over a fatal traffic accident.[23] Insulting Islam remains illegal in Tunisia and virtually all Muslim nations, but there were questions as to the veracity of the accusations. Although Tunisia had recently dissolved many of its discriminatory policies against Jews, Sfez had no chance of a fair trial arguing against Muslim plaintiffs in a Muslim court. The bey ordered Sfez's execution—some say to quell interfaith tensions that had arisen after the bey had ordered a Muslim man killed for assailing Jewish Tunisians.[24] This incident had been an unusual one in Tunisia and garnered attention from French and other European consuls in Tunis, who intervened to spare his life.

Frequently, French and other European consuls supplied indigenous people—particularly Jews and Christians—in various parts of the Arab world with citizenship for no apparent reason. Some people whose parents received European citizenship describe the phenomenon as surreal; decades before many Jewish Arabs would scramble to leave their countries, there transpired what some describe a free-for-all granting of passports.[25] The apparent objectives of the European powers were multifold:

to bolster the number of their citizens in the region and to pressure indigenous governments when their newly naturalized citizens faced legal challenges or discrimination. Oscar's maternal grandparents, who were Egyptian and from a wealthy, possibly influential family, became British subjects, Oscar once told me. He had no idea why. Oscar did not inherit that citizenship, and we have absolutely no known British roots or history in the United Kingdom predating its protectorate over Egypt.

There was at least one instance in which Europe appeared to export its own particular brand of anti-Semitism to the Arab world, and this was used by other Europeans to further their colonial footprint. In 1840, a Franciscan priest from Sardinia who had been living in Syria, Father Thomas, disappeared with his Syrian helper, Ibrahim Amara.[26] Stirred to arms by the foreign Catholic clergy, the Christian Syrian community called on authorities to investigate the Jewish Syrian community over their disappearances. The French consul to Damascus, Benoît Ulysse Laurent François de Paule, count of Ratti-Menton, also pressured Syrian authorities to investigate the Jewish Syrian community, who had fallen victim to instances of anti-Jewish bigotry but never this particular sort of witch hunt. Blood libel, by then a centuries-old European practice, was the accusation that Christian blood was used in Jewish rituals, and in this instance, it was alleged that this was what the Jewish Syrians had done to Father Thomas and Amara. The Syrian government was, at that time, keen to curry favor with their strategically indispensable French allies. Thirteen prominent members of the Jewish Syrian community in Damascus were arrested and tortured to extract confessions. The Damascene Jewish community entreated the

Jewish community of Istanbul for help, which in turn contact-
ed their counterparts in Europe. Meanwhile, French Catholic
newspapers published articles that presumed the thirteen Jewish Damascenes' guilt. The Jewish French community, perhaps
concerned that rumors of blood sacrifices would inspire similar
accusations in France, interceded to help their coreligionists.[27]
Together with a host of Jewish European notables, including
British tycoon Sir Moses Montefiore and Adolphe Crémieux,
then a Jewish community representative to the French government and a noted French lawyer, set out for the Middle East. At
the time, Syria was part of the Ottoman Empire, and in Istanbul
they encountered the officials who secured the imprisoned Jewish Syrians' release.

On that same voyage, in a visit to the Jewish community in
Egypt, Crémieux extolled the virtues of a Western education
as a means of advancing France's colonial project. Crémieux
wrote in a log of his journey to Egypt that Jewish Egyptian
schools taught little else than the chanting of Hebrew prayers.
"I inquired about how the children were raised," he wrote.
"Boys were taught to read Hebrew, to sing it. I did not see a
girls' school. A number of girls belonging to wealthy families
were entrusted to women who supervised them without learning anything from them. These children spent most of the day
in a large room, perched on cushions placed on a large carpet.
They lay there when they were tired of sitting. Judge for yourself
how girls thusly raised would be as wives and mothers."[28] In the
long tradition of European men traveling the region, Crémieux
endeavored to comment on and correct "Eastern" misogyny

only to replace it with his own European misogyny in a triumphalist expression of his own country's superiority over the East. He reinforced his own view that the object of a woman's education should be solely marriage and motherhood.

Jewish Arab education was scarce, according to Crémieux's account of what he found in Egypt, and yet in the historical account of Alexandrian Jewry that Oscar carried around the globe, Taragan wrote that there was always an affinity for institutions of learning in traditional Jewish Egypt. It is likely that there was more than met Crémieux's eye when he parachuted into Egypt to make his informal assessments to support the need for the education system he would import there. There was indeed, as Crémieux observed, no centralized pedagogical ethos, Taragan explained, but "as long as there has been a [Jewish] community in Alexandria, one can say that its administrators have addressed the issue of education."[29] Private tutelage in science and the humanities was common among the Jewish Egyptian gentry and had produced doctors, businessmen, poets, dignitaries, and playwrights. Jewish Egyptians—presumably in the tone with which my grandfather took toward any insult to his homeland—wouldn't stand for Crémieux's insinuation that we had all along been uneducated and uncivilized. At least not at first.

The Crémieux schools were the first institutions responding to the perceived holes in the Jewish Egyptian education system, Taragan wrote. With the exception of the recipients of financial assistance, these schools catered to Jewish Egyptians with funds for tuition. In the 1840s, just after they opened, the schools "found no success and closed down."[30] It was evidently

difficult to introduce new institutions into a community, and it
took nearly half a century, after the entrenchment of non-Jewish
French schools as an institution of the Egyptian gentry, for Crémieux's education system to finally return with the construction
in 1896 of several Alliance schools. These schools would serve
the Jewish Alexandrian community until the mid-twentieth
century.[31]

In 1860, in response to the Altaras-Cohen report and the
Damascus incident, Crémieux founded the Alliance together
with some other Jewish European notables.[32] Europe's new colonies in the Arab world were the main focus of its attentions.
It was, at its core, a manifestation of self-hating Jewry. Early
Alliance literature derides both European and non-European
Jewry and takes for granted that if Jews are occasionally vic-
tims of anti-Jewish violence, state-sponsored and otherwise, it
could stop this by educating them away from their characteristic ignorance, avarice, and usury.[33] The schools would help
raise the profile of the international Jew to one of active civic
engagement.

The Alliance Israélite's general instructions for professors is
one of countless documents in its archives attesting to the way
in which it viewed the students of its schools.[34] "In the first,
[the goal of the Alliance] is to allow a ray of civilization to shine
down from the West on the areas degenerated by centuries of
oppression and ignorance," the document said. "Then giving
the students elements of rational and elementary instruction, to
help them find a livelihood more certain and less detestable than
peddling. And finally, opening their minds to Western ideas,
to destroy certain prejudices and certain outdated superstitions

that paralyze activity and the wellbeing of communities." The teacher was required to treat anything indigenous with disdain, but pupils had to be instructed in a way that would allow them to remain members of the colonized society, the instructions read. Hints of the Altaras and Cohen report on Algerian Jewry seem to inspire this pedagogical vision of a Jewish pupil who, while remaining a member of their indigenous society, has been graced by Western enlightenment—but who still feels an allegiance to fellow Israelites above Arab compatriots.

Beyond education, another important function of the Alliance Israélite was to compile reports on anti-Jewish incidents in the communities where it operated. With these, it would lobby European governments to pressure Arab and other governments to address anti-Jewish violence and discriminatory policy. There was an explicit commitment to save the Oriental Jew. The Alliance's founders argued that human rights and other well-meaning liberal conceptions are universal and that Europe's intrusions were necessary in the name of spreading civilization, but its approach was fundamentally colonial. One of Crémieux's fellow founding members of the Alliance, Isidore Cahen, wrote in 1858, just ahead of launching the organization, "Whether it be the brutal oppression of barbaric peoples, or the more knowing oppression of refined peoples, be it oppression that hits our coreligionists in their material lives, be it an oppression that watches with suspicion their beliefs, be it one ultimately that targets their honor, the Alliance will be a vigilant sentinel from which no wrongdoing will escape, from which an organized power will stigmatize this mistreatment and obtain complete reparations."[35]

The language of the Alliance Israélite was not one of plunder; it was not one that explicitly acknowledged France's goals of conquest in the Arab world. Cahen's use of the term *coreligionist* is important to note. The idea that the Israelites constituted a nation, as opposed to a faith community united by their ancestors' beliefs, was already fomenting in the Alliance; it would prefigure and then nourish the Zionist project. "More than the idea of solidarity, it's the notion of a Jewish people that is at the heart of the Alliance project," French historian Perrine Simon-Nahum writes, noting that early Alliance literature refers to both a single Jewish nation and Jewish people of different nationalities.[36]

In the Alliance's archives are scores of reports of anti-Jewish violence and discrimination that it would use to intercede on behalf of Jewish communities. Instead of local Jewish communities relying on their usual means of addressing threats, for instance, through Jewish dignitaries in Arab governments, they were taught by the Alliance to rely on an interceding hand from farther away. Imagine what it was like to need urgent help and have to go through the Jewish community of France, all so that they could have them entreat local Arab authorities in French or through a translator.

Finally, a decade after the Alliance launched, when Crémieux was justice minister, Paris enacted the Crémieux Decree, which declared that Jewish Algerians were French citizens, legally extricating them from Muslim Algerians and neighboring Jewish North African communities also conquered by France, who remained classed as indigenes.[37] A politic of divide and conquer separated Jewish Algerians not only from their compatriots, but from Jewish Tunisians and Moroccans who remained classed as indigenous to their countries. The shift in status for just a single nation's Jewish population effectively made it less likely for the Jewish Algerian to find common cause with a non-Jewish Algerian, a Jewish Tunisian, or a Jewish Moroccan.

In the brief encounter that Daida had with French primary school education in Tunisia, she attended a school catering to a mixed student body that included lower-income French and other Europeans who could not afford to send their children to boarding schools in France, the so-called Metropole, the center of the now robust French empire. Most of them were economic migrants from around the Mediterranean, especially from Sicily, as well as relatively wealthy Muslim and Jewish Tunisians. The girls learned the French language, French history, and math, but much of their education was dedicated to homemaker studies, such as knitting and sewing.

The most memorable of Daida's teachers at the school was Madame L, a young woman from Corsica whom Daida thought quite pretty. Daida remembered little of what she taught, only that there wasn't a single lesson on Tunisia's history. She did, however, learn of the Sun King, of Versailles. She learned of France's origins, *nos pères les Gaulois* (our fathers the Gauls). One day, as part of a geography lesson, Madame L asked the children to identify their nationalities. Italian, French, Tunisian. Daida answered that she was Tunisian.

"You are not Tunisian; you are an Israelite," Madame L corrected her, firmly. Boukhobza is a common Jewish Tunisian surname, and Tunisia is a small enough country that Madame L had likely already encountered a few Boukhobzas. But she did not say *juive* (Jewish), but *Israélite*. This was at a time when the Alliance institutions were pushing Jewish nationalism and pushing for the formation of a Jewish nation.

"I'm Tunisian," Daida told Madame L, not antagonistically. The implications of the question were not immediately clear to Daida as a young girl, but it was unthinkable in a French colony to observe that she belonged to the Tunisian nation and that a Frenchwoman was the foreigner. France would not suffer Daida growing up thinking she belonged to anything other than a transnational Jewish nation that would facilitate French colonialism across Arabia.

"You're lying," Madame L said. Daida disagreed, perplexed. Daida's punishment was to write on the chalkboard after class, "I will not lie to my teacher" what she felt to have been hundreds of times. In the following days, Madame L asked Daida if she had reconsidered, but Daida insisted that she was Tunisian. Finally, Madame L requested that Daida deposit some coins in the class piggy bank to end the after-school detentions.

Daida's mother, Kamouna, hated Madame L for this. On a separate occasion, Daida asked her parents if she might bring Madame L a basket of large blood oranges from a farm in her father's town of Mahdia. Kamouna asked Daida why she would do such a thing, remarking on how poorly Madame L had treated Daida. Daida ended up giving Madame L the gift anyway, and in return, Madame L filled the basket with chestnuts from her native Corsica. Kamouna, who was a proud person, took Daida out of school not long thereafter to learn how to prepare herself for marriage.

Daida told the story of her run-in with Madame L many times. As she told it when I was young, this was a feminist story about a woman who had managed beyond odds to disagree. In her last few years, it became a story about how the French taught her to feel she was a stateless person. In its final iterations, it was a story of how Daida had early on—reflexively—refused the colonial powers' distortion of reality.

Nonetheless, Daida, like many Tunisians, came to adore France and to see herself, in many ways, as a foreigner in the nation of her ancestors.

The films Oscar and Daida showed me when I was a child may have conveyed to me our Arabness, but those same films conveyed to them an ideal of Arab Western-ness. In Alexandria and in Tunis and throughout the cities of the Arab world, movie houses showed Egyptian films for Arabic-speaking audiences that typically reached toward the West. An Arabic film was good, Daida explained, if it could situate itself between Arabness and Western-ness. A good Arabic film was in Arabic, introduced new Arabic-language songs, and mimicked what Daida described as the class and delicacy of a European film. Deference to Arabic social mores—particularly sexual prudence—were nonnegotiables that faded too as time went on.

Oscar preferred Egyptian movies; Daida preferred French films. To prefer French things was to choose refinement. One of their favorite films was the iconic singer and actress Asmahan's last film, *Gharam wa Intiqam* (Love and Revenge), released in 1944. As in so many other films of the time, the lead, Asmahan, is flanked by often speechless European actors. When I suggested they could be light-skinned Arabs, Daida insisted they weren't. The presence of Europeans was meant to indicate the social status of the star, to signify opulence and liberalism.

At the beginning of the film, Asmahan performs the ballad most commonly associated with her musical career: "Layalee Ons Fi Fienna" (My Joyous Nights in Vienna). Against a European backdrop, the light-skinned men and women sway to and fro. The words are in Arabic and the orchestra features Arabic instruments, but the song is very clearly a European waltz. Asmahan's character has successfully penetrated this European world.

In a later scene, Asmahan performs a song, "Ahwa" (Coffee), at a masked ball, where the costumes are all out of the Arabian Nights. She appears in a traditional Arabic abaya cloak and serves coffee to the guests from a Gulfi Arab *dallah*. Such a cultivated, westernized woman would never wear these Arab trappings in earnest; she does this to entertain her foreign friends. The Europeans in the crowd are also wearing what appear to be film studio reproductions of authentic Arabic dress, smiling with bemusement.

These films were a European colonial education for those who might not be able to afford tuition but who could afford movie tickets. Their message replicated that of the Crémieux schools, the French Catholic schools, and the secular lycées: The more closely you model yourself after the colonizers, the more you will resemble stars like Asmahan and the more you'll have achieved success. If you are poor, it is likely because you have not tried to resemble the colonists enough.

Colonialism took aim at not just what was Arab about Oscar and Daida but what was Jewish. Religion, too, became a means of driving colonialism more deeply into the colonized than a law or violence could, because it aligned the colonial power with matters of the spirit.

André Chouraqui, a French lawyer born in the coastal Algerian city of Aïn Témouchent, is the author of an indispensable history of the Jewish North Africans, *Between East and West*, published in 1968. Chouraqui was a Zionist who served as assistant secretary general of the Alliance and in this and other works he describes—without much skepticism—the Alliance's efforts to promote what is described as the intellectual evolution of Jewish North Africans, whom he seems to agree through their participation in and proximity to mainstream Arab society had become intellectually sedentary, barbaric, and Oriental.[38]

In his discussion of what constituted Jewishness in traditional North African society, Chouraqui finds it useful to address the ever-present question of the Jewish Arab's origins. He acknowledges the impossibility of venturing a single Jewish North African origin story and invalidates attempts at a racial one.[39]

> The successive waves of conquerors and colonizers from all parts of the Mediterranean basin and beyond obliterated and intermingled all separate racial trains among the inhabitants of the region, Jews as well as Moslems and Berbers. To the original Semitic strains of Israelites and Phoenicians were added considerable numbers of Berber converts to Judaism; the later influx of Jews from Spain and Italy introduced European racial strains into the Jewish community. Thus,

while the Jews of North Africa were predominantly dark-haired and dark-eyed, blue eyes and blond or red hair were not at all uncommon; on the other hand, a casual observer would have been hard put to it to distinguish, by facial features alone, a group of Jewish children in North Africa from a group of Moslems or even Christians.[40]

Chouraqui, who was once one of these groups of children himself, is noticeably less bothered by the fact that he was indistinguishable from Muslim Algerians than Altaras and Cohen were in their report.

The high proportion of Arabic and Berber names [among Jewish North Africans] suggests a preponderance of Berber and Arab converts to Judaism among the Jewish population, a hypothesis reinforced by the fact that the Berber surnames are generally traceable to tribal and geographic appellations.

The definition of "Jew" in North Africa must thus fall back on allegiance to Jewish faith and traditions, for it was that which determined, throughout the centuries, the fact that a person was a Jew; once a person had broken all religious, cultural and traditional ties with Judaism, he was in all respects lost to the Jewish community. A sizable portion of North African Jewry thus disappeared during the centuries of Moslem rule by conversion to Islam.[41]

Alternatively, one might say a large number of Muslim Arab-identifying contemporary North Africans are the Jewish Arabs' not-so-distant relatives.

To be Jewish was not a bloodline or an ethnic community apart but a spiritual identity with an experiential component, Chouraqui argues: "The sense of belonging to the community was preserved among the Jews of North Africa with great vigor, reinforced by common faith, and by shared oppression and suffering." Chouraqui's work focuses, almost exclusively, on a history of anti-Jewish violence and discrimination, no doubt inspired by the Alliance's insistence that Jewish history in the non-Jewish world has amounted to a ceaseless pogrom. His fixation on anti-Jewishness distracts almost entirely from any other observation about Jewish North African history (our culture, our own historical figures, our unique belief system) and is rife with contradictions. In one instance, he describes a brutal pogrom against the Jews of Fez and in the next paragraph describes how the launch of the French protectorate over Morocco upset "the equilibrium in which Jews and Moslems had lived."[42] At another moment, he admits that the oppression faced by Jews in North African society was symptomatic of political tumult felt by all: "The arrival of the French marked the end of the oppression of which the Jews had been the chief, though not the only, victim, for the Moslem population too had suffered from the anarchy which had reigned under the capricious, all-powerful" rulers.[43] The modern Zionist concept of the Muslim as the Jewish Arab's aggressor ignores the innumerable Muslims who suffered the same draconian, unaccountable government as their Jewish neighbors.

Altaras and Cohen took none of these nuanced views of what

North African Judaism had meant to Jewish North Africans into account. They were more interested in how Algeria might be subjugated by France through the social engineering of its Jewish community. To that end, they looked to the Jewish Algerian community's apparent veneration of its rabbis. "We must add that the influence of the rabbi is very central, from a religious point of view. Obedience to his orders are demanded by Jewish theology, and at the very least a great respect for his words are demanded of the Israelites. Furthermore, certain principles that are correct but misinterpreted by the public have contributed to furthering [the Jewish Algerians'] almost superstitious veneration of rabbis and popular prejudices that attribute to rabbis an almost miraculous power." Rabbis were useful to the French colonial project, the report found. Just not indigenous rabbis.

> We have found among the rabbis men profoundly educated in Hebraic wisdom and that have mastered a high degree of Jewish philology and can without hesitation develop rabbinic interpretations of difficult religious questions, but we don't know a single one that knows how to deploy to the masses the pure principles of morality and of virtue that the religion of the Israelites professes, these profound dogmas and the relationship to the past and its harmonization with the present; in a word, as we have said about Jewish Algerian government dignitaries, Algerian rabbis are incapable of giving to the Israelite society the powerful and strong impulse necessary in transitional epochs.[44]

If the Jewish Algerians are a mass of occasionally barbaric, unhygienic, primitive Orientals, it's because of the influence of their indigenous leadership. "Without a doubt, the submission [to rabbis] purged of the superstition that perverts the minds of the masses would be a happy one if it were exploited by men of intelligence and of heart, but in the hands of the present rabbis it has results that are more morbid than advantageous."[45]

Altaras and Cohen determined that the French state had to hire a new rabbinical leadership for Algeria. And perhaps unsurprisingly, that leadership must be ethnically French. "What is needed throughout [the country] is a French rabbi that can inculcate his flock with the principles of civilization and morality that France has an interest in developing in Algeria."[46]

The report also recommended establishing a Jewish French sub-administration within the larger colonial administration to aid in the broader colonial effort. Napoleon's emancipation of Jewish French communities—the nullification of discriminatory codes and the communities' elevation to full citizenship—created consistories (councils) in Paris and throughout France to represent Jewish communities and their interests to the government. The report recommended that consistories should be established in Algeria but they "must not be created to represent the Israelite society, but to direct and to expedite its assimilation to France. It's therefore indispensable that the consistory not be subject to that society's influences and, above all, that it not be accountable to that society for the measures that it judges as necessary."[47]

In response to the Altaras-Cohen report, the French government established consistories in Algeria, first a Central Israelite Consistory in the capital, Algiers, and then in Constantine and Oran.[48] Around the same time, France also began to send French rabbis to Algeria as part of an attempt to more closely align Algerian Judaism with French Judaism. Algeria served as a prototype for French dominion in other colonial territories. What happened to the Jewish Algerians was archetypal in France's colonial machinations throughout the Arab world.

It is difficult for me to know how our Judaism changed with the imposition of a new, Eurocentric vision of its practice, first in Algeria and then in the countries whose own physical, intellectual, and spiritual colonization had been incubated in Algiers. Language offers some clues as to how the practice of our religion Europeanized. Before the conquest, the Arabic language—and Islam itself—were central to Jewish North African belief. For instance, as throughout the Arab world, the Hebrew letter *vav* was pronounced "w," because there is no "v" sound in Arabic; for the same reason, the Hebrew *peh*'s "p" sound was pronounced as "b." The guttural *ayin* and *chet* were pronounced as they are in Arabic. Yet in the Passover seders (commemorations of our Biblical exodus from Pharaonic Egypt) that Oscar directed in my youth, he read in the accent of Hebrew officialdom, without these Arabic pronunciations; when he was praying his morning Amidah rapidly and quietly—like the hushed sounds of a gentle babbling brook—one could hear the *p*'s fade to *b*'s and the *vav*'s become *w*'s. Even in his relationship to God, Oscar had multiple identities, multiple accents. The colonists had even driven a wedge into our interactions with God. There was a desirable way of being and a less formal, more authentic way of praying that we saw as more "Oriental" and, implicitly, primitive.

In Daida's time, the older generation did not call the Jewish Day of Atonement Yom Kippur in Hebrew; they called it Leil Kibur, *leil* being the Arabic word for "night" and *Kibur* being the Arabic pronunciation of the Hebrew, since there is no "p" sound in our alphabet.[49] After the arrival of the Alliance in Tunis, Daida's generation began to call it Yom Kippur with a French lilt. Night became day.

Oscar's Jewish Egypt celebrated a series of holidays that have virtually disappeared. An example of a Judaism that celebrated its place in the Arab and Muslim Worlds was Leila al-Tawhid, a holiday celebrated on the eve of the first of the Jewish month of Nissan, the first month of the Jewish calendar. Tawhid is the Islamic faith's principle of monotheism, a tenet held in Judaism as well. There was nothing un-Jewish about tawhid, even as the word itself originated from Islamic theology. At midnight, after the singing of Hebrew and Arabic songs and the recitation of poetry, often to the tune of popular Egyptian songs, the eldest hazzan (cantor) said a prayer in Jewish Arabic that started with the phrase that often precedes Muslim liturgy, *BismillAh il-rahman il-rahim*—In the name of God the most compassionate and most merciful—and lists the names of God (divine attributes like "the Most Patient") in a way that echoes Islam.[50]

Once, as we were walking to our synagogue when I was a child, Oscar thought to teach me a single phrase in Arabic: *BismillAh il-rahman il-rahim*. For my grandfather, it was not heretical to teach me this Muslim invocation, because it was true to us. At one point, it was a prayer we uttered too. We believed in performing actions in the name of God, and we believed that God was Compassion and Mercy. God was the kind of Love

that urged you to find similarities with your Jewish and Muslim
Arab compatriots, to embrace them and to refocus our vision on
the things that unite us.

Outside the singular experience of the Jewish Algerians, whom
France made French with the Crémieux Decree of 1870, the
Jewish Arabs' status was manifest only in day-to-day matters,
such as in clothing, language, and where they lived. Daida wore
dresses and Oscar wore suits. They lived in upscale neighborhoods and encountered upper-crust Tunisians and European
colonists. The more they resembled their colonizers, the more
secure their social status was in a system that treated those more
resolutely relegated to the indigenous sector with indignity and
violence.

In the Jewish French studies of their Jewish Arab counterparts,
North African nationals like Oscar and Daida are referred to
as "Israelite indigenes."[51] In British-dominated Egyptian society, the Jews were often informally classed together with other
Middle Eastern communities—the Syrians, Lebanese, Maltese,
Armenians, Greeks, and others—as so-called Levantines.[52] This
designation meant little in the context of civil liberties. All indigenes were excluded from the British halls of power, and the
British preferred to do business with Coptic and other Christian Egyptians—in a spirit of coreligionist solidarity. The British encouraged Christian Egyptians to school their children at
British public schools in Egypt, even as they were barred from
British social circles.[53]

The Egyptian government began to view Egyptians differently in the early twentieth century, after roughly a half cen-

tury of British dominion. Cairo began to count "race" in its censuses of the Egyptian population, which employed European census techniques.[54] In the 1919 census, Jewish Egyptian subjects were divided into two puzzling categories: "Jews by religion," which comprised a modest majority at about 63 percent just after Oscar's birth, and "Jews by race." The implication of this nonsensical distinction is that the Egyptian census takers determined—likely by sight—which Jewish Egyptians were ethnically Egyptian and which were racially Jewish and not Egyptian. How did the census takers understand the Egyptian race in a country as diverse as Egypt? Were my ancestors perplexed and amused by the census takers' decisions or was it totally intuitive to them? Were some Jewish Egyptians more purely Egyptian?

These new designations didn't immediately give any more rights to Oscar than to the rest of the Egyptian population. Jewish Egyptians had to earn those rights on a daily basis, in terms of how they looked and where they went. The Altaras-Cohen report had recommended an "absorption" of Jewish Algerians into French and European communities.[55] One of the ways they could achieve this was through dress. "All the eminent men of Algeria agree that a change of dress would be an important advancement for the Jewish [Algerian] race," Altaras and Cohen wrote.[56] The new outfits "would awaken in the [Jewish race of Algeria] the instincts of human dignity by allowing them to be mistaken for part of that family of civilized people that France has created in Africa."[57] Yet the Jewish Algerians' status was not that of the European, arguably even after they were given French citizenship en masse. These Europeanized Jewish Algerians would buttress the status of the white Europeans and influence poor indigenous Muslims to aspire to a similar kind of social elevation. Moreover, the Jewish Algerians wearing "clothes identical to the French will double in appearance the numbers of the European population which will present to the indigenes thenceforth a compact, strong mass against which it will appear impossible to fight."[58]

Absent of any special legal protections, one's address was another means of ensuring elevated status in the colonies. Before her death, Daida drew me a map of the Tunis of her youth. The Jewish cemetery and the Grand Synagogue of Tunis are planted squarely in the European districts, abutting enclaves such as Little Sicily and La Residence, the building from which the French colonial authority exacted its rule. Her family lived, for most of her youth in Tunis, in the neighborhood still known by the name granted it by its French overlords—Lafayette. Her apartment building, where they lived on the first floor, was located near Église Sainte-Jeanne-d'Arc, Saint Joan of Arc Church, and a surrounding area that in those times was called Place Jeanne d'Arc, Joan of Arc Place. After independence, it was renamed Place d'Afrique, Africa Place, but for many Tunisians still living in Tunisia, for whom aligning with France still bears a centuries-old cultural cache, the name sticks. Also on Daida's map, there is a depiction of an old-fashioned Arabic-style city gate—Bab el-Bahar (Gate to the Sea), which under the French colonial regime became the Porte de France (Gate to France). The colonial task of renaming city streets and monuments was never especially subtle. Behind that gate, and not included on the map, was the *medina* (the city), Tunis's indigenous sector, where the Muslims lived. Beside them, also on the

wrong side of the Gate to France, were the poorer, more traditionally minded Jews whose manner resembled the Muslims
more than the French and their Jewish Tunisian collaborators
who lived on the right side of the gate. Poorer Jewish Tunisians
always lived in the indigenous sector of town, whether it be
in Tunis or Alexandria, or in faraway Baghdad, often in small
enclaves called *haraat al-Yahoud* (literally the Jewish neighborhoods) or *hara* (neighborhood, singular). The Jewish *haraat* had
historical antecedents—in most cases, they existed as a vestige
of an era when, under more discriminatory periods of autono-
mous Arab rule or amid heightened interfaith hostility, Jewish
indigenes were sequestered in their own ghetto.

The people from the *medina* and its Jewish *hara* segregated
themselves often along color and class lines. It was rare to see
a person from the other side of the gate try to move to the
European and Europeanized side. By most accounts, they were
either ignored or looked down on with disdain by the French
and other Europeans.[59]

Daida's family lived in a building where their extended family were the only other Jewish Tunisians; the rest were French-
speakers of European origin. Daida's family never spoke to their
neighbors. Beyond one Italian girl whom she met in her brief dal-
liance with schooling, Rosy Petuzzi, she had no European friends
and had never entered a European home—not even the home
of the Jewish Spanish, Italian, and Portuguese families who had
lived in Tunis for centuries. She believed they found it easier to
involve themselves in European circles, even though anti-Jewish
sentiment among the French in North African was notorious.

Daida was in her teens when once, sitting on a tram that ran from the Tunisian sector through the European sector, a Tunisian wearing a *jebba*—a Tunisian cloak—climbed aboard, to the shock of the other passengers. Moments later, after some commotion, he was arrested in a scuffle with the authorities. One of his *baboush*—traditional Tunisian slippers—was left behind in the tram's aisle. To Daida, this incident came to signify the violence of the colonial regime.

But her sympathies were not always with the indigenous Tunisians. Frequently, Daida remarked to me that one of her younger brothers had married an insufferable, low-class woman, who was given to wearing countless bangles and rings of gold in an old (Arab) style that, in practice, had become nouveau riche and tasteless when viewed through a Europeanized lens. "She was from the *hara*," Daida would say. Explaining what she meant by this, she said that the *hara* Jewish Tunisians' "manners were *fellahi*," the Arabic word for peasant-like. Many Arabs with rustic roots use this term out of pride, to denote an ancestral and a spiritual connection to the land; my grandmother as a proud Tunis woman always used this term derisively to signal ignorance and backwardness. What Daida meant by *fellahi*, she said in a conversation just before her death, was that they had Arabic manners and frequently spoke only Arabic or at best broken French. They were incapable, due to their poverty and ignorance, to act French, or, as Altaras and Cohen wrote, to allow themselves to be mistaken for French. Daida often seemed to take greater liberties in criticizing fellow Jewish Arabs than Muslim Arabs in this regard—a reflection of the social norms of the time.

Wealthy Jewish Arabs habitually looked down on poor Jewish Arabs in the same way that they had been taught to look down on poor Muslim indigenes. The popular image of the Jewish Egyptian among Jewish Egyptians was more educated, wealthy, and Europeanized than that of their Muslim and Christian counterparts. Oscar modeled himself after that shirtless musical genius and author of Arab revolutionary and romantic song Mohammed Abdel Wahab. Abdel Wahab was Muslim, light-skinned, and from a middle-class Cairene family. He spoke fluent French, and commanded respect in the "Oriental" cabarets in France, where he had performed. Abdel Wahab was better equipped than poorer Jewish Egyptians to enter the European world and partake of the spoils of empire.

One day, the young Oscar encountered a beautiful young woman on the streets of Alexandria with a Jewish name. She had jet-black hair and large eyes and a light rose-colored dress, he wrote in his journals. "How's your mother?" he sang, pretending to be a family acquaintance in order to strike up a conversation. "She's fine, thank you!" the woman exclaimed in surprise. "This conversation went on for several minutes," he wrote, ever the scoundrel. "The girl believed I knew her mother!" She agreed to meet him that night for a stroll.

The Jewish girl worked at a laundry in the city center. Every evening for about a week, Oscar met her at her work, and they would go for dinner and a movie or a stroll. "One night, I told her I wanted to take her near her home, but she told me not to. I followed her trying not to let her see me. Unhappily, she noticed me and after that she never wanted to see me again. The reason: Where she lived was a slum," Oscar wrote. Her family lived on a street with poor, mostly Jewish Egyptians, who like his own grandparents wore the traditional clothes of our community.

Their children did menial jobs, but they still found it necessary to wear light rose-colored frocks and speak introductory
French. "She was embarrassed to let me see where she lived,"
Oscar wrote. "I was living at our house at Ramleh, compared
to her apartment it would have been Beverly Hills to Watts. I
couldn't care less. The girl was nice and I was sorry our friendship ended there." And it did end there.

The division between wealthy and poor Jewish Arabs was,
as for my grandparents, enforced and self-enforced by imaginary boundaries. You had to have money to benefit from the
politics of divide and conquer that separated—and in some ways
elevated—some Jewish Arabs from their Muslim and Christian
and other Arab compatriots.

It is commonly accepted in historical accounts that across the
Arab countries, the Jews allied themselves with the European
colonists. That's not an entirely false picture; the data, although
collected by the French, who were not above wild fabrication
to support their conquest, illustrates widespread support. In the
French Grand Rabbi of Algiers Maurice Eisenbeth's 1936 demo-
graphic study entitled *The Jews of North Africa*, he wrote that
among the Jewish Algerian population in 1934, a vast majority
taking a survey did not respond to a question asking if they were
"Israelites naturalized as French" by the Crémieux Decree of
1870. Rather, most had replied "yes" to the question "Are you of
French origin?"[60] So profound was the effort to allow the Jewish
Algerians to be mistaken for part of French civilization in North
Africa that by the 1930s, it appeared the Jewish Algerians had
quite literally mistaken themselves for French. Their forefathers
were not Algerian, not Israelite, not Jewish, but Gallic.

This portrayal may not be inaccurate, but it fails to ask, most importantly, why more Jewish people did not actively oppose the colonial regimes, as though complicity with the French were a foregone conclusion. Daida never grabbed a torch and pitchfork and advanced on the Residence with throngs of others who believed in Tunisian self-determination; Oscar never stabbed a British soldier. In many ways, they both benefited from those regimes and never gave much thought for what their family—what I—would lose, namely ourselves and any sense of belonging in this world. That's not to say they weren't thinking anticolonial thoughts; it's to say that they felt powerless to act and, what's worse, had been convinced of their inferiority. They understood that they were considered an underclass in their own homelands, that they had been so effectively separated from the Muslim and poor sectors of their own societies that they were lulled into bourgeois complacency.

Any association with Arabs or Muslims and their culture was itself an act of subversion. Jews were not intended to be part of the fabric of their societies, even as the Alliance established vocational schools, ostensibly to make them useful to their societies. In reality, it was to make them more useful to the new French administrators. For a Jew to celebrate their Arab homeland's national holidays or to partake of a Muslim or Christian Arab holiday was a contravention of the Altaras-Cohen report.

But still, despite no decolonial uprisings in solidarity with non-Jews, the Jewish Tunisians remained Tunisian. For many, each year was marked by the slaughter and barbecue of lamb on Passover and then another family's lamb or at least sweets at mosque festivals in celebration of Eid al-Adha.[61] Holidays and weddings were an opportunity for Jews and Muslims to share in each other's lives, even as French policy endeavored to separate them. Part of what arguably facilitated the continuation of these Muslim-Jewish relations was that many Muslim Tunisians also willingly underwent a process of acculturation and entry into the colonized gentry. The Ben Rhomdane family of Mahdia—with its long history of friendship with Daida's family—were indeed Muslim and involved in Tunisian government, but habitually sent their sons to study in France and marry Caucasian French women who—if only nominally—converted to Islam.

There were some Jewish Arabs who advocated for their nations' liberation. But very often, they paid a price for their valor. Two Tunisians come to mind: Habiba Messika and Georges Adda. Habiba Messika, the Jewish Tunisian singer born in 1903, we've already discussed. Nicknamed *h'bibat el-koul* (the beloved of everyone), Messika was known to have traveled from party to party, flanked by a throng of Jewish and Muslim men nicknamed *il-asker il-leil* (soldiers of the night). Her patriotism was well documented, and in her song "Baladi ya Baladi," she sang of the prospect of "living in freedom" in Tunisia at the height of the French dominion over Tunis.[62] Tunisian director Salma Baccar's 1995 film about Habiba Messika, *La Danse de Feu* (Fire Dance), portrays a legendary moment in 1928 when, wrapped in the Tunisian flag, she sang a liberation ballad, "El-watan, il-shehaada il-houriya" (Homeland, Martyrs for Freedom) to an audience of tarboosh-wearing Tunisian gentlemen, and French authorities stormed the concert hall, dragging her and her comrades off stage to prison.[63]

Georges Adda, a onetime leader of the Tunisian Communist Party, joined the party in 1934 and was imprisoned multiple times by the French authorities for conspiring against the French occupation.[64] In the documentary *Un printemps 1956: L'indépendance de la Tunisie* (Spring 1956: Tunisian Independence), Adda recalls one occasion when he was imprisoned with hundreds of other dissidents who, as key figures in their movement were executed, began to sing the Tunisian anthem.[65] "The walls of the prison that are one meter wide trembled, they moved with this song, with this hatred that we had, with this furor," he says. Later in life, Adda writes, "Tunisia is my country, and the Tunisian people my people. All the women and all the men who suffer political and social injustices are my sisters and brothers. For the liberation of my country, I knew prison, concentration camps, and deportation by the French colonists. Today, I must offer my support to the martyred Palestinian people."

Daida met neither Adda nor Messika. She had been taught to be obedient and to busy herself with laundry and other menial chores for a large family. Once, Daida's cousin Aziza, whose parents were more relaxed, invited Daida to a dance party. When Daida returned home late and her parents found out that she had been associating with men who were not related to her, her father hit her for the first and only time in her life. For her, it would have been impossible to attend revolutionary meetings in the dead of night with a group of unwashed, Marx-reading, free-thinking Tunisians.

Egypt had figures comparable to Adda and Messika. Yaqoub Sanuaa—also called Abou Nadarra a-Zarqa, a nickname alluding to his signature blue-framed spectacles—was born in 1839 to a prominent family employed by Mohammed Ali Pasha around the time of the growing French and British presence in the country. In 1877, he launched a satirical publication that accused the ruler of Egypt, Ismail Pasha, of selling the country out to the Europeans. In one famous cartoon, Ismail Pasha is seen auctioning off the Sphinx and pyramids in Giza to a throng of ravenous European bidders.[66] Abou Nadarra also coined the slogan "Egypt for the Egyptians," which was employed in rebellions against the Egyptian leadership.[67] He was exiled for his pains. A 2016 *New Yorker* article compared the many Egyptian dissidents who, after the 2011 revolution, have left the country to him.[68]

Oscar was not tied to the hearth like Daida, but he greatly feared possible reprisals from authorities cracking down on dissidence. Even in America, he often advised me not to criticize the government to anyone over the phone. Once, when I returned home from protesting the beginning of the war in Iraq with my mother, he waited for us at the door. "Are you crazy? Do you want to be put on a blacklist?" he shouted. "I forbid you from going to more protests." As Oscar would find out later in Egypt, citizenship was something that can easily be taken from you, despite constitutional guarantees of freedom of expression and of assembly.

Remember the scene in *Casablanca* where the Nazis have commandeered Rick's Café and they're chanting the Die Wacht am Rhein, the Nazi anthem? Victor Laszlo marches over to the orchestra and instructs them to play the Marseillaise, and Rick approves the request. Then the Europeans in the café risk their lives to sing the French national anthem in defiance of the newly arrived Nazis. It's easy to forget in such a well-crafted bit of cinema that there are no Moroccans or even people attempting to play a Moroccan in this scene. Their absence doesn't matter. There's a single Arab character in the entire movie, and his is a bit part—and he's a thief and a scoundrel. It's easy, in the tugging of heartstrings, to forget that the anthem should never have been played in Morocco. Ever.

The scene is emblematic of how my grandparents and their compatriots lived under European dominion. They were forced into a war started by the Nazis, a war that spread to our region as a consequence of European imperialist expansionism.

When the Italians and Germans began bombarding British-occupied Egypt in 1940, his time had come, Oscar often said. He continued working at the pharmaceutical company during the day, but he began attending night courses on poison gas, which were sponsored by the Egyptian government. When he graduated, he became a volunteer air warden. He was issued "a metal helmet, a gas mask, a special coat, and a flashlight," he wrote in his journals, and was given a special identification card, a piece of folded beige cardstock signed in regal Arabic calligraphy by the director general of the Department of Civil Protection from Air Strikes. Oscar added his name in both Arabic and in English in own majestic hand—generous, fanciful hoops and hamzas on a document he would present to the authorities in case of emergency. For place of origin, he wrote not Egypt, but Alexandria—the crown of the country, as far as he was concerned. The card bears a photo of a foppish, angular-faced Oscar, with furrowed brow, looking purposefully into the distant future, not unlike the high school yearbook photo of a future statesman.

Oscar now went on government-sponsored trips to Cairo

every month. This was jet-setting, to him. He had only been
to Cairo on occasion, as a child after his mother's death, a few
times to visit relatives and go to Luna Park, and then again in
1938, when train tickets were discounted in celebration of the
wedding of King Farouk and Queen Farida.[69] In his unit, Oscar
found colleagues and friends among fellow Arabs of all faiths.
A photo of Oscar and his colleagues from the wartime years
shows a group of men at the Alexandria harbor, wearing suits
and tarbooshes—valiant men who ran out into the streets in
an air raid, yelling to people to turn off their lights. After the
air raids, he went to traditional Egyptian cafés to smoke shisha, drink tea, and eat *bassboussa*. Naguib Mahfouz's 1947 book
Midaq Alley revolves around one such café, and perhaps Oscar
and his friends also listened to the stories told by professional
hakawati—Egyptian storytellers—as they celebrated their hero-
ism well into the night.

But in 1941, as Europe's war raged on, a friend told Oscar
that the British-run St. John's Ambulance Brigade was accepting
applications for volunteer medics. Oscar jumped at the chance.
As he writes in his Price Club autobiography and often made
clear to me, he never intended to quit the Egyptian volunteer
position, but it seemed that over time his sense of responsibility to the British grew. The Egyptian government could not
compare to the British, who provided vaccinations, a uniform,
a book with a military code of conduct. The British also issued
Oscar an identification card that was almost identical to the
Egyptian one in size and color, except it was in English. According to the card, which he filled in himself, his nationality was
Egyptian, his eyes were blue (they were dark brown), his hair

was auburn (it was black), and he was 5 feet 12 inches (he was 5 feet 7 inches, if that). He kept both cards throughout his life, and while there are infinite little creases in the Egyptian card, there isn't one on the British card. It remained immaculate.

The volunteers had access to the British Navy, Army and Air Force Institutes (NAAFI) and its rations shop, where he was able to purchase British and international "cigarettes, candy, canned fruits, cocoa, towels" at a low cost. As a volunteer with the British armed forces, he could afford to provide for his family and take care of the younger of his sisters, Viviane, who had become his surrogate mother, and whose health was deteriorating. He would feed his family cocoa and canned fruits and sell the rest— mainly the cigarettes—on the black market.

With great privilege came great responsibility. A St. John Ambulance Brigade Overseas Membership Book—also immaculate—shows that Oscar passed an annual exam, and over the next few years, his "number of drills" and "hospital attendances" would grow exponentially. Almost every day after working at the pharmaceutical company, Oscar rushed to the 64th General Hospital, housed at the British-run Victoria College, another of the famous foreign schools. Some of Oscar's duties were medical and undoubtedly fulfilled some of his dreams of being a doctor; he took temperatures and pulses. But "for the most part, I helped the nurses serve tea and later, at around 7 or 8, dinner," he writes. Like the nurses, he wore white overalls, and he helped them "do the beds." Oscar had become an unpaid domestic worker for the British occupation.

Once after a shift at the hospital, hanging around the NAAFI, a royal marine bought Oscar a beer. When the marine stepped away, the cashier told Oscar in Arabic, "Whatever you do, don't lend that man any money." (It is unclear whether the shop worker was a Muslim, a Christian, or a Jewish Egyptian—or just a friendly foreigner who'd learned some Arabic.) "Don't worry, I know what I'm doing," Oscar said. As anticipated, Oscar's new friend asked him if he could borrow several Egyptian pounds, and Oscar obliged. "You'll never see that money again," the cashier said. "You should know better than to lend someone money in a war." Perhaps he did it because he was enamored with British soldiers, the sort he might have seen at the movies, with their slicked-back hair and gentlemanly manners. No one questioned their worth, and the European ladies fawned over them. In Egyptian high society, Jewish and otherwise, Oscar had been nothing. Now he was rubbing elbows with the British.

Several weeks passed and Oscar heard nothing from his new British friend about the borrowed money. His fellow volunteers, some of whom had found themselves in similar situations with the soldiers, finally convinced Oscar to go to the marine's barrack and ask for his money back. At the barrack, the marine chatted with Oscar as though nothing happened and eventually went to a drawer and retrieved a pistol, with which he began to tinker as he spoke. He appeared to clean it, all the while talking about Egypt and the weather and London—polite small talk.

"I was really scared and my hands started to go up little by little all the time thinking he could kill me and pretend that the bullet was inadvertently triggered while he was cleaning his arm," Oscar wrote. "I had to remain cool and [convince] the marine [that] playing with his revolver could cause an accident, and eventually he put it away," he continued. "Thank God he didn't shoot!" Oscar left "a wiser man: Never lend a soldier money and never in a war," he wrote. That had been the only lesson after almost dying over a few pounds. That was the worth of his life, prostrated before a British marine.

But Oscar was devoted to the British, to the point that, at his funeral, we played a cassette tape of bagpipes that Oscar loved with permission from our usually strict rabbi. "England has always been special to me," he wrote, "because in Egypt during World War II, I spent most of my afternoons between 1941 until 1945 in the military and naval hospitals with the wounded British soldiers. Some of them were not so friendly. For instance, some considered themselves too special for the likes of me, but there were the exceptions. There were those who thought the privilege of buying items at the NAAFI should be reserved only for the armed forces. Most of the wounded soldiers were nice and often talked to me of their town in England. The Scots were friendlier. The Scots were known as Jock, the Welsh as Taffy, the Irish as Paddy."

Oscar relished his duty to the British. He helped them heal their wounded without question and with a passion so fervent that when the war ended, he received a medal and a certificate "in recognition of devoted service to the cause of humanity during the Second World War." The head of his division, W, sent him a letter in August 1946, that opens, "Dear Hayounski." Oscar recalled that once one of the British supervisors of his division suggested that he was a Muslim and he corrected him. The only Jews the British supervisor had encountered were the Jewish British Londoners of European extraction. And so Oscar Hayoun earned a Slavic suffix and a nickname, born of a stereotype.

"I should like to thank you for all your keen and loyal support of the Division," W continued. "I personally have very highly admired your friendly cooperation. Wishing you all the best in the future." And that was it—the sum of Oscar's payment for four years of labor in service of a war that, if it had to happen, should have remained in Europe where it started.

For much of his life, one of Oscar's favorite movies was the 1939 classic *Gunga Din*, but later in life, he suddenly couldn't stand it when my mother suggested that she play it for him. The film, based on the Rudyard Kipling poem of the same name, is about a dutiful indigenous Indian who sacrifices his life in service of the British occupation. Gunga Din is a slight brown man—portrayed by Sam Jaffe, a white actor in brownface—enamored with the pomp, regalia, and valiance of arrogant British soldiers. He is repeatedly rejected and mocked by the British, until he finally dies to help them subjugate his own people. The reasons why Oscar loved Gunga Din were obvious, and my mother, Nadia, would say when I was young, "He was Gunga Din." Oscar's friends were Arab and the non-Arabs who participated in Egyptian society—the Greeks, the Armenians, and the Maltese—and yet he worked for the British for years without pay. He believed they had to win their war because the Axis forces would have invaded Egypt and slaughtered its Jewish communities as they had in Europe. But all my grandfather had to show for his labor was a small tin medallion with a cross, his name crudely etched into the back, a certificate of completion, and a letter of thanks topped with a bigoted nickname.

———

In Tunisia, ahead of the war, things were good for Daida's family. Her father, Sami, had made enough money working for a European-owned winery to start his own small-scale wine-barrel factory with a young farmhand at the winery with whom the family had become friendly, Ali.

Then, in 1939, as they huddled around a radio they would later need to submit to the Jewish community leaders, the Boukhobza family and Ali listened to the French president announce that France was at war, as were the people sitting around that table. Tunisia was plunged more deeply into the conflict than Egypt. Where Oscar only ever encountered German prisoners of war, wounded in stretchers at the hospital, Daida now encountered Nazis on the streets of Tunis.

As in Alexandria, wardens were assigned to make sure windows were entirely blacked out at night so that they weren't targets for bombardment. Sami, the only Tunisian man in the building and the only blue-collar worker, agreed to build a shelter for the building's tenants in a nearby vacant lot. Over the course of Tunisia's half-year involvement in the war, the shelter was gradually enlarged to serve several neighboring buildings. When the sirens rang, Daida was charged with grabbing her youngest brother, Guigui, who was still a baby, as well as a knapsack that Kamouna had prepared for the family with chocolate and a change of clothes. She had to run to the shelter, where she sat crammed together with neighbors. For the first time, she came face-to-face with the Europeans alongside whom she'd always lived.

In the first few years of the war, the family contended with occasional air raids. They were terrifying, but they were not a constant interference in their lives. "I remember one night, we decided to stay home and a bomb fell about two blocks away. It felt worse than an earthquake—my teeth were chattering. It took me a good half hour to calm down with the help of my father," Daida wrote. The next day, the apartment building a block away had crumbled. Daida vividly recalled seeing the drapery. The home had been opened to the world, like a life-sized dollhouse.

One morning in November 1942, Kamouna asked Daida to go to a grocer on the Avenue de Paris—what has since become Liberty Avenue—around the corner from her house, to buy a half kilo of salt. The grocer was opposite the French gendarmerie, the law enforcement headquarters. Just as Daida was stepping into the grocery, two men in strange uniforms pulled up to the gendarmerie, rang the doorbell, and began to speak emphatically with the officer who answered the door. Passersby whispered to each other in shock, "My God, those are the Germans!"

Daida had just witnessed the start of the Nazi occupation of Tunis. "I ran, I did not walk, my heart beating very fast," she wrote. "I told my parents that the Germans are now in Tunis. From that day, the war was in our daily life." The next day, the Nazis began to make a series of demands of Jewish community leaders. First, they demanded money and a list of hundreds—about eight hundred, per Daida's recollection—of young male conscripts to go on foot to a makeshift labor camp fifty miles away in the port town of Bizerte. The Jewish leaders compiled a list of young men exclusively from poor families. Her uncle François, from a wealthier branch of the Boukhobza family and a fervent believer in socialism, offered to take the place of one of the poor young men on the list. After the war, he would later recount how one of the young men, born with one leg shorter than the other, was shot dead on the long march as he lagged behind the rest.

After they took the young men, the Nazi authorities began to confiscate radios, arms, and other assets—entire businesses, sugar mills, farms. In what my grandmother described as Tunisian obstinance, Sami gave a fine Arabian racehorse he had purchased before the war to a Muslim family friend. He sold his wine barrel factory to his former boss, the Swiss vintner, for a nominal sum before it could be requisitioned by the Germans. He dismantled the family's radio and hid it. He buried the rifles he used to go hunting on horseback. When time came to turn items in, the Boukhobza family had nothing to give. It was as though they had, in all those generations of government dignitaries and farmers and entrepreneurs, subsisted on air.

Ali lost his job, and for lack of options moved in with Sami and his family to become a domestic servant to the Boukhobzas in exchange for room and board. He suddenly found himself living on the European side of the Bab el-Bahar divide, eating with and adopting the dress and manners of a Jewish Tunisian family. I have no records of Ali's life, of his feelings, of what it meant to be a young Muslim from a low-income, rural family, suddenly thrust into the European part of town. Did the young Daida resent him? Did her family regard him as a Tunisian like them?

The allied bombs aimed to liberate French territory from the Axis, not Tunisian bodies from occupation. It is indeed lucky for me that the Allied forces prevailed, even if neither Axis nor

Allies should have come to my family's homeland in the first place. If the Allies hadn't won our family clearly would have been slaughtered, but am I to be thankful for the war effort? Was it the goal of the Allied forces to fight for the safety of Tunisians?

Food was scarce at that time. The German soldiers stole rations from their Italian collaborators, Daida often joked, since German food was fairly flavorless—even in times of plenty. At the market, where people stood in line from 2 a.m. until it opened at 8 a.m., the only bread available was a sort of black loaf, already molding by the time they received it. Daida's mother, Kamouna, would habitually gather scallions she found on the market floor, soak the black loaf in water, remove the mold, roughly chop the bread with the tails of the scallions, mix both with her harissa and eggs, ball and fry her concoction, and put it in a tray and go with Ali into the center of town to sell it to the German soldiers on a street corner. Her sons, coming in from the streets where they played, would try to eat them, but they were forbidden. These aren't for you, she'd say. The balls were immensely popular with German soldiers, terrible as their rations seemed; within moments, they were gone, and the soldiers seemed not to know that they were eating scraps. With the money Kamouna earned, she bought edible food on the black market, including Arabic bread made in a *taboun* oven.

Still, this was the time that Daida first knew hunger, she said. And compounding that stress, she and her family were waiting to see if they would be deported to Nazi death camps in Europe. Daida later said she had thought she would never end up leaving Tunis, but for the first time, she was made to imagine a life— and a death—abroad.

In the way that the French occupying force had been not altogether malicious, there were moments of friendliness between the Boukhobza family and the Germans. Kamouna and Sami continued to take their early morning coffees, even as bombs fell and Nazis marched through the streets. A German officer at their café had purchased some traditional Tunisian slippers that had already torn, and Kamouna, who before the war did seamstress work for the European families to bring in extra income, repaired them. The next day, the soldier came to the café with a small box. In it was a jar of strawberry jam and bar of chocolate. Back home, Daida inspected with wide eyes this luxury food that had been "very scarce since the start of the war." She noticed the labels were in English, and realized the gifts "were probably both taken from an English soldier. But we certainly had a feast. It was some time since I saw jam or chocolate."

Despite these exchanges, their house was often ransacked by the German authorities, who would go through drawers taking anything they deemed to be of value. The wise Kamouna learned that if she bundled up the children and Ali and pretended they were ill, the Germans would pass over their home, fearing feverish plague within, in what for them was still an exotic land.

Eventually, the family heard on a radio purchased on the black market that the British would heavily bombard Tunis. Kamouna had an uncle in the town of Hammam Lif, not far from Tunis, who had a room free in his house where at least twenty people slept on the floor on blankets for weeks: Daida, her parents and siblings, her uncle's side of the family, Ali, and another Muslim Tunisian friend of Sami's. By the end of their stay, everyone had a cold, and everyone had lice.

———

World War II affected Egypt and Tunisia in different ways. In Oscar's Egypt, it drove a wedge between the Jewish and Muslim populations. Some among the Muslim Egyptian majority welcomed a Nazi invasion for a number of reasons: as a means of loosening the British grip on their country and of obstructing a nascent Zionist movement that aimed to occupy Arab land. I am disgusted by the Egyptian Arabs who did not reject a Nazism that would have killed their compatriots and other humans. But I also reject the suggestion by opponents of the Jewish Arab identity—and proponents of the denigration of Arabs—that the Nazism of some Egyptian Arabs during the war serves as proof of the division between the Jews of Arab nations and their compatriots. Still, it is important to note, not in their defense, but as a means of better understanding how some Egyptians came to support Nazism that no one, including Daida and Oscar, yet understood the depth of the horrors the Nazis were perpetrating at death camps north of the Mediterranean. The Egyptians who did support the Nazis in the war erred in favor of backing the enemy of enemies. Still, Oscar and the rest of Egypt did know that Hitler was rounding up Jews across Europe and that if the Nazi invasion succeeded his family would face a terrible fate. As a result, many Jewish Arabs, Oscar included, began at this time—in Oscar's case, for the first time in his youth there—to feel estranged from their homeland.

In Oscar's ancestral homeland of Morocco, King Moham-med V—grandfather of the current monarch, Mohammed VI—rejected the Vichy government's pressure to enact discrim-

inatory laws against Jewish Moroccans, for which he is still venerated today. Moncef Bey, the sovereign in Tunis, also rejected
extreme pressures from the Vichy government to inscribe the
forced labor and discrimination of the Jewish Tunisians into law.
Both took a stand against Nazism on the principle that Jews
were equal subjects of their North African kingdoms. At a time
when North African palaces were overrun with foreign dignitaries in suits, forcing the two sovereigns' hands on any number
of measures, the safety of the Arab subject was a red line that
even Hitler himself could not cross.

In France, the Grand Mosque of Paris forged records for
dozens of Jewish North African families that attested to their
Islamic faith. Among them was Salim Halali, the famed Algerian singer, born Simon Halali to a Jewish family in Annaba.
Halali had, during the war, become a presence in the popular
"Oriental" cafés in Paris, where he sang Arab and Andalusian
songs. Si Kaddour Benghabrit, the Moroccan founding rec-
tor of the Grand Mosque of Paris, hid Jews at the mosque and
gave Halali and others their forged certificates for dozens of
Jewish North African families, engraving a false name on a
grave in the outskirts of Paris to help fend off suspicion that
Halali was Jewish. Halali ended up living, for the majority
of his life after the war, in a countryside home in Morocco,
where he kept an elephant in his backyard. Many recount that
Halali performed once in Jerusalem for a community of Jewish North Africans living there, but after he took the stage, he
announced in Arabic, "Long live the Arab nation," and was
promptly booed off stage.[70]

For some in Egypt and closer to Palestine, which was on the brink of occupation, the Nazis further separated Muslim and Christian Arabs from their Jewish compatriots, teasing out existing divisions wrought by French and British colonialism. For others, the urgent need to resist genocide and the promise of liberation from European rule inspired greater solidarity. The diverse responses to World War II were a testament to the political diversity of the vast Arab world and the improbable resilience of some in the face of unrelenting European occupation.

Qaid Ibrahim Shemama, Daida's ancestor, in his Tunisian royal regalia.

Oscar's grandfather Issrail.

Young Oscar in a schoolboy uniform.

A photo of Oscar as a schoolboy. He cut himself out of the class picture.

Daida's maternal grandparents, Ba Kiki and
Ma Julie (misspelled "Jouli" usually—as they
would've pronounced it).

Daida's family in a horse-drawn carriage in
their neighborhood of Tunis. Left to right:
Daida's brother Max, Daida, Daida's mother
Kamouna.

Oscar looking crispy.

A postcard from a friend in Egypt featuring a neighborhood near the rue Zahra, where Oscar lived (Ramleh).

One of Oscar's British IDs from his wartime volunteering.

One of Oscar's Egyptian IDs from his wartime volunteering.

A postcard featuring the Grand Synagogue of Tunis a few blocks from where Daida lived.

Allied soldiers with Daida's family. Daida is the second from the right, her mother is third, her aunt Emna is fourth.

Daida's cousin Aziza with her husband,
Maurice.

A funny photo of Daida's family. Top, left to right: Unknown first
cousin, Daida's brother Guigui, Daida's father Sami. Bottom, left to
right: Daida's aunt Emna, Daida's mother Kamouna.

Daida in a field.

This is the street in Tunis where Daida grew up, formally la rue Beulé, now nahaj Libya.

Daida's aunt Emna.

Daida and her daughters in Paris.

Oscar and Daida visiting Oscar's family near Tel Aviv. Top, left to right: Oscar, Oscar's sister Viviane, Daida, Oscar's father Yaqoub. Bottom: My mother, Nadia.

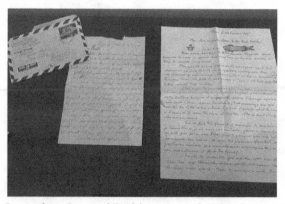

Letters from Oscar and Daida's parents to the United States. Oscar's father wrote in Arabic script. Daida's parents wrote in transliterated Arabic and French and drew little superstitious emblems in the marginalia. They had the habit of writing "555555" around the names of loved ones to ward off the evil eye.

New Year postcard from Tunisia.

A photo of my mother, Nadia, looking a bit
ill at ease with a Santa in Los Angeles.

Daida (second row from the bottom, second from the right)
graduating from night school in Los Angeles.

Oscar's records from Egypt and Los Angeles.

4

المنفى / Exile

I was on a bus between Cairo and Alexandria. The seat beside me was empty. Oscar had been dead for four years. We never ended up going back together, certain as he seemed in his promises that we would. In every generation, a person must see themselves as though they left Egypt. So reads the Passover Haggadah, the recitations of the holiday that commemorates the Biblical Jews' Exodus from Egypt. I looked out the bus window at golden land and the occasional green valley. *Wadis*, in Arabic, I recalled in that moment, from Oscar's lessons. I tried to see the land through Oscar's eyes as he traveled this road between Cairo and Alexandria countless times during and after the war, selling medicine to lone pharmacies out in the middle of nowhere. This was how he was rejoined to his land, and this was where he and the land retreated from each other.

———

The Alexandria of Oscar's youth prided itself on being a bastion of European modernity, relative to Cairo to the south. It was the center of that cinematic world in which Arabs spoke Arabic but affected Western mannerisms and dress. For the Alexandrines, to leave the city limits, even to go to Cairo, inspired dread. When Oscar's manager at the pharmaceutical company—the Greek girl, as she's called in his accounts—first gave him a list of forty-three small towns and villages to visit as a representative for their company and sell their war wares to local doctors and pharmacists, his heart sank. It was "this or nothing," he wrote, and so he accepted. "I regretted leaving the Alexandria I loved, but going to those villages was the most interesting time of my life," he wrote.

Leaving Alexandria, the train would stop at Damanhour, then Kafer el-Zayat, where it would slow to cross an old bridge. There, Oscar would jump from the train—or "alight," as he wrote—and take a bus to Basyoun, then Kafer el-Sheikh. On another train from Kafer el-Zayat, he'd head first to Tanta, then to Mansoura. Oscar made these trips with frequency from the start of the war in 1939, until he left Egypt a decade later. Oscar remembered the names, even of small hamlets, nearly a half century later. He must have expected that I'd return to trace his steps. He took great care to map out the precise routes he took and the tricks he used to get back to Alexandria as quickly as possible.

There were teams of traveling salesmen in those days, among them the Egyptian representatives of foreign-owned pharmaceutical companies sent to capitalize on a rural population suffering from a parade of epidemics. Oscar frequently saw the same faces sitting on that train as it pulled away from the station, and he befriended several other young men, also Alexandrines. Most of them were Jewish or Coptic, he wrote, who spoke European languages well enough to be employed by the European companies and Egyptian Arabic at the native level necessary to sell foreign goods in the small towns where most Europeans dared not go at all. Most foreigners saw these towns as dirty, malaria-ridden, and lawless places, but that didn't stop them from taking their residents' money.

It became necessary for Oscar and his fellow traveling salesmen to coordinate their trips. Egypt had strong transportation infrastructure, compared with other nations in the Arab and indeed the entire world of the time, but navigating routes from trains to buses to shared taxis necessitated teamwork, even for the locals who spoke Arabic. One of the most remote villages among Oscar's forty-three was located a train ride to Mansoura, from where, with three Coptic Egyptian colleagues, he took a car to the bus stop on the edge of town and from there a series of buses. It was, altogether, a two-and-a-half-hour trip.

Many of the jokes and stories Oscar told came from these travels. They ran the gamut from funny to odd to frightening. In one of his stories, he found himself having breakfast in a town a few hours by train from Alexandria. The second floor of the restaurant where he ate wrapped around the interior of the building so that diners could see and shout orders to the open kitchen on the first floor. In the kitchen was a gigantic vat in which the chefs prepared the traditional Egyptian breakfast of *foul mudammas*—fava beans soaked in brine, cooked, smashed, garnished with eggs, and doused with lemon juice and olive oil.

That was all they served, their specialty. At a table on the second floor, an old man in a galabeyah was eating breakfast when suddenly one of his slippers fell into the vat. Oscar stopped eating, paid his bill, and left, disgusted.

In another instance, Oscar was sitting in a bus crammed with farmers. He was wearing his usual suit and tarboosh. Suddenly, he felt a tap, tap, tap on his shoulder. Looking up at the overhead luggage compartments, he saw a strange liquid, thick like syrup, dripping from a suitcase onto his tweed jacket. The suitcase belonged to an old woman sitting behind him, who said, "'Don't you worry an instant, my son. It's butter,' which meant it was 'good stuff,'" Oscar wrote in a Price Club notebook. To Oscar's mind, this was hilarious.

Other stories were more touching. In 1947, Egypt was battling a cholera epidemic. One of the first villages Oscar visited with his briefcase of sample medicines had erected a makeshift barricade against any outsiders, where the doctors were vaccinating everyone as Oscar arrived. Oscar had left his vaccination record at home and he had to submit to a second vaccine, with the rest of the village. He sat with the villagers for hours, chatting and waiting, and after he had visited the pharmacy, one of the families in the village, with whom he'd become friendly, fed him a home-cooked meal and asked him about life in Alexandria. Such is the Arabic culture of empathy and hospitality, in the countryside as in Alexandria. Oscar's sisters baked cakes, and to be caught by a guest without a nice cake or rice pudding with rose water to offer would reflect poorly on our whole family.

Oscar could have hit scores of pharmacies in just a week, but that's not the style of the Egyptian countryside, where the phar-

macist or doctor will likely invite you to have tea, and more
often than not a bite to eat—and even more often, several bites.
On one trip in 1948, Oscar traveled with two other pharmaceutical salesmen friends from Alexandria, both Coptic, to a
small village. The doctor there happened to have a full lamb
barbecuing behind his home, where he also saw his patients.
Happy to receive long-awaited drug shipments, he invited Oscar
to partake. Lunch with the pharmacist devolved into hours,
which turned into the rest of the day. "We spent most of the day
joking, eating," Oscar wrote. When the Alexandrian salesmen
spoke to Oscar, they suddenly addressed him not as Oscar but
as Boutros, the Arabic version of Peter. They were disguising
him as a Coptic Christian out of fear that his Judaism would
put the three of them in danger. "It would have been dangerous for me in the small villages during the Arab-Israeli War,"
he wrote. A coalition of Arab armies, including Egypt's, was
fighting Zionist soldiers, armed with munitions supplied by an
expansive network in the Soviet Union, Western Europe, and
the United States. Young Egyptian men were dying in defense
of the Palestinian people and Jerusalem's Al-Aqsa Mosque, the
third-holiest site in Islam. In the past, our family members had
occasionally hidden their faith at moments of hostility to Jews.
But so too had religious and other minorities across the Arab
world, including members of Muslim sects and Christians.
Oscar's Coptic friends reflexively hid his identity during their
trip to the countryside. But Oscar found himself taken aback by
this. In the course of these hours spent eating and chatting under
a pseudonym, Oscar realized that as a Jew, he was no longer welcome in these villages, where people felt powerless in the face of

Palestine's occupation and where their only means to fight back was to harm any Jewish person who crossed their path, even if that Jewish person was also Egyptian.

Meanwhile, in Tunis, the Germans had disappeared. After about three days of bombardment, when all of Tunis had been ordered to remain home or be shot in the streets, the inhabitants peered through the holes in their boarded-up and blacked-out windows to see the Allied forces. The Germans were declared prisoners of war and they were taken away, roughly six months after they had first arrived. "The occupation by the German came to an end— before doing too much harm to the Tunisian," Daida wrote. It was unlike either Daida or Oscar to focus on the negative. There is a sort of nobility to this silence; they did not want to speak of victimhood. Or perhaps, too, it was yet another consequence of living under a colonialism that made Oscar and Daida overlook any indignities. They were too concerned with surviving.

The British replaced the Germans, and many of them blatantly pursued local women, Daida remarked with disgust. She never went into detail as to why. The American soldiers she encountered left a better impression, which later served as one of the reasons to go to the United States. "All the empty lots around our neighborhood were turned into army encampments, occupied by the Americans," she wrote. "From time to time, in the evening, they had outdoor movies. Many times we were invited to watch the latest pictures from the U.S. Mostly they were musicals with a love story. I became acquainted with Diana [Dinah] Shore, Betty Grable, Harry James, Benny Goodman, etc. . . . and especially all the songs of the time—Bessame matcho [Consuelo Velázquez's 'Bésame Mucho'], Begin a Begin [Cole Porter's 'Begin the Beguine'], and others."

For the gregarious Boukhobzas, the war and its aftermath were a time for encountering all sorts of foreigners, whom they welcomed into their home. Sami, Daida's father, befriended a young Jewish—non-Arab—American soldier, Albert, a well-educated man who spoke French, and a Native American soldier, Chancey Pete, for whom Albert translated. Albert and Chancey Pete became fixtures at Boukhobza family dinners and parties, and when on furlough, they would stay at their home in a room with Daida's brother. Conversation with Chancey Pete enthralled the Boukhobzas, raising questions for them about the Native Americans the Boukhobzas had seen in American films. When she learned that he had a daughter, Daida knitted her a sweater, which he took with him when the Allied forces departed. It is possible that there was an element of survivalism in their choice to befriend the Americans and engage with their culture as they had engaged with that of the French. Perhaps after so many consecutive white conquests, the Boukhobzas knew they needed to befriend their occupiers to survive. Or maybe it was our own North African concept of karma. The money you spend on friends comes back double, Daida often told me, in the manner of a Jewish Arab Emily Post. The Boukhobzas were generally generous and, even in times of rationing, never starved.

As the dust from the bombardments settled and the sky over Tunis took on its familiar turquoise hue, life returned to normal and the Tunisians resumed their positions in the old order under the French, whose dominion of Tunisia endured for more than a decade after the end of the war. Daida's father was once again in charge of his small barrel-production factory. Ali was working a normal job and returned home to live with his family in the outskirts of Tunis, although Daida insisted that he was a member of our family. Daida's parents continued to encourage her to meet potential husbands, the candidates now slightly older and less attractive than before, for her prospects had diminished as she hit her mid-teens. Daida wanted to leave the endless laundry behind, but she knew that a husband and children would mean another sort of servitude. She found fault with all the matches the marriage brokers brought and she weathered her parents' shouting. Finally, her mother stopped prodding. Maybe she had reconciled herself to Daida's early-onset spinsterhood, or maybe she had just grown accustomed to Daida's housekeeping.

Daida's year was once again punctuated by a series of Jewish and Muslim holidays and a few other family celebrations. "The only birthday my family celebrated every year was that of my older brother," Daida told me. Guests at the birthday party dressed in traditional Tunisian outfits, or customized versions of them, somewhere between Orientalizing themselves and harkening back to a time when Tunisian clothes were the standard of elegance. Kamouna sewed sequins into a veil for Daida and prepared foods rich with meaning, stuffing fish with eggs and other symbolic treats to represent long life and abundance and guard her precious Youssef against the Evil Eye, for who would not be envious of such a son?

As a practical joke, Sami paid two men to dress in Tunisian royal regalia and to knock at their door at around nine in the evening. When Kamouna answered, they declared they were

there at the request of the bey. Perplexed and tipsy, Kamouna "was really trembling, running to serve them, but the two
men gave themselves away when they started laughing," Daida
wrote. At around midnight, an exhausted Daida retired to an
empty bedroom while the party raged on—such events were
meant to continue until dawn, if they could. Daida's father, who
felt ill, followed, entreating the partygoers to continue without
him. He lay down next to Daida and while they slept through
the laughter and the drunken shouting, she felt an intense fever
radiating off him from across the bed.

Early the next morning, and with little sleep, they went to
the family doctor, who had Sami admitted to a hospital, where
he would remain for an entire month. It was polio. Sami lost
the use of his legs and, soon after that, he lost the barrel business. There was no hope of successful treatment, let alone a
cure, in Tunis, the doctors said. For all the supposed benefits of
the French protectorate—the education, the new buildings, the
tramways—the best doctors and the latest medical advancement
remained in France.

Zionism is described by Zionism as a reaction to the constant
bigotry faced by all Jews everywhere always. The Zionist project reaped what the Alliance had sown in Jewish communities
throughout the Arab world—the view that the rest of the world
had continually brutalized us and that the only answer was to
unify with people beyond our immediate countrymen to form
an international Jewry as envisioned by European Jews. The
Alliance taught this in Tunis and even in the British colonies
like Iraq where the Alliance had operated schools. The Zionist

project simply redirected Jewish Arab attentions away from France and toward Palestine.

The Alliance and the Zionists were, at first, at odds. The Alliance had engineered an ouster of the old rabbinic leadership in Algeria, promoting the replacement of older rabbis with Alliance-friendly younger rabbis. The Zionists, most of whom at the outset were Jews of Germanic origin, then appeared to plot against the Alliance in much the same way, advocating for the replacement of Alliance-supporting community leaders with Zionist counterparts.[1] The Zionists and the Alliance were in a tug-of-war over the Jewish communities throughout the Arab and Muslim worlds. "Oriental Judaism became the chessboard on which the fight [between the French and German camps of colonial Jewry] played out," writes historian Esther Benbassa, whose research has focused on the Alliance and the history of Jewish people from Muslim-majority countries.[2]

Theodore Herzl, the man who turned modern Zionism into the movement that led to the foundation of Israel, was born to a German-speaking family in Budapest in 1860, the year the Alliance was founded. Budapest was then part of the Austro-Hungarian Empire, which was deeply hostile to France at the time, and Herzl believed that Germany, not France, should be the guiding light to world Jewry. He personally attacked the Alliance in his newspaper *Die Welt* (The World), claiming that it did not serve the interests of the international Jewish community but those of France.[3] The Alliance's top brass, for its part, attempted to undermine the Zionist organizations that sprang up in Europe, North Africa, and the Middle East, scoffing at the premise of Palestine and not Paris becoming the center of world

Jewry.[4] Where the Alliance had hoped to keep Jewish communities as integral members of their societies, operating as agents
of French empire, Zionism suggested that they would need to
leave their homes—for a destination in what the Alliance determined was a fundamentally backward Middle East. How could
the future of world Jewry aspire to such a lowly place and not
in their home countries, with attentions and allegiances turned
toward France? German, Yiddish, and modernized Hebrew
were the Zionist movement's languages, not French.

Early hostilities aside, it is crucial to note there was always
a Zionist—or at least Jewish nationalist—camp in the Alliance that took Zionism as a natural conclusion to the Alliance's worldview. One of the Alliance's founding members was
Charles Netter, an early proponent of a Jewish settler colonialism in Palestine, where he died in 1882.[5] Netter was convinced
that many of the Alliance's students in the Middle East would
adopt Zionism despite the conflicts between the two sides.[6] For
many Jewish Arabs, the Zionist project appeared to be a logical conclusion to the Alliance's project of unifying international
Jewry through victimhood. If the world's Jews were indeed unified by a common struggle against bigotry and existed as a transnational people, as the Alliance taught, then they clearly needed
to safeguard themselves from hatred with borders and a military.
"Had the Alliance, in its education, led the way for Zionism?"
Benbassa asks.[7] In the Jewish Arab experience, it most certainly
had. Zionism would have had a hell of a time convincing Oscar's
and Daida's communities without the Alliance and the ideas it
impressed upon their societies. Transnational Judaism was not
naturally intuitive to many Jewish Arabs. They weren't born

thinking that all Jews are one, even if the Bible spoke of a nation of Israel, and they weren't taught that by their communities. For many, this was a concept introduced by the Alliance. People who didn't practice a North African form of Judaism were considered by Oscar's and Daida's ancestors to be non-Jews to the point that the Jewish Italians who arrived in Tunis centuries before Daida's birth were seen by many Jewish Tunisians to be peddling an apocryphal, Christianized Judaism. A flavor of that old spirit of separation was passed down to Daida.

Oscar's family viewed Jewish Europeans in the same way. Oscar disapproved of my attendance at Ashkenazi synagogues. Once, we attended an Ashkenazi Reform synagogue service together, and Oscar commented, with distaste, that the congregants and the use of musical instruments on Shabbat more closely resembled the Christian Evangelists he'd seen on TV than anything he was accustomed to in Judaism. To be fair, such comments were in retaliation for what seemed to him to be the frequent Jewish European suggestion that Jewish Arabs knew less about Judaism than their counterparts in Europe. Judaism had originated, Oscar would remind us angrily, in the Middle East, not in Germany or Russia. In Egypt, Oscar resented the presence of Jewish refugees from Eastern and Central European nations, largely because they cloistered themselves off and viewed North African and Middle Eastern Jews, as well as Iberian and Italian Jews who had emigrated to the region, as inferior. Even if the Jewish Egyptians were wealthier and better educated, by Oscar's estimation, the Jewish Europeans never welcomed them in their circles. Organizations such as the B'nai B'rith of Alexandria, which was part of an international network of philanthropic groups launched by Jewish German Americans, pushed Zionism, touting the very same ideals of transnational Judaism that Oscar had first learned at École Harouche, which was linked by its founder to the Alliance. Were it not for the Alliance, Zionism would have had to work from scratch, convincing the likes of Daida and Oscar that they had more in common with Jewish Russians and Germans than the Muslim and Christian Arabs with whom they grew up and shared customs, a language, and a history.

In Tunisia, in 1920, only a decade before Daida's birth, about a dozen Zionist organizations—a hodgepodge of mostly European-administrated religious societies, charity groups, and media—launched the Fédération Sioniste de la Tunisie (Zionist Federation of Tunisia), which obtained the official recognition of the Tunisian authorities.[8] They did little, at the time, to encourage Jewish Tunisians to settle in Palestine. Instead, as Jewish Tunisian historian Paul Sebag describes it, theirs was a "Zionism without realization." In other words, they advocated for a new nation for European Jews without any intention of actually leaving their homelands.[9]

The sympathies of poorer Jewish Tunisians were more easily won at the time, according to Sebag. Those who had little instruction and maintained a traditionalist religious fervor were easier to convince of a Zionist project to fulfill Biblical prophecies of a Jewish return to Canaan, even if the Messiah had not yet appeared. But for all its activism, Zionism won few converts among the more affluent segments of Jewish Tunisian society, at least while Daida was still in Tunis. Only a small contingent of Tunis's educated class half-heartedly supported Zionism; in the tug-of-war between the Alliance and Zionism, the majority of Jewish Tunisians from the posher classes still looked to France.

The Alliance had also instructed the social elites in French supremacy, and in Oscar's Alexandria, until after World War II, few Jewish Egyptians were convinced of political Zionism and, if they were, they fell in the "Zionism without realization" camp that Sebag describes—they approved of the Zionist project but had no intention of emigrating to Palestine. Zionism in Alexandria was, as in Tunisia, little more than a series of social clubs. In the history of Alexandria that Oscar carried around the globe, Taragan paints a picture of the Zionist movement before the war in a section entitled "Literary and Athletic Organizations."[10] These social organizations met in the homes of committee members—the vast majority of whom had distinctly Jewish European, non-Arabic surnames like Schlesinger, Staraselsky, and Goldenberg—or at the Ashkenazi (Jewish European) Synagogue of Alexandria. The first such organization was Benei Zion (Sons of Zion), launched in 1908 by David Idelovitch, the second, Tseyerei Zion (Young Zion), started by Simon Zlottin. The membership of these two groups was comprised of youth "among the Russian immigrants" in Egypt.[11] Taragan writes that they were less about settling in Palestine than about repatriating "our unfortunate Eastern European brothers fleeing pogroms and persecutions."[12] They had little or no real personal implications for Jewish Egyptian lives.

Among the later generations of Zionist organization leadership, there are also a few Sephardi names among the committees and leadership of Egypt's Zionist social organizations, like Taragan himself, for instance, who was a member of the Sons of Zion.[13] At its earliest stages, Zionism had hoped to purchase Palestine from its Ottoman administrators. The Sephardi community was historically closer to the Ottoman Empire's leadership than its indigenous North African and Middle Eastern counterparts because of the sizable Jewish Spanish community in Istanbul, and so their support was especially important to the Jewish European Zionists living in Egypt and likely elsewhere.[14]

Socialists and communists—their exact numbers are unknown because their activism necessitated subverting colonial authorities and their supporters in the Egyptian government—opposed Zionism on the principle that they were not Jewish nationals but Egyptian nationals and that to build a state on religious principles would undermine the prospect of the eventual international workers' revolution, in which the Palestinians were also to participate. According to Jacques Hassoun, a Jewish Egyptian Marxist historian and psychoanalyst, "Communism and Marxism provided a coherent vision, a theoretically coherent possibility of being Jewish and Egyptian at the same time without any major contradiction, at least until the 1950s," when Egyptian authorities declared all Jews were Zionists and, driven by fear, many Egyptians began to embrace Israel as a potential refuge.[15]

As in Tunisia, Jewish Egyptian support for Zionism was divided along class lines. "In general, the Jews that became communists were either from the middle class or even the upper class. Very few poor Jews became communists. Zionists, on the other hand, were never from the upper class. They came from the middle or lower classes," Hassoun said.[16]

Oscar was uninterested in politics and even less interested in penetrating the ranks of the Jewish Europeans who had suddenly begun to invite the Jewish Arabs and Jewish Iberians and Italians who had long been in Egypt to join their cause.[17] And yet, in his last years in Egypt, Jewish friends introduced Oscar to HaShomer HaTsair (the Young Guard), a European-launched international Zionist-Marxist organization (at the time, people still believed socialism and Zionism to be compatible).[18] Oscar attended a few meetings, where he was instructed in the tenets of Zionism and its necessity for Jewish Egyptian youth, particularly as Arab society, knowing what Zionism meant for Palestine, grew more hostile to its own Jews. They would meet in private homes or in the recreational centers of synagogues, where leaders gave speeches and distributed flyers, and Oscar was brought around to the cause. When the time would come for his family to leave Egypt, Oscar set his sights on Palestine. France, which Oscar and his family had always looked to as a beacon of civilization, had lost its allure after the French Vichy government's wartime collaboration with the Nazis, and Jewish Egyptians no longer seemed welcome in their homeland. Only Palestine remained.

Oscar would frequently travel to the city of Tanta, which served as his base while he made treks out to several villages in Tanta's orbit. There, he would get a room at a hotel—a simple room with a bed, and a bathroom shared with other guests. The hotel owner was "a Greek" who Oscar never saw. The manager was Egyptian, a friend who always reserved a nice room for Oscar. The manager's religion is not mentioned in the Price Club notebooks.

In the run-up to the Arab-Israeli War of 1948, Oscar occasionally encountered some trouble visiting the villages around
Tanta, where everyone seemed to know each other. Once, on
a bus, a plainclothes police officer—"you recognized them very
easily," Oscar wrote—approached his seat.

"Where are you going?" the officer asked.

Oscar gave him the name of the village pharmacy.

"What are you?" the officer asked.

"I'm Egyptian."

"I know, but what are you?

"Oh! I am a Christian," replied Oscar (that's to say, Boutros).

"And what's the purpose of your visit?"

"To sell medicine to the pharmacy there."

"Wait there for me at the pharmacy."

When Oscar arrived, he was panicked and told the Muslim
pharmacist that he'd had some trouble with a police officer. He
didn't tell the pharmacist he was Jewish. Another traveling salesman, who was already there, overheard Oscar's story and said,
"Don't worry, I'll talk to the cop."

When the officer arrived, the salesman, who visited the
village more frequently and knew the officer well, explained
that Oscar was a friend, and the officer left. Then, while the
pharmacist was in the back room, the salesman who had saved
Oscar a night in a small-town Egyptian prison said in French, "I
know you're also Jewish." (French was spoken exclusively by the
Egyptian middle and upper class.)

The Jewish community in the Egypt of Oscar's youth had
never had to hide their faith, save from a small group of Muslim
fundamentalists. But as time progressed and tensions escalated,

subterfuge seemed to be the only way to live in Egypt, and the friendship of non-Jewish Egyptians became indispensable.

Oscar stayed in the hotel in Tanta countless times over the course of a year. At the counter, he and the manager would talk about each other's lives and Oscar's wartime adventures. Then, one day in 1948, the manager showed him a letter from the local chief of police. Do not allow Oscar Hayoun, a non-Muslim, to stay at this hotel, the letter read. The hotel's owner was also a non-Muslim, probably Greek Orthodox, but the police chief here meant Jew. "The manager had been my friend and was sad indeed to tell me this," Oscar wrote. "I was saddened by this and at a loss about my work in this town, probably the most important one with about 15 pharmacies."

In a development almost as improbable as a plot twist in an Egyptian film, a young porter at the hotel approached. "I know!" the porter said. "Come with me!" Oscar followed him across town, past the European edifices of the city's center, past the city's iconic, sprawling Al-Badawi Mosque, to a district of Tanta that Oscar had never seen. The two entered a pharmacy there, where "there was a druggist, a Lebanese or a Syrian, who was friends with the chief of police." In the back room, the pharmacist's friends "enjoyed opium," Oscar wrote.

The porter explained Oscar's troubles to the pharmacist. "Simple," the pharmacist said, "go next door and have a cup of coffee. When you're done, stroll by as if by chance. I'll call out to you to say hi, and you tell me how upset you are after what happened at the hotel." The pharmacist had called the police chief to stop by for a visit. Oscar did as he was told, and everything went as planned. "Come on, let this man do his job in peace," the pharmacist entreated the police chief, who in turn asked Oscar for his work papers to certify that he was an employee of an Alexandrine pharmaceutical company. Oscar dutifully obliged, and the police chief wrote, "Inspected," on the work papers and signed his name. "Thank you," Oscar said, referring to him with the royal honorific, "bey." "I called him bey because every official and especially a Chief with a capital C was treated by the people in those times as a bey like we say, or a king. A pasha, and this kind of officer enjoyed flattery. Although that chief may have been the son of a peasant, becoming the chief made him as a lord."

Oscar returned to Alexandria and told his boss what had happened. Before Oscar set out again the following week, his boss gave him a bottle of Coty cologne for the bey. "When I arrived in Tanta, I crossed paths with the chief of police [who] greeted me in a cheerful voice as if we had been friends for a long time. 'Hello, Mr. Oscar!' the chief of police said, and I gave him the cologne." Oscar continued to stay at the Tantawi hotel.

On the road, particularly where there was no bus or train, the only way to get from one point to another was to hail a ride in a shared cab. In the immediate aftermath of the Arab-Israeli War, all of Egypt was talking about what had transpired in Palestine, and in one trip he took in a shared cab, Oscar found himself listening to a conversation among the other passengers about how miserable the situation was. When one suggested that they should kill all the Jews, Oscar said, "Let's not talk of politics, but pray," and he recited one of a series of Muslim prayers that he had memorized for these circumstances.

After the creation of Israel, Jewish Egyptians had to fear not only the authorities, who had turned on them, but the entire population. Often during his last months in Egypt, Oscar encountered the same man who would just stare at him. Does he know? Oscar wondered.

"One day, we began to chat," Oscar wrote, "and everyone was talking about the war with Israel at the time, so I did everything to talk just about work and not about what was happening." The man went to the bathroom and asked Oscar to look after his belongings. Oscar glanced at his "season book," the booklet given to train travelers who purchased tickets at a monthly rate. "I saw his family name was Fedida, an Arabic Jewish name. When he came back, I said, 'Your name is Fedida! I thought you were a Muslim!' He turned to me and said, 'I thought you were a Muslim!'" They were both relieved.

What frightened Oscar on those trips to the Egyptian countryside around the time Israel was established on the ashes of Palestinian civilization had originated much further afoot. Anti-Jewish sentiment was growing in response to what was happening around the Arab world at the time.

Jewish Arabs had already begun to emigrate to Israel to increase the Jewish population there, even as the Israeli military was engaging in a campaign to raze Palestinian towns, killing hundreds and driving hundreds of thousands more from their homes. If there is little discussion of the Palestinian Nakba here, it is in the hope that you will endeavor to hear not me but Palestinians tell it. For too long, that story—of Palestine's past and future—has been told by non-Palestinians.

Jewish Arab colonists went to Palestine for a variety of reasons: sometimes it was out of fear of the rising animosity toward them in their homelands; sometimes it was out of a genuinely felt religious or political commitment to the Zionist project. Others were taken there in what many have called human trafficking by Zionist agents; they had no clue where they were headed when they were spirited away on buses and boats in the dead of night. Zionist agents were engaged in a multipronged effort to inspire Jewish Arabs to move to Palestine, sometimes even by firebombing Arab capitals and pitting those countries' national security apparatus against them. In the way that the Islamic State and similar terrorist groups have relished Western Islamophobia because it supports their dualistic, clash-of-civilizations world-view and supports their drive to draw more recruits, Zionists did nothing to stop the criminalization of Jewish Arab communities. Instead, they appeared to provoke it unabashedly, despite risking Jewish Arab lives. Even long after Oscar left the Arab world, a deluge of events continued to plant a wedge between Jewish Arabs and the societies in which they lived, who began to fear and resent their very presence.

What nuance there had been in Jewish Arab political identities very quickly disappeared under the onslaught of Zionist efforts in Arab states. In 1947, there was a violent clash in Cairo between the Zionists and the Anti-Zionist League, an advocacy group started by Jewish Egyptian communist Ezra Harari on decolonial principles and concerns that the colonization of Palestine would turn Egyptian society against Jewish Egyptians. King Farouk's government, however, determined that anti-monarchal communists were the greater concern, and the League was banned.[19]

Beginning in 1948, a year before Oscar left Egypt, the Israeli intelligence's Operation Goshen smuggled about ten thousand Jews out of the country into Palestine to bolster the number of Jewish settlers there.[20] The operation indicated the extent to which early Israeli intelligence had already infiltrated Egypt and other Arab nations. Zionist agents reportedly received instruction in codes transmitted on Israeli public radio, and many of the Jewish Egyptians traveled via Swissair to Palestine.[21] Once more, Europe proved central to dragging Jewish Arabs into a colonial project.

Daida's family felt themselves divorced from these international politics by more individual family concerns. Her eldest brother, Youssef, was the first of her family to leave Tunisia for France not long after the war, with the help of an uncle from the Bellaïche family who had already long established himself there. In Paris, Youssef, now Joé, managed, through his sheer charm and the education Daida's parents had provided him, to ingratiate himself into a circle of young, wealthy French people, the sort who frequented Paris's Oriental cafés and found Joé to be handsome and droll.

Many Jewish Tunisian families had applied for French citizenship under the protectorate; Daida's had not. Among the permissions Daida and her family needed to go to France was a passport, which proved difficult to obtain. In 1948, Daida and her mother submitted applications for their family's passports at the gendarmerie and were told processing would take at least a month, due to high demand. A month had passed when Daida returned to find the passports had not yet been processed. "From that day on, I was told to come tomorrow and tomorrow and many tomorrows passed with no passports ready," she wrote. "Finally, the door policeman told me, 'I saw your passports. They are ready. Come in the morning next day.'"

But the next day, the clerk said the passports still hadn't been processed. Daida asked the officer at the door, and he said, "I know the passports were ready, but they disappeared." He could not say anything more.

Meanwhile, Sami's health was declining. The once tall and jovial man was now hunched, gaunt, and dispirited. His health continued to deteriorate, and he was intermittently hospitalized. The need to emigrate became increasingly urgent.

"Go see the Ben Rhomdane family," Sami told Kamouna and Daida. Several members of the Ben Rhomdane family were involved in public affairs, not just in Mahdia, but in the Tunisian government. One in particular had been a childhood friend of Sami's.

Daida and Kamouna traveled from Tunis to Mahdia by taxi. It was the last time that Daida Boukhobza would see Mahdia, the town of her father—the last time she would hear the waves crashing against the back wall of her father's family home on the sea, where they stayed. The next morning, Kamouna and Daida went to the vast Ben Rhomdane estate. They were greeted at first by a domestic worker. "As soon as he heard who we were, he received us right away," Daida wrote, referring to her father's friend among the Ben Rhomdane. "We introduced ourselves and explained our situation."

The Boukhobza family did not customarily ask for favors; it is better to give in abundance, take nothing, and never find oneself in anyone's debt or the butt of anyone's joke, was the philosophy in their family as it was in Oscar's. When Sami's friend heard that he was ill and in need of help, he was eager to oblige. But on one condition. It was around 1950, and Jewish Tunisians were beginning to join the occupation of Palestine via France. "He asked us to promise that we were not going to Palestine, but to France—which we did." Daida had followed the Arab-Israeli War in the news with ambivalence. She had no personal interest in Palestine. She wanted to go to France. Daida viewed everything east of Tunisia that hadn't been influenced by the French as backward. Arabness, Judaism, Israel were irrelevant. For many young Jewish Tunisians like Daida, the Alliance had triumphed over the Zionists; Paris was the future.

Daida and her family agreed to Ben Rhomdane's promise, and he wrote them a letter on the spot. "As soon as we presented the letter [to the French authorities back in Tunis]—ten minutes after, we had all the [passports] in our hands," she told me. Such was the rule of the law in the colonies. It could be bent with a flick of the pen from a privileged few.

A few days later, an article appeared on the front page of the newspaper *La Dépêche Tunisienne*, revealing that the chief of police had for months been withholding and burning all passports bearing Jewish names. From the outset, the French authorities had made it clear that Jewish Arabs were unwelcome in France, where many opposed what they feared would be a postwar flood of North Africans trying to savor the fruits of empire.

By 1949, Oscar was determined that his family would move to Israel. His trips outside Alexandria, his run-ins with the police, had impressed upon him that hostility against Jews in Egypt was only going to grow. It wouldn't be long before it would reach Alexandria.

Like Daida's family, the Hayouns had not made any moves, even as Moroccan nationals, to gain French citizenship. Previously, when the French consulate had announced that all Moroccan nationals in Egypt were eligible, the family decided there was little point: Egypt was their home. Morocco, even though they ate Moroccan food and spoke a Moroccan Arabic dialect at home, was a place they had never been to. They were proud Egyptians. But the world they had known was changing very rapidly. In a world that had not even really begun to reckon with revelations on the Holocaust, Oscar and his family feared what a surge in anti-Jewish sentiment could do.

Oscar had heard that some Jewish Egyptians were traveling to Israel via Marseille. His father, Yaqoub, at first rejected the idea. This likely wasn't based on any sort of allegiance to Palestinian Arabs. He just thought it was absurd to leave Egypt, where the Hayouns had established themselves for generations. Moreover, Yaqoub's wife, Rosa, and his parents, who had lived in the small apartment behind the house on rue Zahra, were all buried in the Jewish cemetery in Alexandria, in Egyptian soil. How could he abandon them? For our family, not to visit the graves of loved ones would be a source of shame.

Yaqoub, who had visited the Jewish holy sites of Palestine while it was Palestine, considered Egypt, Morocco, and a great many places in the Arab world to be central to his faith. Restoring the Biblical nation of Israel without the Messiah was to take divine matters into human hands. It was hubris.

Before their departure, Yaqoub had encountered the Jewish Europeans who had fled the Holocaust for Egypt. He had
already experienced their preference for their own fellow Europeans and how they viewed local Jews. He foresaw being a
second-class citizen.

In the end, as news of anti-Jewish violence became more frequent, Yaqoub relented and agreed to move to Palestine. The
Hayouns found it necessary to bribe someone at the French consulate to give them fake Tunisian passports with a temporary
travel permit to France. It cost the equivalent of about $25 per
person for these documents, Oscar wrote in his notebooks in the
1990s. Cheap documents that would be confiscated by Israeli
authorities when they arrived in Palestine.

Egyptian auteur Youssef Chahine's classic 1979 film *Alexandria,
Why?* is set in the twilight universe of Oscar's Alexandria, the
golden city under British colonial rule. In it, the patriarch of
an Egyptian Jewish family, portrayed by the iconic Egyptian
Muslim actor Youssef Wahby, expresses doubts about Zionism:
How could a prominent Jewish Egyptian family dream of leaving Egypt? There is a fervor with which the Egyptian of any
faith loves Egypt. There were practical considerations, too: it
was during World War II, and the Nazis were gaining ground
against the British in northern Africa. The film understands
that, despite the devastation occupation would wreak on Palestine, the fear of the Nazi regime was overwhelming to the Jewish Egyptians. The family eventually moves to Israel.

The family's daughter, Sara, is portrayed by Naglaa Fathy,
who is a vocal Palestinian rights advocate. One character tells

Sara that he will travel to America to study film. He asks Sara if he might contact her brother, David, who has gone to the United States to study at a military academy. Sara does not respond, the implication being that David has become so brainwashed by Zionism that he won't associate with his old friends from Egypt. Sara has a child from an affair with a Muslim Egyptian. At the end of the film, Sara leaves Israel and returns to Egypt, when her lover meets their child for the first time, and remarks that his baby looks like a foreigner. Israel has made Egypt's children— the Jewish Egyptians—unrecognizable.

Oscar watched this movie when I was a child. I was somewhere in the same room, probably drawing or playing with toy cars or Pocahontas figurines. Oscar said nothing to me of this film. And he did not mention his own departure from Egypt to Israel in his Price Club notebooks. On his initial displacement, Oscar was virtually silent.

Some of Daida's extended family would never leave Tunisia. Others would leave decades later after the War of 1967 between Israel and the Arab states provoked more violence against Jews. Many of the family who moved to France retained their Tunisian citizenship or neglected to apply for French citizenship for reasons that were not immediately apparent to us. Perhaps it was the realization that our Tunisian-ness was more than just a detail of history or a cultural legacy that we recall in the music we play and the food we eat at our bar mitzvahs and weddings. It was everything we are, although less recognizable to us with each generation.

"I left all my toys to my cousins (I was keeping them to give to my own children)," Daida wrote. She had never imagined leaving Tunis. Perhaps she never did, in some parallel universe. I imagine her now, standing outside the Grand Synagogue on the former Avenue de Paris, now Liberty Street, on Yom Kippur with her husband and children, smelling an apple punctured with cloves in the shape of the hand of Fatima, or waiting for her husband to come home so they could break the fast.

With the little money they had, Daida's family purchased boat tickets to Marseille. "The trip on the boat took us two days and one night everyone on board was seasick, but my family and I were constantly on deck, looking at the sea. Many of the other passengers were young men on their way to Israel. They tried their best to persuade us to join them to no avail." And her life in Tunis came to an end. They arrived in Marseille and took the train to Paris, where her brother Youssef had already rented them a hotel room near Porte de Clichy.

"A new beginning," she wrote.

Oscar hung on for a while, carousing as though his days weren't numbered. He was a little older than thirty when he left Egypt, the age that I am as I write. He submitted his notice to his pharmaceutical company several months in advance. In the last weeks of his work, as he traveled from village to village, he had a companion, a younger man, also a Jewish Egyptian, also wearing a suit and tarboosh, learning the ropes of Oscar's job. Oscar taught his protégé the train and bus routes. He taught him to stay at the hotel at Tanta, to give the district chief of police a bottle of Coty when things went south, and not to sweat the small stuff—a little melted butter on the lapel hurts no one.

Three sisters from Cairo, the eldest named Lina and the youngest named Nadia—my mother's name—were visiting Oscar's neighborhood friends. Lina was a beautiful girl, and Oscar was a romantic. Even knowing that he would leave, he fell for the woman who'd represent his last bout of youthful lust in Egypt. He wrote her love letters, posted them in Alexandria for her to read in Cairo. To what end? Oscar knew he would soon leave the country and that Lina would remain. In his last months in Egypt, he took several trains down to Cairo to see Lina, likely not for sex. Lina was presumably a virgin from a high-society family, just Western enough to leave home for dalliances with a foppish young man in Cairene parks. Lina's religion was not mentioned in the Price Club notebook account of her. She was probably non-Jewish, because Oscar observed that while he was on his way out, she would surely stay. On one occasion, they were strolling through Zamalek, the wealthy district of Cairo, not far from her family's mansion, through the shade of its greenery at dusk. At a pastry shop, a young server girl exclaimed to Lina, "Oh, how beautiful you are!" And the words imprinted themselves in Oscar's mind, with a photo of this woman of Egypt, *bint beladna* (daughter of our nation, a compatriot), whom he would leave there. "In fact Lina was one of the most beautiful girls I ever knew. I had a photo with me of Lina, but it disappeared when I was with Daida," Oscar wrote.

Weeks before she died, Daida told me she had ripped and thrown away the photo of Lina, fed up with Oscar's Casanova tales of romance and debauchery. She told me with an expression like a gangster. And with that, she breathed a fiery pride

into my gut, which was not uncommon for Daida Boukhobza.
After he left Egypt, Oscar would correspond with Lina from
France, but eventually he married and stopped the letters. Lina
faded into a sea of forgotten faces from a land before time.

Before their departure, the Hayouns sold the home on rue
Zahra before the government could seize it. But that did little
to prepare the family for their journey. They were only allowed
to bring three hundred Egyptian pounds per person with them;
the rest had to be confiscated by the government. So they bought
some plain gold bangles and one bracelet in the shape of a snake
with ruby eyes. They planned to sell them abroad. They never
did; I wear one bangle today. I will die with it, all that's left, not
of our family fortune but of our family. I hope that the Egyptian
revolutionary government gave our family's money to a peasant family. Maybe it kept a child alive, and that child was the
great-great-great-grandmother of someone who will free our
Arab world, once and for all. Someone who will prove to their
children and theirs that to be Arab is a thing not of great sorrow
or of exile or of the past, but of progress and beauty and solidarity.

Two or three months before they departed, the Hayouns
rented a room in the home of a Jewish Tunisian woman whose
surname was Messika—of no known relation to Habiba Messika, the Jewish Tunisian star of Arabic song and symbol of Arab
national integrity. "Our balcony in the rented room was looking
at an open-air cinema where they were showing Arabic movies," Oscar wrote. "The good part of it was we got to see free
movies. The bad part was we had to see a movie 1,000 times—
the same movie." The last thing Oscar saw of Egypt was the one
that existed in those movies, the maddening repetition of the

same songs over the course of months. And within each song, a good line, dripping with agony, repeated twice, three times.

At the port, passing the authorities to board the *Adriatica*, an Italian ship to Marseille, where they would stop before continuing on to Palestine, the family signed documents revoking their citizenship, bequeathing their remaining assets to the government, and promising never to return. Oscar never wrote of these documents. He told me of them only once or twice, and never at length. Much as Daida promised never to go to Palestine—not by choice, but by circumstance—Oscar unintentionally kept his promise never to return to Egypt.

The *Adriatica* set sail. A pair of dolphins appeared to accompany the boat, hours into their departure, Oscar wrote, after they'd pulled away from Alexandria's harbor and all of Egypt and the Arab world shrank from view.

There in the middle of the sea, Oscar saw no land at all. For Oscar, who'd just signed away his nationality, this was the beginning of years of not just figurative but legal statelessness.

Much as the trajectory of our nation—Egypt and the Arab world surrounding it—the number of devastated possibilities is dizzying. Oscar was deeply handsome and, everyone remarked, had his father's voice when he chanted our Passover prayers and sang along to his old, scratched Arabic records, sitting in his chair, hand tapping against his armrest. Oscar could have been his generation's Mohammed Abdel Wahab, if not for the French, the British, the Alliance, the Zionists, 1948. I would, of course, not be here. But Oscar could have lived a marvelous life, if only he had stayed—if only he had been let alone by the Zionist project and allowed to stay. The Hayouns had left Morocco, but remained within the boundaries of the Arab world in Egypt, and the abroad that Oscar had imagined before 1948 was in Beirut, within their world. But now, he set off on a long road farther and further into the West. The Arab world was being made impossible for him and so many others.

In 1950, unknown parties bombed a series of Jewish community sites in Baghdad. Some, including Jewish Iraqis living in Baghdad at the time, believe that the attacks were perpetrated either by Israeli intelligence or other Zionists hoping to push Iraqis to leave for Israel.[22] Both the Iraqi government and the British Embassy to Iraq agreed that Zionist activists had perpetrated the attack.[23] Mordechai Ben-Porat, a native Iraqi born with the Arabic name Murad Kazzaz (like many Jewish settlers in Palestine, he took a Hebrew name), was an Israeli intelligence agent in Baghdad at the time.[24] Decades later, as an Israeli politician, Ben-Porat sued a journalist for suggesting he played a role in the attacks.[25] Historical sources differ on Ben-Porat's involvement, but by the time of Israel's founding, any number of Zionist-sympathizing organizations could have taken it upon themselves to engage in an act that would provoke Jewish Iraqi fears about remaining in their ancestral homeland.[26] Correspondence between Israeli intelligence agents, now public, indicate that those particular agents had no knowledge of the source of the attack, but Israel's newspaper of record, *Haaretz*, notes that this does not conclusively disprove official Israeli involvement in the attacks.[27]

One of the consequences of these attacks was that Baghdad legislated a Denaturalization Act allowing Jews to depart if they signed away their citizenship and their assets to the Iraqi government. The law paved the way for similar measures in other Arab nations with large Jewish populations, like Egypt, which were suddenly caught in the push and pull of their government and Zionist operatives taking cues from Israeli intelligence.[28] Over the next two years, in Operation Ezra and Nechemia—also dubbed Operation Ali Baba—hundreds of thousands of Jewish Iraqis were airlifted to Israel.

In 1954, at least nine Jewish Egyptians recruited by Israeli intelligence firebombed key locations in Alexandria and Cairo, specifically targeting foreigners. They apparently aimed to pin the attacks on non-Jewish Egyptian groups as part of Operation Susannah, which sought to sour the relationship between Egypt, Britain, and the United States. The operation's purpose was also to create unrest that would keep the British military on Egyptian territory at a time when it was preparing to withdraw, removing from the region what Israel considered to be a buttress against the Egyptian military.[29] Two of the nine operatives were hanged after a highly publicized trial that corroborated the view of many non-Jewish Egyptians that their Jewish compatriots posed a national security threat and that they had to be expelled from the country. The attacks "raised fundamental questions about their identities and loyalties," writes Stanford professor and noted historian on the Jewish Egyptians Joel Beinin.[30] While the trials appeared to still treat Jewish Egyptians as separate from Zionist Egyptians, that nuance began to fade in popular Egyptian understanding of its Jewish religious minority.[31]

In 1956, France and Israel solidified their alliance in the Suez Crisis, with Paris supporting Tel Aviv against Cairo in retaliation for Egyptian president Gamal Abdel Nasser's support of the Algerian movement for independence.[32] The Alliance would become a resolutely Zionist organization, and France and Israel's colonial interests intertwined. On the heels of the crisis, with Egyptian casualties far outnumbering the canal's Western invaders, the Egyptian government finally declared that all Jewish Egyptians were Zionists and had to be expelled or face imprisonment in concentration camps.[33] A small community of openly Jewish Egyptians remained (and still remain to this day). Others converted to Islam or pretended to come from Muslim stock. What the darkest hours of Arab history had not managed to do to the Jewish Arabs, the colonial project had done—these Jewish Arabs were no longer Jewish.

That same year, Algeria's independence movement, the National Liberation Front, sent a letter to Jewish Algerian community leaders, urging them to reject French imperialism.[34] It was a call that went largely unheard, and as the French ramped up their violence against Algerians fighting for their independence, the Jewish Algerians were classed with the French and targeted in several fatal attacks.[35]

In 1961, Israeli agents conducted Operation Yakhin in Morocco, whereby they paid Moroccan authorities to smuggle Jewish Moroccans to Palestine at a time when the nation was emerging from French rule.[36] Questions abound as to whether the Jewish Moroccans transported to Palestine were fully aware of what was happening and that they were essentially purchased from Moroccan officials for as little as $100 per person.[37] I've heard it from Israelis that the Jewish Moroccans had been heavily integrated into mainstream Moroccan society, and they only decided to leave because of a deeply felt religious attachment to Palestine. That's a trope that continues today that serves to gloss over signs of human trafficking, and it feeds the notion that the Jewish Moroccans were zealots who left to the holy land for God, while the Jewish Europeans left for the practical, scientific objective of building a safe haven for world Jewry.

In 1962 came a high-profile espionage case that appeared to underline the dangers of allowing Jewish people to continue to live in Arab societies. Eli Cohen—a Jewish Syrian from Egypt—moved to Syria, assumed a Muslim name, and befriended high-profile government officials, delivering intelligence to Israel that would prove crucial to the occupation of the Golan Heights.[38] Israeli intelligence depended on the physiognomy of the Jewish Arab in order to subvert Egyptian and Arab territorial integrity and autonomy. Cohen was eventually discovered and executed in Syria. In both the Egyptian Operation Susannah and Eli Cohen's Syrian plot, Israeli missions in Arab lands served multiple purposes: while they lasted, they supplied crucial military intelligence to the Israelis, and when they were foiled, the missions made it impossible for Jewish communities to continue to live in their homelands without being suspected of treason. Such was the effect of Zionist terrorism in the Arab world amid Israel's launch.

5

חושך / Darkness

From Marseille, Oscar and his family were bused to Saint-Chamas, a sleepy, picturesque French town without Alexandria's grandiose architecture and cosmopolitanism. Save for the few Roman ruins that it had in common with Alexandria, it was an unremarkable place where, decades later, residents would vote overwhelmingly for the extreme-right, anti-immigrant National Front led by presidential candidate Marine Le Pen.[1] The Hayouns didn't see much of Saint-Chamas. Before they had a chance to be tempted to stay, they were funneled—in Oscar's writing, it is unclear by whom, Zionist agents or the local authorities—directly into a relocation camp with other Jewish Egyptians from Alexandria, Cairo, and Tanta, who were en route to Palestine.

They were among the earlier Jewish Egyptians to leave Egypt. Many at the resettlement camp had only known the comforts of the middle and upper class, and for the first time, they had only a few hundred Egyptian pounds and a single suitcase to their names. They slept not in stately houses and apartment buildings, but in tents with the winds rattling the tarp as they tossed and turned in their cots and ate strange rations. "Nights were extremely cold although it was August," Oscar wrote. There had been harsh winds in Egypt—it was common practice to wear fresh newspaper inside one's shirt as a barrier against the cold—but there had been nothing quite like the Mistral of southern France, the wind that emerges like a ghost from the Mediterranean.

Finally the group was taken back to Marseille and, from there, to Palestine.

Oscar wrote little of what happened on their arrival in Haifa, but he did tell me. They were greeted first by Israeli authorities who sprayed them and their belongings with dichlorodiphenyl-trichloroethane, or DDT, an insecticide that some say can cause neurological disorders, depression, and anxiety in humans.[2] Many European new arrivals were also sprayed down with DDT, but the majority of those had emerged from concentration camps, where they had lived in subhuman conditions and in ramshackle transit centers with poor sanitation. Yaqoub, on the other hand, was a distinguished-looking man in Western dress who had lived in a stately home on the Mediterranean that was governed by our family's characteristic germaphobia. He had come from a brief stay in a transit camp with other such people. Imagine his shirt wet with chemicals intended to kill vermin. Imagine the beads of DDT on his glasses. Imagine him watching Europeans speaking languages he didn't understand as they sprayed his children. This was an image Oscar painted for me and my mother, Nadia, several times, with great anguish. It was a moment indicative of how Jewish Europeans viewed North Africans and indigenous Middle Easterners. For them, however much Egyptians bathed, their country was not the modern, cosmopolitan nation with an ancient history that it in reality was. A North African or Middle Eastern person, at their cleanest, was essentially seen as dirty. It is of course the case that no one— European or non-European—should be deloused like an animal with toxic chemicals. But the decision to delouse Jewish Arabs coming from regular homes in societies that never experienced a Holocaust was significant. Our homelands were the backward places of Ali Baba stories, teeming with lice and vermin. The Europeans had gleaned their worldview from Orientalist writings and their respective homelands' colonial policies. The way in which Zionism is portrayed by Zionists as the culmination of an age-old international Jewish struggle against anti-Semitism obscures how it is a continuation of colonialist white supremacy.

After spraying Oscar and his family with DDT, Israeli authorities confiscated their ill-gotten passports and forced them to exchange their Egyptian pounds for Israeli shekels, which were virtually worthless anywhere else.

Each of the new arrivals from Egypt was briefly interrogated by the Israeli intelligence in the first of a number of interrogations over the coming weeks. Oscar wrote, "They invited every one of us to answer some questions while our memory was still good, regarding all the military installations that we knew of, radar etc. It was interesting. They paid us a lunch plus some extra money enabling us to buy some chocolate bars."

Our kingdom for some chocolates. One of the Egyptian movies Oscar rented from our bootlegger in Los Angeles, newer movies featuring unknown stars with muttonchops and feathered bangs, was the 1978 classic *El-Saoud ila el-hawiya* (Climbing to the Abyss), which offers a fictionalized account of the life of Muslim Egyptian spy for Israel, Heba Salim.[3] Salim, from a wealthy Cairene family, studied at French schools and, entranced by the West, eventually moved to France, where she is hired by the Mossad to gather intelligence on Egypt's national security. At the close of the film, Salim is arrested and returned to Egypt on an empty plane. She sits in a window seat, dressed in the trappings of a high-society French woman. As she touches down in Cairo, the Egyptian intelligence officer handling her extradition points to the country below and says: "Those are the pyramids. And that's the Nile. This is Egypt, madame."[4]

That scene resonates with me in my reading of Oscar's interrogation on Egypt. In the film's account of her, Heba Salim had also sold Egypt for her French fur and colonized view of sophistication. Absent from the moment of Oscar's life when he was made to sell our homeland for a shack and some candy was our memory of poetic strolls along the Nile, the family photos before the pyramids.

By then, the Hayouns were living in a tent city, about an hour and a half south of Haifa by bus, in a place called Beer Yakov. They ate rationed food and awaited relocation to more permanent dwellings. "Imagine me having nothing to do after a busy life in Egypt. It was not a life in this place," he wrote. "I used to roam around the villages in the company of a younger boy looking for citrus groves, picking sweet lemons and oranges. All the groves were owned by Arabs who had fled." These were ghost towns pillaged and still unsettled by the invaders, the Palestinians who had grown those fruits either slaughtered or made homeless before their harvest.

One day, Oscar borrowed a bike and rode to nearby Ramleh, which shares a name with the seaside neighborhood Oscar called home in Alexandria. Perhaps that's why this town interested him. There, he found the remains of a city from which Zionist military commanders, Yigal Allon and Yitzhak Rabin, who was later known to the West as a venerable peacemaker, had driven out tens of thousands of Palestinians, killing at least several hundred.[5] The incident amounted to what some historians have called ethnic cleansing.[6] When Oscar arrived, only a few hundred Palestinian survivors remained.

Several listless months passed. There was no hope of employment, no immediate promise of relocation to a home where they wouldn't have to live in cramped quarters, and this propelled Oscar to leave Palestine and return to France. He fought bitterly with his father. Oscar was the one who had pushed the family to go to Palestine, and now he was leaving his father stranded with his daughters and their families out of what seemed to Yaqoub to be boredom. For Yaqoub, his son's departure was an act of flagrant selfishness, but Oscar argued that in France he could make money to send to his family and ship them the basic necessities they couldn't afford in Israel, even though the state paid to feed the people what rations it could afford in the camps.

Oscar was adamant and he obtained the necessary travel permits and left Haifa with the equivalent of $15 in his pocket, he wrote in the 1990s. Back in Marseille, for the first time in months, he wasn't corralled into a resettlement camp but walked about town as he used to in Tanta and Mansoura. Oscar always believed in the curative power of a meditative evening walk, in seeing the world on foot. Now, he was racked with guilt for leaving his family behind. Whatever bitter words his father had used to convince him to stay swirled in his mind.

"I spent the first night in a hotel room full of bed bugs," he wrote. "I couldn't sleep all night and I cried—this was the first time away from home and all my family. I panicked. The next day, I was ready to start my new life, and a few days later I went from Marseille to Paris." For Oscar, to admit that he cried was not a light matter.

In Paris, Oscar stayed with a friend from Egypt until he found a room in a slum just outside Paris—the sort where many immigrants from the African continent continue to live today. Eventually he found work selling textiles in an outdoor market. At night, he played the Egyptian Cairophone records he had brought with him from Alexandria. He had no money, no indoor plumbing, but somehow he managed to get his hands on a record player, and he'd lie in bed at night, smoking cigarettes and listening to the music, staring into nothing.

In Paris, Daida, her parents, and two of her three brothers lived crammed into a single room at a residential hotel on rue Tholozé in Montmartre. To wash, they paid to use the public baths and, at other times, they cleaned themselves with a rag over the sink in the shared toilets located on every other floor. Like Oscar's family, even on arrival in Palestine, they were militantly tidy people. Youssef, the beloved eldest son, lived on another floor, in a larger room than the rest of his family, with a stove the family used to cook food that they would take back to their floor to eat. The grocery shopping had to be done on a daily basis, not just because there was no refrigerator but because rats would get to any food they didn't immediately eat.

On one occasion, Kamouna broke into sobs when she learned Youssef, who had only just found a job, would have no money until he received his first paycheck at the end of the month. How would her family eat? Guigui, Daida's baby brother who was about seven years old, went to a nearby Algerian grocer and told him that his family had newly arrived from Tunis and, with a father suffering from polio, they would go hungry. His mother was in tears, he said. The grocer asked Guigui if he could speak to Kamouna. He proposed to her that she buy food for the month on credit, no interest. Like Judaism, Islam prohibits usury.

Montmartre itself was as picturesque as an American caricature of Paris: cobblestone streets, cafés flanked by boutique booksellers selling special editions of Oscar's beloved *Les Misérables*. Just out of the view of the Sacré Cœur, the iconic church overlooking the neighborhood, there was the Moulin Rouge, with its burlesque dancers doing the cancan, and its little sister, the Moulin de la Galette dancehall. There were streetwalkers and struggling artists, and there were pockets of immigrants from France's African colonies, trying for a small piece of an economy built on their backs. For their part, the Boukhobza family wanted treatment for Sami's polio.

On their first day in Paris, Daida and Guigui wandered Montmartre. Dizzy with the lights and other sensory stimulation,

WHEN WE WERE ARABS

they kept walking until they found themselves far from home
and lost. Daida stopped to ask a man on the street for help. "Go
check a metro map," he shouted, without stopping. "Since that
day, I learned never to ask for directions in Paris," she wrote.

There were other North Africans living at the hotel in Montmartre, but the most colorful of the Boukhobzas' new neighbors were the *Français de souche* (French by origin), white French
people. There was an escort in one room; a lesbian couple, one
much older than the other, who always seemed from what they
could hear through the hotel's paper-thin walls to be fighting and pleading with each other; and an old woman who was
mentally ill and wandered the halls, frequently knocking on the
Boukhobzas' door to mutter incomprehensible things. *Allah yis-
ter* (God help us), Kamouna, Daida's mother, would say, shaking
her head or throwing her hands up after she had encountered
one of her neighbors. But if the managers of the hotel had been
particular about their tenants, they would never have rented to
the Boukhobzas, who still carried with them the perfume of
Tunis. Such is the racism in France against the peoples it had
colonized. Cost of living, unequal opportunities, and denied
rental applications force immigrants to cling together, and they
are then blamed for segregating themselves.

Eventually, Youssef found Daida a job at a candy factory, where
she worked with a handful of other young women, mostly white
French. A separate team molded orange-flavored chocolate in
the shape of orange segments, and it was Daida's job to count out
a given number of segments, assemble them into a ball, and wrap
them in a piece of orange foil. Food was scarce, and there was
no money for sweets, so when she started at the factory, Daida

would sneak a few chocolate segments into her apron pocket and eat them for lunch. Soon enough and for the rest of her life, she came to hate chocolate, even just the smell of it.

Unsurprisingly, the boss at Daida's factory took advantage of the young women, paid them miserable wages, and counted their bathroom breaks. All the money from the job went to Daida's family, except for a metro pass and an occasional croissant for breakfast. Daida had a single dress that she washed and hung up each night and ironed in the morning, as well as a set of pajamas, and a coat. Tunis placed no restrictions on what Jewish Tunisians could take with them, but this was all she had brought in the way of clothes. Other than that, she had a few photos from Tunis, a *warka* pan to make the dough for Tunisian *brik* fritters (a rather large object), and a Passover prayer book (Passover had been her favorite holiday) with translations in Jewish Arabic and French that is now falling apart in a Ziploc bag in L.A.

One evening, Youssef asked Daida to accompany his girlfriend to the *brit* (bris, as it is better known in the United States) of a friend's son. Youssef couldn't attend, and he pitied his little sister who worked long hours for the family. Youssef's friend was Daoud, a Panamanian of Jewish Palestinian and possibly Egyptian origin. Having lived most of his life in Panama and speaking French with a thick accent, he still spoke Arabic as a first language and that was the language in which he conversed with Daida. Daoud had just had a son with a much younger Jewish Tunisian, a beautiful woman but, according Daida, from the *hara*, the poor and very traditional indigenous Jewish community of Tunis. Most Tunisians who had left by that time were middle- and upper-class families who could afford a move to

France. From a poor family, the girl's prospects were slim so she'd had little choice but to marry Daoud, who was amiable and wealthy, if not young.

It was at the party that Oscar met Daida. Oscar, as it so happens, had encountered Daoud through mutual acquaintances, and they were fast friends. Oscar was struck by Daida's beauty when he saw her, a small North African factory girl more than a decade his junior, sitting alone in the single frock she had for all occasions. With her black curls, full lips, and large eyes, she resembled many of the women in the Egyptian movies he loved. As the guests chanted the traditional Jewish Arabic *taalil* songs, blessings in Arabic mixed with Hebrew, and everyone became fairly inebriated on Ricard, a French anise liquor, Oscar asked Daida to dance.

Within a few hours, Daida knew that she would marry him. "I met an Egyptian, and we're getting married," she told her mother that night when she returned home. "My mother thought I am crazy," she wrote. But Daida wasn't crazy. It wasn't love at first sight. Daida was born too mentally strong for such delusions. She liked Oscar, but more than that she wanted to leave her parents' home. By then she would have married anyone, and she would have learned to love him in the way many women of her generation learned to love men to whom they were matched. But she was always adamant to note that she hadn't been matched. She had decided when she would marry and whom. To Daida, reflecting on her life, this was a victory.

Days later, a great-uncle, a half brother of Kamouna's who was living in Paris, welcomed Daida's parents, Daida, and Oscar to his apartment, which was more presentable than the Boukhobzas' since he owned a small business. Daida served tea and remained silent as her elders arranged her future, as was the custom.

Daida had some trouble understanding Oscar's Egyptian Arabic at first. When she asked if he would like more tea, Oscar said *bidoun zyada*, which means "no more." Struggling to understand him, she heard *bizyada*, "more," and continued to pour, even as Oscar reflexively covered his glass. Daida mistakenly poured some hot tea on his hand, but he was not seriously burned. The others laughed, nervously. How well would they fare as newlyweds if Daida couldn't even understand him enough to serve him a cup of tea?

Daida's parents approved of the marriage, most likely because it meant one less mouth to feed and one less body in that cramped room at the hotel. And Daida, at nineteen, was no longer in her prime, at least in Tunisian culture. Still, they very clearly disliked Oscar. Her parents, until their deaths, even when Oscar and Daida moved into their own apartment at the same hotel in Montmartre, never referred to Oscar by name. They called him "the Egyptian," even to Daida's face. Decades later, when Daida visited France, her nephew, a young child whose parents were both Tunisian, exclaimed, "You're the one who married the Egyptian!"

On Oscar's side, his father sent him a letter in Arabic urging him not to marry Daida. For Yaqoub, the marriage was a sign that his son would likely settle in Paris for good, never to return to Palestine. He wanted desperately for the family to be reunited. "Tell her that you are coming back to visit your family for an indefinite period," he wrote. "And I suggest you destroy this letter after you read it." He wouldn't chance causing a rift with a woman who might, against his will, become his daughter-in-law. He must not have known that Daida never learned to read the Arabic alphabet.

They were, however, married a few weeks after they had met. Oscar saved Daida from her factory and her family and, in turn, Daida's uncle did Oscar a favor. Oscar didn't have French citizenship, not even through marriage to Daida, who had obtained a passport and a French residency permit but wasn't a citizen. Oscar had by then overstayed his work permit and faced having to return to Israel. But Daida's uncle wrote a letter explaining to the French authorities that Oscar was one of his employees, and Oscar was allowed to stay.

Israel's Polish-born founding father and first prime minister, David Ben Gurion, was especially vocal in his denigration of Jewish Arabs, particularly North Africans. He referred to the Moroccans, like Oscar's family, as "primitive" and as "savages."[7] In one instance, Ben Gurion spoke of how "the immigrant from North Africa, who looks like a savage, who has never read a book in his life, not even a religious one, and doesn't even know how to say his prayers, either wittingly or unwittingly has behind him a spiritual heritage of thousands of years."[8]

In Israel's first few decades, its leaders repeated calls against Jewish Arabs, and their hatred seemed to infiltrate the Israeli mainstream, which they maintained should uphold Eurocentrism, or white supremacy, at all costs. Israel's founding father Abba Eban, a South African of Lithuanian origin, said that "one of the greatest apprehensions that afflict us when we contemplate our cultural scene is the danger lest the predominance of immigrants of Oriental origin force Israel to equalize its cultural level with that of the neighboring [Arab] world."[9]

Golda Meir, who served in the nation's top offices before becoming prime minister in 1969, was similarly transparent in her distaste for Jewish Arabs and her preference for Europeans. The more closely they resembled her own eastern European roots—Meir was born in Kiev, when it was part of the Russian Empire—the better the new immigrants were. In a 1964 address in Britain she said: "We in Israel need immigrants from countries with a high standard, because the question of our future social structure is worrying us. We have immigrants from Morocco, Libya, Iran, Egypt and other countries with a 16th century level. Shall we be able to elevate these immigrants to a suitable level of civilization? If the present state of affairs continues, there will be a dangerous clash between the Ashkenazim who constitute an elite and the Oriental communities of Israel."[10] This attack on Jewish Arabs and other non-Europeans became a guidepost for her administration in the early 1970s, when she reportedly commented that new waves of Russian émigrés were "real Jews" and her administration showered them with benefits withheld from Jewish Arabs and other non-Europeans.[11]

Indeed, their total disdain for all things Arab, a disdain necessitated by their imperative to build their fledgling society atop an Arab one, manifested itself in the allocation of public resources, at a time when jobs and housing were decided by the state. Many Jewish Arabs were left to languish for years in *maabarot* (transit camps), while European newcomers were quickly settled in affluent neighborhoods. Enough time passed without Israeli leadership seeking to uplift the Jewish Arabs from tents and shantytowns that eventually these became so-called development towns, where many Jewish Arabs remain today.

Jewish Arab stereotypes persist in the films still accepted as Israeli classics today. In a childhood Hebrew class, teachers showed us a film released in 1964, a few years after Yaqoub's death. *Sallah Shabbati* stars *Fiddler on the Roof*'s Chaim Topol, who, like all but one of the actors portraying Jewish Arabs in the film, is of European Jewish origin. Topol's character, Sallah, sounds and acts like a caveman who, while sometimes a lovable oaf, is uneducated, unclean, abusive to his wife and children, and unconcerned with living in cramped squalor. He is also criminally lazy. He is content to play backgammon with his fellow Jewish Arabs in the shantytown where the pioneering, hardworking whites have settled them.

Sallah Shabbati's depiction of our arrival in Israel, the *maabarot*, and subsequent North African and Middle Eastern enclaves where we lived are portrayed as Frantz Fanon describes the colonizer's imagination of the colonized—squalid dens of barbarianism. "The colonized's sector, or at least the 'native' quarters, the shanty town, the Medina, the reservation, is a disreputable place inhabited by disreputable people. You are born anywhere, anyhow. You die anywhere, from anything. It's a world with no space, people are piled one on top of the other, the shacks squeezed tightly together. The colonized's sector is a famished sector, hungry for bread, meat, shoes, coal, and light. The colonized's sector is a sector that crouches and cowers, a sector on its knees, a sector that is prostrate. It's a sector of niggers, a sector of towelheads."[12]

Eventually, Sallah's daughter Habouba is lucky enough to marry a white Jew; integration is possible through assimilation. Sallah's son of marrying age, however, doesn't find a white woman; that would have been unacceptable in Israel at the time. In Judaism, religion passes through the mother's line, but ethnicity—Ashkenazi-ness, Sephardic-ness, Mizrahi-ness, as Israelis describe it—is typically inherited through the father, almost as a patriarchal retort to the faith itself. For a white man to marry a Jewish Arab woman not only fulfills an Orientalist appetite for dominance, it effectively waters down the Jewish Arab line. At the same time, the young Jewish Arab male is taught to fantasize about integrating into this society; he's taught to appreciate white beauty, but in the end it's a cocktease that keeps him compliant. "The gaze that the colonized subject casts at the colonist's sector is a look of lust, a look of envy," Fanon writes.[13] "Dreams of possession. Every type of possession: of sitting at the colonist's table and sleeping in his bed, preferably with his wife." The discrimination and racism that defined these early days in Israel persisted in large part because they were ingrained by its founders in the nation's society and economy and transmitted from generation to generation. Yaqoub and his children may have heard the Moroccan song, in the traditional Moroccan *shaabi* (folk) style, called "Lishkat Avoda" (Employment Agency, in Hebrew), one that explains that generation's feeling of being left on society's margins. The

song was penned in both Moroccan Arabic and Hebrew in the
1950s by Jo Ammar, a Moroccan émigré to Israel:

> *I came to the employment office.*
> *The man asked, "Where are you from?"*
> *I said, "Morocco."*
> *He said, "Get out of here."*
> *An Ashkenazi went to the employment office.*
> *[The agency] asked, "Where are you from?"*
> *[The Ashkenazi] said, "From Poland."*
> *[The agency staff] said, "Come on in. Come on in."*[14]

There are also allegations of even more horrifying acts: pro-
grams, potentially sponsored by the Israeli government, to
remove the newborn babies of thousands of Jewish families with
origins across the Arab world—from Tunis to Aden—and to
place them with Jewish European families. The Israeli government has denied that this transpired and blocked a push by the
children removed from their families to find their birth parents.[15] Those children who were only removed from their parents were perhaps the luckier ones. Israeli press reports in 2017
revealed that some Jewish Arab children were used for medical
experiments.[16] Among those experiments was one that aimed to
prove that Yemeni children had African blood.

This was the Palestine that awaited Oscar. This was why, as
bad as things became in Paris, Oscar stayed put.

Years passed with the Hayouns split between Paris and Israel.
In the early 1950s, at the onset of the war for Algerian independence that would help unravel the French empire, it seemed

there was no way for Oscar—with an Arabic surname, a North African countenance, and an Egyptian accent—to find work in Paris to support his new bride and, about a year after their marriage, their first child, a daughter named Rosy after Oscar's mother. While Daida became a homemaker, Oscar continued to sell textiles at a street market. He was among the best-educated of the stall workers, a polyglot with an Egyptian French high school diploma, years of experience selling pharmaceuticals, and a certificate proving his service to the British.

Meanwhile, the Israeli authorities had settled his father and sisters' families in a moshav—a collective agricultural settlement—where Yaqoub complained that the Jewish European directors reserved the most dilapidated, confined living accommodations for the Jewish Arabs.

With what money Oscar made beyond covering the bare necessities of day-to-day life in Paris, he would ship Yaqoub groceries, household items, and medicines that the new Israelis found scarce. Oscar often sent goods for Yaqoub to sell to his neighbors. On one occasion, it appears from Yaqoub's letters, written in Arabic on Israeli airmail stationary, that he was having some trouble with the delivery of some sort of oil. Then Yaqoub wrote again, saying the functionaries had asked for the brand of the oil and a shipment number, assuming that Yaqoub was trying to claim someone else's delivery. "You know that if it were a [Jewish European], they would have tossed the package to me from a window on the second floor," he writes, with a sense of exasperation frequently echoed by his son in our conversations decades later. "I will get the bottle soon, InshaAllah [God willing], but you have to tell me the name of the make, if you remember it."

Between the money generated from this and other schemes over the course of a few years, Yaqoub purchased a modest home in a Tel Aviv suburb for his family. For him, to have everyone together in the same building and a quiet place to recite psalms was all that mattered.

Not long after that, Yaqoub suffered a debilitating fall, not unlike his own father. He wrote to Oscar: "If you moved here, I would certainly be a lot better." Oscar's sister Viviane entreated her brother in a separate letter, "With your certificate from the British, you would surely find work here!" In reality, employment as a young Jewish Arab male was not only uncertain but unlikely, and Oscar's family knew it. "These lands of Israel are not for the [Jewish Arabs]," Yaqoub wrote in 1953. "It's for the Yiddish. They work—the husband, wife, and children—where in a [Jewish Arab] family of 7 or 8, not a single one can find work. And the taxes [on food and other necessities] keep going up. One day bread was sold at 7 piastres, and the next it was 18." A piastre, it is important to clarify, was not an Israeli but rather an Egyptian monetary unit, and "Yiddish," the language spoken by some Jewish European communities, was how Yaqoub referred to Jewish Europeans. Yaqoub described the news touting the advancements made by the Israeli administration to develop its fledgling state as "false propaganda," when in reality Jewish Arabs were being systematically degraded. In an earlier letter, he wrote: "There is not 1 percent of [Jewish Arabs] who like living in Israel and we wait for the whatever little chance we have to be able to leave. After having come to the Holy Land, we prefer our cities and our countries."

The North African community in which Oscar and Daida lived in Paris also found itself marginalized, and as a result they embraced Arabness with less reserve and self-loathing. They went to watch Arabic movies, they sat in Arabic cafés where they listened to live music, and their friends were almost exclusively Arab: Muslim, Christian, and Jewish. Oscar and Daida themselves were never politically active and would discourage me from activism—but at this time, they were acquainted with communist activists, both Arab and non-Arab, who advocated for the freedom of France's colonies, and there was an aura of excitement around North Africa's impending independence.

Many of Oscar's friends at the time were Algerians and other North Africans, some Muslim, some Jewish, who were also eking out a living there, and from them he learned to support the cause of Algerian liberation—ironic, perhaps, since he never expressed any strong feelings about the need to liberate Palestine. Were Algerian lives more worthy because their customs, their food, their language, their particular history of occupation, their faces more closely resembled our own? Or was Oscar attracted to the Algerian cause by fashionable Parisian progressivism of the likes of Jean-Paul Sartre and Simone de Beauvoir, who also envisioned freedom for Algerians but supported the occupation of Palestine?[17]

When I was little, they told me a story—one that seemed too wild to be true—of how the Paris police rounded up a crowd of protestors against the occupation of Algeria and shot scores of them in the courtyard of a police commissary, disposing of their bodies in clandestine graves. It wasn't until the fiftieth

anniversary of the massacre that, reading about it, I realized this
hadn't been a tall tale.[18] How Oscar and Daida knew of this and
whether they knew any of the dead, I never thought to ask.

In 1954, Oscar and Daida decided it was time to visit his family
in Palestine and for Daida to meet her in-laws. They had been
married for a couple of years and were living in the residential
hotel in Montmartre with Daida's family, in an apartment on
another floor. Theirs was a single room for what had become
a family of four: they had Rosy, nicknamed Rozeza, and now
my mother, Nadia, or Nadina. (Oscar resigned himself to never
having the son he wanted and he stopped trying.) Both Rosy
and Nadia were born stateless, since at the time Tunisian citizenship could only be inherited from the father.

They decided to go for several weeks. Daida went first, traveling by boat from Marseille to Tel Aviv with Rosy. Oscar
followed a few weeks later, with Nadia. Daida's father- and
sister-in-law, Yaqoub and Viviane, picked Daida and Rosy up.
Yaqoub embraced Daida and told her in Arabic that his son
had married a woman the color of a peach. From this moment,
Viviane, who had a darker complexion, appeared to resent her.
One evening, Viviane showed Daida a photo of a Christian
Syrian woman with whom Oscar had a fling in Egypt. How
beautiful she was! Viviane exclaimed. What she had meant,
Daida told me, was that the Christian Syrian looked more pass-
ably European than Daida.

Viviane also seemed to be embarrassed to be seen with a
Tunisian. Egypt was the epitome of sophistication, not Tunisia,
not Algeria, and not Morocco. But then Daida felt the same of

Tunisia. And a great many other Jewish Arabs have expressed to me the same feelings of exceptionalism for their own ancestral homelands and derision for other Arab nations with similar histories, languages, and families. For many, a unity of Jewish Arabs was not intuitive. Viviane's own grandfather had moved his family from Morocco to Egypt, and Morocco was a part of Viviane's identity, but she had tucked it away in the past where Israeli society couldn't find it. When Viviane introduced Daida to her friends—mainly Egyptians, some of whom the Hayouns had known since Egypt, some since the resettlement camp at Saint-Chamas—she introduced her not as Daida Boukhobza, because Boukhobza was a North African Arabic surname, but as Daida Levy. Daida found this odd. Hayoun is also an Arabic-language North African name, but it was perhaps the distinctly Arabic prefix *Bou-* of Boukhobza that stopped her from using it.

Before Oscar's arrival with Nadia, Viviane traveled with Daida and Rosy by bus to Jerusalem. Standing in line at the bus depot in Tel Aviv, Daida saw one of her father's brothers waiting for a bus for the northeast city of Tabarriya. He was wearing traditional Tunisian clothes—the vest, draped *sarouel* pants, and the chechia hat. "*Aami* [Uncle]!" she shouted in Arabic. Heads turned. It was like a scene from a Tunisian soap opera. Daida embraced her uncle, tears in her eyes, and his wife and children, all dressed in the clothing of their town, Mahdia. "Imagine what it was for me to see a familiar face on such a trip," she wrote of her experience in a strange place where she felt so uncomfortable with her new in-laws. But before they could talk at length, Viviane pulled her back into the line of people waiting to go to Jerusalem and told Daida explicitly that she had embarrassed her in public by speaking to this strange man. "He's my uncle!" Daida exclaimed. But Viviane was still upset. Daida promised her uncle she would look him up. On the bus Viviane remarked "how old fashion and backward my relatives were," Daida wrote. That was the last time Daida ever saw her uncle and his family.

In our home in Los Angeles sits a photo—enlarged from the original—of Viviane's grandfather Issrail, wearing a tarboosh, a galabeyah with a sash, and a cloak. "Look at the photo of your grandfather's grandfather!" Daida would punctuate this story by saying. "He was dressed completely in the Arabic style!" What she meant was that although they are Tunisian, vests and pants aren't as much of a departure from sensible Western clothes as a galabeyah. What Daida didn't know was that as soon as Issrail died, his children demolished his small apartment behind their home and everything he owned save the photo we have of him in Los Angeles today.

On that trip to Jerusalem with Viviane and Rosy, Daida saw a group of Palestinian Bedouin men staring at the bus from a distance. No doubt they saw a bus transporting Jewish settlers from one colonized city to another. At least in Tunis, the colonizers remained in the big cities. Here there was nowhere that was safe from the forced migration and massacres that Israel used to gain more land. As the bus approached Jerusalem, Daida's mind returned to Tunisia, where her father would take her to his Bedouin friends in the desert, from whom he purchased food. The Bedouin here stared at her in anger, Daida wrote. "It was not as in Tunis. We were the enemy now." She had become one of the colonizers.

When Oscar arrived, Daida was relieved. The atmosphere in the house was tense. Try as she did to be liked, Oscar's sisters did not approve of her. At one point, Viviane asked Daida to explain to her Egyptian friend why her son should not marry a Tunisian. Daida responded with silence, perplexed by this hostility.

Oscar arrived in Tel Aviv. Yaqoub embraced him, but there was still much resentment for Oscar having left. They bickered; until Oscar and family left, they were continuously bickering. Oscar had carried with him several packages for his father's hustle selling French luxury items to early Israelis. Chief among them was an expensive, baroque crib requested by a friend's acquaintance. When Oscar delivered it, he arrived in an opulent home. The Jewish European woman who had requested the bassinet was cooking hamburgers and onions and it smelled delicious. As Oscar assembled the crib, she asked, "Your family is Moroccan?" Oscar replied, "Yes, but from Egypt." The woman remarked that she'd heard there were a great many North Africans living in France, as in Israel. Your family must go to the Arab synagogue nearby, she said with an air of derision. She didn't offer him any of the food she was cooking or even a glass of water, Oscar said, and to his Arabic sensibility the absence of hospitality, especially after he had lugged the bassinet across the Mediterranean, was an affront. Oscar finished putting together the crib, took the money, and left. He believed that the woman had acted the way she did because she needed to feel superior to a man who lived in France. But she had nothing on him; he was from Paris. In his mind, it was better to live in a slum in Paris than the finest home in Tel Aviv.

At that time, to call a Jew from an Arab country an Arab was to insult them for being uncivilized. To link Jewish Arabs to the conquered Palestinians was to question whether they deserved to live in Israel, and this further estranged Jewish Arabs from Arabness. The French had dispossessed the North Africans of their Arabness by claiming they were part of a distinct Israelite nation. The Israelis dispossessed the Jewish Arabs of their Arabness by weaponizing the term in the same way that the Yiddish insult *schwartze*, black, weaponized dark skin and encouraged Jewish people of color to make themselves as white as possible, both physically and figuratively.

Later photos show Viviane, her hair dyed an ill-suited, unnatural blond. To her mind, as to the minds of so many non-Jewish Egyptian and Lebanese and Tunisian women I've encountered, this blond would exonerate her from her insufferable brownness and all the untouchable things she was made to believe were associated with it.

Ben Gurion's view of Moroccans as primates didn't die with him. When I was a young child in Hebrew class in Los Angeles, our teacher taught us a song composed in 1966 by Polish-Israeli songwriter Haim Hefer for the musical *Kazablan* (Casablanca) about an interracial relationship between a European and a Moroccan Israeli. The Moroccan is accused of a crime committed by another European, but justice prevails and the Moroccan is found innocent. The song, "Koulanou Yehudim" (We Are All Jews), is about the need to overcome racial bigotry in order to realize an Israel where "all Jews are friends," as the song goes. Perhaps ironically, in 2002, Hefer caused a stir when, in an interview, he described Moroccan Israelis as evolutionarily underdeveloped.[19]

Places like Sderot and Dimona, once the sites of rundown transit camps and then development towns where North Africans and indigenous Middle Easterners found themselves mired in poverty, are still slums where people from those backgrounds languish. The Adva Center, an Israeli policy research organization, found in a 2017 report that a "significant" wage gap persisted between Jewish Israelis of Ashkenazi (European) and Mizrahi (Middle Eastern and North African) origin. Europeans earned 31 percent above the national average and Middle Eastern and North Africans earned 14 percent above the average.[20] Non-Jewish Palestinian citizens of Israel earned about two-thirds of the average. The numbers may fluctuate as the global economy and regional conflict affect everyday lives, but the social order along ethnic lines remains the same.[21] And it reflects historical and continued Israeli attitudes toward the Arab world.

It's not a situation that's likely to get better anytime soon. The Israeli press lambasted education authorities in 2015 after Israel's Central Bureau of Statistics revealed a staggering gap in educational attainment: Native-born Israelis with European roots top the list for obtaining academic degrees, at around 50 percent.[22] At the bottom of the list were Jewish Middle Easterners and North Africans, at around 30 percent. Middle Eastern and North African people born outside of Israel were actually more likely to have obtained degrees, if only by a small margin.

Something about Israel is actively hindering the personal and professional development of its citizens of North African and indigenous Middle Eastern origin. In the Jewish North Africans' and Middle Easterners' case, perhaps it is that they are still so uniformly associated—in casual references, for example, to their hotheadedness and superstitions—with the uncivilized, the primitive. Such views don't just vanish as time passes, and when you are continually told by the people who sit at the head of society that the best you can aspire to is vocational schools for blue-collar work, as is the case for many in Israeli development towns, you believe it.[23] Israel's top brass continues to say heinous things about Jewish Middle Easterners and North Africans, but, generally speaking, they hide their feelings toward all things Arab under a veneer of political correctness. In 2017, Ashkenazi prime minister Benjamin Netanyahu, apparently meaning to say that he had suffered from a surge of anger, said "my Mizrahi gene burst"—a petty, nasty jab that generated some commotion and eventually led to an apology.[24]

Today, many Jewish Arabs in parts of Occupied Palestine complain that the police stop them to check their papers more frequently than their European counterparts. Some say this is because Jewish Arabs are traditionally associated with petty crime, but it is also part of efforts by law enforcement to make Jewish Arabs feel less welcome in their own towns through discriminatory policing because they resemble a part of the population that Israel believes should be discriminated against—the non-Jewish Palestinians. Sometimes the confusion of Jewish Arabs with non-Jewish Palestinians turns fatal.[25] In 2015, at a time when the Israeli government restricted Muslim Palestinian access to their holy sites, there was an escalation in street violence between Israelis and Palestinians, the latter without a single viable political means of fighting for social justice. At the time, several Jewish Arabs with full Israeli citizenship were targeted in violent attacks by fellow Israelis.[26] You would be hard-pressed to find a more powerful illustration of the absurdity of both the concept of phenotypic race and the murderous anti-Palestinian racism not just perpetrated by individual Israelis but fostered by Israel's administration.

Nevertheless, many voters for the far-right Likud Party are Middle Eastern and North African. The potential reasons for this are manifold, and none is conclusive. Some make the infantilizing argument that, coming from the Arab world, Jewish Arabs can only respect the rule of strongmen.[27] Another, less frequent argument is that colonialism, in Palestine and across the pillaged Arab world, has necessitated a kind of Stockholm Syndrome: every step closer to the prevailing power is a step away from being a target.

In official Israeli surveys, the Jewish Arab is given a status distinct from that of the non-Jewish Palestinian. They are never classed as Arab; they are more often Mizrahim. As in their income disparity, Jewish Arabs are engineered to be in their own social class, far above the non-Jewish Palestinians and far below the nation's white minority. Representations of ethnicity and power in film continue to reinforce the socioeconomic benefits of whiteness in a society still dominated by Europeans, despite the number of Jewish Arabs now occupying high-level positions in government. These circumstances are not particular to Israel. White supremacy is an international phenomenon, but in Israel's case it is woven into the country's very foundations. All attempts at social progress will be as effective as spraying a dumpster with Febreze.

The only way forward is to decolonize, and since a great many of Israel's citizens can still choose to identify as Jewish Arab, that decolonization could start from within. There are signs that Jewish Arabs are standing in solidarity with their non-Jewish fellow Arabs in Palestine and with our legacy of belonging to the Arab world. Jewish Arabic music is seeing a resurgence among our communities in Israel with groups like A-Wa, a band of three Moroccan Yemeni sisters that performs traditional Yemeni music, modernizing the Arabic musical tradition in a way more integral to Arabness perhaps than Mashrou' Leila, a Lebanese alt-rock band that ironically sounds a bit like the U.S. band Beirut. There are advocates like Reuven Abergel, a Moroccan taken to Israel as a child, who cofounded the Israeli Black Panthers (its name drawn from the Black Panthers in the U.S.). The Panthers demanded civil rights and social equality for Jewish Arabs in the 1970s but were ultimately crushed by the Israeli administration under Golda Meir and her successors.

Perhaps A-Wa, Abergel, Daida, myself, and others rejecting the separation of our Jewish community from a larger Arab whole—either expressly or in reclaiming the Arab cultural heritage—bespeak a trend toward reclaiming Arabness. Abergel put it beautifully in a short biographical film by Rebecca Pierce, who is an advocate for Jewish people of color.[28]

Abergel admits the role of the Jewish Arab in the colonization of the non-Jewish Palestinian. "The Jews from Arab countries

that we find here who became soldiers in the army, they are
partners in the oppression, of the Palestinians and also of themselves. . . . But that's not to say that we, the Mizrahim, are sitting
in silence today. We are always pushing forward in the struggle
against white dominance," he says. About young Jewish Arabs,
he adds, "Even with the situation here, they know that they are
missing something. They've had their identity and their culture
taken away. And today there is a renaissance of youth returning
to the Arab culture."

Among Yaqoub's letters from Israel, one in particular catches my
attention. Written on the back of the letter, as though it were a
whisper, were three lines:

> *Shamaa from Alexandria escaped from Israel back to Egypt*
> *They caught him and put him in prison for four days.*
> *They asked him everything about Israel and finally kicked*
> *   him out [of Egypt] and sent him to Italy.*

I have no way of knowing who Shamaa was, or why he
"escaped" Israel—if he'd committed a crime there and sought
refuge in the land of his birth. Maybe he went back to Egypt
out of longing for his homeland and a disillusionment with
Israel.

What's more certain is the point of this letter. Yaqoub was
warning Oscar against returning to Egypt, as difficult as the
West became. You can't go home again. Practically speaking,
he would be imprisoned, likely tortured and interrogated, and
then sent back to Europe because, with Europe's support for

the creation of the state of Israel, Jews had suddenly been associated with Europe and the Jewish Europeans who launched and initially orchestrated the Zionist project. The letter is dated April 18, 1951. It marks one of so many points of no return.

At around sixty-seven years old, Yaqoub suffered a major heart attack and died in Occupied Palestine, without his son and without much of anything, except for the house he'd built for his daughters—and for his son. "Every night I dream of him and wake up crying. Poor papa," Viviane wrote, in French. Viviane spoke pityingly of death: poor thing. But maybe he doesn't need her pity. Perhaps Yaqoub has been freed from his longing for his son, for his city, and for his country, his wife and parents buried across an un-traversable border in Egypt. Maybe we all return to some point of origin. Maybe Yaqoub is in Alexandria or in eastern Morocco or in the Arabian Gulf, in Biblical Canaan thousands of years before, in the prehistoric Amazigh land of Tamazgha in North Africa. Then again, maybe there is only his absence.

After his death, there were no more Arabic-language writings in our family; only the Arabic that my grandfather would endeavor to teach me and the Arabic he scribbled on cassette tapes of Arabic songs and movies and the transliterated Arabic that peppered Viviane's French: *Je vous souhaite un très heureux mabrouk!* (We wish you a happy *mabrouk*). The Arabic *Mabrouk* means "May it be blessed," one of those invocations that is about as religious as Merry Christmas has become and is shared by Jewish, Christian, and Muslim Arabs.

———

Back in France, later in 1954, Oscar was failing to provide for his family once more and began to consider leaving. Yaqoub's death was the clincher. Palestine was out of the question. There was nothing there for Oscar and his family.

Daoud, the Panamanian of Jewish Palestinian origin, had suggested Panama. He had an import-export company where Oscar would work, and he had introduced Oscar and Daida to the Panamanian ambassador, who told them the couple would easily settle into society there because they would be indistinguishable from their new compatriots. For a remarkably modest sum, they could buy Panamanian citizenship. But in the meantime, Daoud, who had returned to Panama, wrote that his business had taken a turn for the worse and that, like many of their mutual acquaintances, he was considering emigrating to the United States. That was the last Oscar and Daida heard of him, and so Oscar canceled their arrangements with the Panamanian embassy. Daida often told me, marveling jokingly at the randomness of life, we almost became Latino—Jewish Arab African Latinos. It would have been easier, she often said; no one in France, Israel, or the United States seemed to welcome her as much as the consuls at the Panamanian embassy, and she had heard that many Palestinians, Lebanese, Jewish Russians, and others had settled comfortably in cities across Latin America, from Mexico City to Buenos Aires.

The only alternative in a world of dead ends was the United States. Sick of struggling to make a living, Daida's brother Youssef moved to New York "to find a better life" than in Paris, Daida writes. As charming as he was, there weren't enough jobs for the French, let alone Jewish Tunisians. But he returned to

Paris not long after his trip, met an attractive European woman, and remained there.

Since before her departure from Tunis, Daida had continued to correspond with Albert, the Jewish European American soldier who with the Native American soldier Chancey Pete had been a frequent guest at the Boukhobzas' dinner table. Albert agreed to sponsor Daida's new family while they tried their luck in America. In the States, few knew what North Africans were or associated them with a disintegrating empire. Unlike in France, they were not linked to waves of immigrants seeking the spoils of empire and burdening ill-equipped social services.

Daida had insisted that the family—herself included, for she still had to apply to the Tunisian authorities in Paris for her birth certificate and other official documents—make a request for full naturalization. Not long before their departure for the United States, Oscar and Daida and their children were finally naturalized as French. They have a copy of the publication listing their names, together with many other Arabic North African names, some typically Muslim, some typically Jewish. But even as their place in the Republic had been secured, theirs was a feeling of social and economic estrangement. France was not the paradise of their colonized imaginations. There was no pride in the pretense of finally legally belonging to it while in practice they continued to feel like rejects. Stories abounded of discrimination and slurs against North Africans, Jews, and immigrants. In contrast, they had learned that America was built by minorities. They knew New York to have black people, and Asians, and Latinos. There were many people of Jewish faith there and of faiths they'd never known existed. None of the places they had been had accepted them—not their homelands after the Zionist project had been realized, not Palestine, not Europe, and it suddenly began to appear that America was the only realistic option.

6

الذاكرة / Memory

When they arrived in New York in 1956, it seemed to Oscar and Daida that there weren't very many Arabs—Jewish or otherwise—in the city. In Paris, they quickly found the Arab French communities scattered across the city, but in New York, these communities were more difficult to find. There were of course many Arabs. The earliest communities of Lebanese and Syrian New Yorkers, mostly Christians and Jews, had already been there for generations. But they would meet in their mosques, churches, and synagogues, and Oscar hadn't found a Jewish Arab congregation where he would have learned of businesses catering to their community, such as the Arabic bakeries in Brooklyn, on Atlantic Avenue and in Bay Ridge. Daida and Oscar stayed almost exclusively in the Bronx, where they lived, and Manhattan, where Oscar worked, doing the books for a textile company owned by a friend of Albert, the soldier Daida's family befriended after the war. It was Albert who had sponsored the Hayouns. He was filled with an improbable love for this strange family, and he had found them their apartment and Oscar his job.

As for the Jewish community, the Ashkenazi Americans Oscar encountered seemed to want nothing to do with him. Once again, he found himself shocked and disappointed that the notion of universal Jewry taught at the Alliance schools and at the Zionist meetings he attended in Egypt did not exist in practice. Oscar prayed alone, at home, without a *minyan* (the minimum ten men required to recite certain prayers).

Oscar knew some English from working for the British in Egypt, but Daida only spoke Arabic and French, the language she used to communicate with Albert. Daida's first new friend in America was a Puerto Rican woman she met in her building who also spoke very little English. That woman, Daida recalled, looked Tunisian, whatever that meant, since Tunisian-ness, and Arabness more broadly, contains multitudes. There was probably something familiar about the woman's appearance, and, coming at a moment in Daida's life when she'd traveled so far from anything she had known to a place without even the Arabic cabarets and movie houses she had known in Paris, she drew comfort from seeing this woman. At first, Daida and her friend communicated with hand gestures and through the odd French or Spanish word they had in common. Often, they found themselves at an impasse, which had them in fits of laughter. Daida and her friend attended an ESL class and learned to navigate the city together. Then one day, Daida's friend, who had found a job at a tie shop, gave Oscar a tie as a present. This was unacceptable to Daida, who felt the woman was making a move on her man. Even so far from Tunis and her parents in Paris, the social mores of her childhood remained intact: there are two mutually exclusive worlds, one for adult men and one for women, and when they overlap, it leads to illicit behavior. By the same logic, Albert and Daida were never alone together when he came to dinner, despite having known each other for so long. Albert understood full well the family's old-fashioned Arabic prudence and remained at arm's length.

The cooking and cleaning were more exhausting for Daida than they had been in Paris. It seemed there were no ready-made Arabic foods here, as there had been in France. The Arabic bread had to be made from scratch, without the traditional *taboun* oven that gives it its unmatched deliciousness. The couscous had to be made from scratch too, and repeatedly steamed before serving, and the fava beans had to be soaked in brine to make the *foul mudammas* breakfasts that only Oscar enjoyed—the Tunisians prefer broad fava beans to the Egyptians' small beans. To make a single couscous and vegetable soup for Friday night, Daida had to start preparations on Wednesday. But she had to make it. The family was suffering from a kind of year-round depression in those first few years, she explained. Daida was happy, she said, to thrust herself into work that reminded her of home. Nadia's earliest memories are of Daida preparing the couscous for Shabbat, singing along to a record of songs from Asmahan's last movie, *Gharam wa Intiqam.*

At that time, in the late 1950s and early '60s, Oscar and Daida spoke only in Arabic, with the occasional words in French. Often, in the morning when she was preparing him coffee, Oscar, like the *hakawati* (raconteur) of the Egyptian cafés, would tell her the same stories of Egypt that he wrote down in his Price Club autobiographies. Daida prepared coffee in a *kanaka* (a small stovetop pot) they had brought from Paris. She would pour a teaspoon of coffee grinds into the pot, some cardamom, and a sugar cube; then she filled it with water and set it on the stove. She would also prepare the pita bread, or *khobz shami*, as our family called it. To heat it, Daida put it directly on the stovetop, over a small flame, and stood there for a few moments, waiting until it puffed up. Then she'd flip it and repeat the procedure. Their apartment in South Bronx became a small *ahwa* (coffeehouse) every morning.

After about a year in New York, in 1957 the family moved to Los Angeles and Oscar got himself a job bookkeeping for two different companies. Their first apartment was in a predominantly immigrant neighborhood near downtown L.A., where Oscar worked. After work, the whole family would meet him in Pershing Square at night for sandwiches in the park, until they realized that even in the late 1950s and early '60s, Pershing Square at night attracted some colorful and downtrodden characters.

My mother, Nadia, was now in school, where she was called "charcoal face" and "monkey." Oscar had forbidden his daughters from shaving their legs or wearing makeup until they were adults. Before the arrival of other Jewish North Africans and the construction of the temple Oscar attended, there were no other girls like them, whose fathers thought makeup was for hookers, so they eventually resorted to applying makeup in secret.

While Oscar and Daida spoke in Arabic between themselves, they spoke mostly in French to Rosy and Nadia. Rosy and Nadia were entirely uninterested in the Arab culture. In the 1960s, America didn't celebrate difference in the same way many of its communities do now, in after-school specials on polite, progressive society. On the occasion of Rosy's thirteenth birthday, Daida decided to throw her daughters a party to help them make friends, and she prepared a selection of Arabic dishes for it. But her daughters invited none of their classmates out of embarrassment that their family was different, and so Daida ended up setting the table and waiting for some time before her daughters sheepishly revealed they hadn't told anyone to come. To them, Oscar and Daida may as well have been Martians. "What did you do with all the food?" I asked. Daida threw it all out in anger, at a time when our family never wasted a crumb. Nonetheless, this incident and others spurred Daida and Oscar to Americanize. One consequence of this is that Daida and Oscar occasionally affected slang—Come on. You got to be kidding me. Oh, brother—yet with an unmistakable Arabic r's and gutturals. On one occasion, Nadia mused, they purchased a case of Crest toothpaste because they'd seen a commercial suggesting that's what American families did. Still, Daida and Oscar found it impossible to forget who they were in the United States.

As soon as he purchased a car and found a Jewish Arab congregation of friends to point him in the direction of Arab shops, Oscar began trekking to the farthest reaches of the greater Los Angeles area, looking for things that made him recall Egypt. Interspersed with his records from Egypt are ones he purchased from a specialty record shop in Los Angeles. Many of his newer records bear a golden sticker from the store Silwani and

Company, an institution when Oscar arrived in Los Angeles. In *Asmahan's Secrets*, a stunning biography of Daida's favorite Arabic singer and actress, the author, Sherifa Zuhur, paints a vivid picture of the store.[1] If I associated Oscar more with Arabic pop culture in my youth, it was because Silwani's wasn't the sort of place that Daida would have visited; it would have been unseemly for Daida to hang out with *al-shabab* (the dudes) there. At several of the stores Oscar and I would frequent together when I was a child, Oscar would sit and converse, sometimes over tea, with the Arab storeowner, who was often Armenian, while I wandered around. Oscar sought out the company of other Arabs, but he never told any of them that he was Jewish. If they were Christian, he allowed them to assume that he was Muslim to avoid questions on Christianity; if they were Muslim, he was Christian. Implicit in this was the fear, born of the Alliance and of Zionism, that everyone non-Jewish hates Jews. Or perhaps born of the view that, after 1948, he couldn't claim he was both Arab and Jewish.

Daida found work selling toys at a department store in downtown Los Angeles. From their neighbors, who were also new immigrants, she learned about night school. Without having completed a French elementary school education in Tunisia, Daida took business and administration courses, and owing to her French and Arabic, she was hired in an entry-level position at a bank, in their international loans division. By the time she retired in her sixties, just before I was born, she had risen to the division's assistant vice president and had been numerously awarded for her contributions to the team. She was offered the position of vice president, but her success had already strained her relationship with her husband, who, although he encouraged her, was visibly disheartened by how much easier she found her way in this new society. She turned it down.

Daida and her husband, after saving for a long time, moved to North Hollywood and into a resolutely middle-class neighborhood. I was born to Nadia and raised in her parents' home. Oscar, perhaps more than Daida, was perplexed that his daughter would have a child out of wedlock, but like good parents everywhere, he got over it with time. In me, he had the son he had so desperately wanted.

Nadia wanted to be a foreign correspondent, but the family had no money for such luxuries as a risky, fulfilling career, and so while she was finishing high school her parents enrolled her in a dental assistant training course. While Nadia was working to support us—which was for much of my childhood—Daida and Oscar were my parents. They picked me up from school, fed me, played with me, and often put me to bed. Oscar would stand at the gate of my elementary school together with the other parents. In first grade, a young white boy named Thomas greeted me when I arrived in class with an *Hola!* Confused, I asked what he meant. "Your grandpa is a Mexican," he said. It seemed that Thomas hadn't meant this with malice; *Mexican* was often used in the 1990s for anyone Latin or brown. It's interesting, in retrospect, that I was not considered by Thomas (or his parents) to be Mexican. He hadn't said you're Mexican; my grandfather was, and so he offered me a well-meaning little *Hola*. I didn't say to Thomas, no, he's Jewish or Egyptian or Moroccan or Arab. I knew him to be some of those things, at the time, but not all.

As a child, playing with Pogs, little cardboard discs decorated with images of the Power Rangers and other things that were popular in the 1990s, my mother bought me a pack with international flags on them. Nadia—off on Tuesdays and Sundays—showed me the Tunisian, the Egyptian, and the Moroccan flags and said: "This is where we are from." But beyond that, how does one convey to a child a sense of those places? To me, the stars and crescents and eagles and bright crimsons and jet blacks and emerald greens—they meant nothing.

Early Saturday mornings, at around 8 a.m., Oscar would arrive home from temple, where he would open the door for the early risers with a special key bestowed upon him by his friend, the rabbi's brother. This was his weekly act of self-sacrifice: waking at 5 a.m. and driving his car to a spot where it would remain unseen and un-judged. Many of the congregants did the same, all but an especially devout Yemeni family who found a home adjacent to the temple. From the side of the temple, where in the late 1990s anti-Jewish graffiti and a series of trespassers had been discovered by the synagogue security guard, Oscar would unlock the door, turn on the lights in the main prayer hall, and wait for his friend Youssef. There, they would speak in Egyptian Arabic, which they thought superior to the Moroccan and Yemeni Arabic of the other congregants, until the few other staunch members of the congregation, who sacrificed their weekend sleep for God, joined them. Mostly, Oscar and Youssef would complain about their grandsons. Nadia, who adored her father, forced me to go to services on Friday and occasionally Saturday against my will. But Oscar frequently complained that I wasn't complying with his efforts to bring me up in our faith. I believed in God and the Jewish path to being close to that God. And yet I always felt I was a depraved and truant spirit, and I told

Oscar that I didn't feel that God was there. For Oscar, that didn't matter. To his mind, religion meant fulfilling clerical responsibilities. Warm, fuzzy feelings of spirituality were for the hippies and fancy college graduates on American television.

But maybe Oscar was satisfied with Friday nights. His complaints weren't always sincere. It was Oscar's custom, owing to his fervent belief in the Eye, to complain about anything or anyone he loved dearly to avoid the jealousy that he thought brought misfortune. For Oscar to say of his grandson that he was not observant or obedient enough was, to Oscar's mind, an attempt to save me from Youssef's envy. That's not to say that Youssef was a bad man; he was Oscar's closest friend and as one of few Egyptians in a majority Moroccan congregation a precious, rare reminder of his homeland. Youssef was no doubt aware of this custom of throwing off the Evil Eye. Youssef, who once gave me a prayer card with a large Khamsa/Hand of Fatima, must have known the drill and was remarkably not offended by the insinuation that he might be jealous of Oscar's grandson, who did go to Friday services more frequently than Youssef's grandson, who was also a filial boy.

Oscar would arrive home from temple, after the predawn services, wearing the tweed flat cap and matching jacket that a great many Middle Eastern and North African men of a certain age would wear. He smelled of 4711 eau de cologne, which reminded me a great deal of *bukhoor*, the fragrant wood chips that we, like other Arabs of all religions, burned to keep evil spirits away. Asked to describe the smell, Daida said only one word. *Clean.* So too have many other non-Jewish Arabs I've asked. As I smell a box of premium *bukhoor* I have from a shop on

Atlantic Avenue in Brooklyn, I hear all those Arabs I've known say it in unison, *Clean.*

When Oscar arrived home, Daida was typically at the women's gym or the supermarket. It was my responsibility to pour an opened can of Sahara-brand *foul mudammas* into a casserole and turn on the stove. To turn on a stove on Shabbat is a transgression in Judaism, but both Daida and I were significantly younger than Oscar, and so, he said half seriously, we'd have more time to repent. Once the *foul* was heated, I would pour out some of the brine and then put the beans on a plate and, using a fork, crush them lightly—not into a paste, but to a consistency where they were still identifiable as beans. Oscar would add olive oil and squeeze of half a lemon, and we would both peel our own single hard-boiled egg. Daida had warmed store-bought pita— by then, it was readily available, as there were many Middle Easterners in the United States—which I'd retrieve from the oven, and together we would use the pita to scoop the *foul mudammas* from this plate.

"*Foul* in the morning is for the kings!" Oscar would declare, in the way some Japanese people say *Itadakimasu* and some international Christians say grace. Sometimes he'd say the rest, "*Foul* in the afternoon is for the peasants. *Foul* in the evening is for the horses." And we would laugh. Daida often got home from her women's gym midway through breakfast. She occasionally joked that in Tunis, Egyptian-style small fava beans were for the horses at any time of day. The Tunisian way was the superior way of doing things. And she would often shake her head at the sight of Oscar and me eating with our hands from a single plate. "Terrible," she would say, shaking her head with disapproval. "Like two barbarians."

The rest of Saturday was filled with all sorts of activities. Within walking distance, Oscar had befriended an Armenian Lebanese tanner and he would take me to wander the man's shop, bored silly, while they had coffee and told Arabic jokes. Sometimes we went to museums. Sometimes Oscar would load me into a car and head for Glendale or West L.A. to buy some Arabic ingredients at a Greek, Armenian, or Persian supermarket. Very often, the three of us went to stamp conventions. Oscar had been a philatelist since Egypt, and in a room full of vendors with catalogues of stamps, Oscar would purchase stamps from Egypt, particularly those commemorating well-known figures and historic moments—certain pashas or the liberation from the British, with a proud King Farouk standing below the old Egyptian flag. Oscar's white whale was a stamp of his favorite singer and actor, Mohammed Abdel Wahab, strumming an oud. For years we scoured conventions and shops to no avail. Daida was bored by stamps. She would take long walks in the neighborhoods where the conventions were held, often Pasadena, and occasionally have a drink. From the men at her bank, she had learned to enjoy a glass of Galliano. "On the rocks," she would say.

In the evening, we would watch our hour of *Arab American Music Television* as we ate mezze on a foldout table in our den. This was our weekly fête, we would call it. My mother would arrive home from work toward the end of it—on one occasion, as we were dancing. I would happily miss play dates for these fêtes.

One Saturday, in high school, and following a conversation on our identity with a Jewish Moroccan American girl—from an honest-to-goodness Sephardic family with documents attesting to her family's expulsion from Spain—I asked Oscar and Daida if we were Arabs. The Jewish Moroccan American girl had told me she was, and I was unsure.

Daida reacted as though I'd insulted her character or threatened her life. She silenced me with the aggression that many Jewish Arabs would show today if someone suggested they were Arab. To them, it was a slur. "You sound like the Aseknaz" (how Oscar and Daida pronounced *Ashkenazi*), she said.

"Well, what are we then?" I asked, and she responded that she was Tunisian, but that in Tunisia there are many kinds of people.

"But Tunisia is an Arab country," I ventured. Her anger was visible. It grew as I continued. She was no longer listening to me.

Oscar, ever the contrarian, but in a tone I believe to have been in earnest, looked at Daida and said, "Yes, what else are we?"

Daida was even more upset, now with both of us.

"Why are there Muslim Arabs and Christian Arabs, but the Jews are only Jews?" I asked her. "Do you hate Jews?"

And what then of this American-ness we had adopted? Were Jews only Jewish here, too?

"Jews can be Egyptian and Tunisian, but not Arab. From Biblical times, there were Jews and Arabs," she answered. "I am Tunisian, and I am Jewish, but I am not Arab."

There are a great many Muslim Tunisians in Tunisia today—and in Lebanon, and Egypt, and indeed across the Arab world—who do not identify as Arab. The Arab identity is a choice, and what incentive does the Arab have to embrace Arabness? It is a term that has been maligned and degraded by Europeans since the Crusades, and most tangibly in the 1800s, when the Arab became a slave to European conquest, detested, unwashed, and segregated in their own neighborhoods.

Even today, there is very little that is celebrated about us, even within the Arab world, by those who have drunk the colonial Kool-Aid, and it is tricky, in this age of populism, to recall the beauty of a degraded people without promoting something akin to a Make America Great Again mentality. How does one champion an ethnic identity without falling into the pit of tribal nationalism? It is important to note that mine are not arguments for an Arab supremacy but to restore to humanity a people so deeply disfigured by white supremacy that we have lost all semblance of self and of dignity. It is in this context that I say we—the Jewish Arabs and the entirety of Arabs, continually disgraced and destroyed—are a beautiful people, from Rabat to Manama. The Jewish Arabs, and the Arab people to which we may choose to belong, and the countless other peoples who are debased. We belong to them, too.

In the aftermath of the terrorist attacks on 9/11, our family made a conscious effort not to speak any Arabic in public. Even a *"HamdelA"* (thank God) elicited a look of fire from my mother at the supermarket. Oscar's summertime Arabic lessons at our kitchen table stopped, as it was clear Arabic would no longer be useful to me. Where earlier in my youth there had been a concerted effort to teach me about Tunisia and Egypt, I don't recall us ever speaking of the past anymore. If we played an Arabic record, we turned it down low so that our Republican neighbors wouldn't hear.

Our family purchased two American flag decals for the windows on the front and side of our house. We were thankful to and proud of our adopted homeland—our family had certainly lasted longer there than in any place since our exile circa 1948 from our homelands—but this was also a gesture born of fear—fear that neglecting to express patriotism in the form of the American flags would mark us out.

A Moroccan family from our synagogue had spent what for them was an enormous sum of money to bring a cousin to the United States from Morocco. That cousin was deported in the immediate aftermath of 9/11, when boundless authority was bestowed on the Department of Homeland Security. To my grandparents and members of their synagogue, it was absurd that a Jewish man was deported on suspicion of Islamist terrorism. At least the French had understood the Arab countries better; they had known we were not all Muslims. For the Jewish Arabs I encountered at the time, it became useful to underline their apparent separation from Muslim Arabs, one that had been engineered for centuries by the French and British and then the Israelis. The post-9/11 backlash against Arabs and Muslims in the West—and the terrorism that inspired it—has continued to distance us from ourselves. I remember, too, how some of the Israelis in Los Angeles I knew rejoiced after 9/11. Now people understood what the Palestinians were, they argued, comparing the Palestinians to the hijackers.

We were often afraid that we would feel the impact of government scrutiny in those times. For a few years following the enactment of the Patriot Act, I was unable to check in to flights electronically and once, when I was flying Southwest from Oakland, a worker told me that I had a special Homeland Security designation on her computer requiring me to check in at the counter. The reason for this, as for much of what the Department of Homeland Security does, remains shrouded in mystery. When I returned home from that trip, my grandparents were frightened. "Don't they know that we're Jewish?" they asked. Oscar and Daida came to the conclusion that it was both good and bad that our passports did not identify our religion. In a situation where authorities and ordinary people were attacking Muslims, Jews were also unsafe. In such circumstances, it became difficult to see beyond one's situation to the countless non-Jewish Arabs facing similar scrutiny.

If Oscar and Daida reflexively distanced themselves from Arabness after 9/11, it wasn't just in response to the failures of U.S. policy to deal with terrorism in a way that didn't dehumanize innocents and turned some Americans into second-class citizens. It was also a reflexive response to colonial cues deeply embedded in them. The reason they recoiled from Arabness stemmed from an understanding that their country of origin marked them out for scrutiny and potential harassment by the authorities. As with Oscar's Egyptian-ness, one's identity may traverse seas and oceans but one's citizenship can be dissolved in a minute.

I had my bar mitzvah not long before 9/11. I read from a Torah in the shape of a minaret, which was contained in a hard cylindrical case with a top in the shape of a dome you would commonly find in traditional Islamic architecture. At our synagogue, the women remained in the back, as they did in many American mosques.[2] Nadia and Daida could hardly see the service.

One of Oscar's Egyptian friends had prepared a large pot of *foul mudammas* on a low-heat hot plate the evening before so as not to break the Shabbat prohibition on starting flames or doing any work, and he served the *foul* to the guests in the court-yard behind the prayer hall. Among them was a Jewish studies teacher of Jewish European origin. "Is this kosher?" she asked loudly enough for the rest of the congregants to look at her with great disdain and for some to say, in hushed Arabic or French, a few choice words about this Jewish European woman. No one understood what led her to assume that food prepared in a synagogue might not be kosher. Many of the families at that synagogue had arrived in Israel only to find that a great many Jewish Europeans, in the top brass and in society, did not seem in earnest to believe in the international Jewish community that had inspired the Zionist project in the first place. Israel's first leaders had derided our intelligence, our humanity, and fre-quently our religion. For this woman to insinuate that we didn't know basic Jewish dietary codes was a trigger, perhaps. I had heard similarly ignorant comments in school before. An Ashke-nazi American friend, who often visited Israel, told me that Jews from Arab countries can be clever, but never intelligent. To his mind, only the European was capable of intelligence. I suppose Jewish Arabs belonged in the souq, eking out a living haggling for belly dancers and snake charmers. "They want to own our religion," Daida said years later.

On the night of my bar mitzvah, at a hotel ballroom in Sher-man Oaks, California, Oscar's friends from his synagogue looked on in pride as I and my friends and a belly dancer we had hired from a local Moroccan restaurant performed Arabic-style dances

to the Arabic pop music popular at the time: the Egyptian singer
Amr Diab's "Amarain." It was a far cry from the Backstreet Boys
and Britney Spears of the other bar mitzvahs and quinceañeras I
was attending around that time. On the dance floor I was sur-
rounded by the men, as it is our custom, as in religious Muslim
households, for men to dance together. A couple of guys, younger
men born in Morocco, tied napkins together and twirled them as
they danced. A Jewish Persian friend explained to another guest,
a Jewish European American, that this is how Middle Eastern
people have bar mitzvahs: there's a belly dancer and someone's
uncle makes it rain. In our family's case, perhaps different slightly
from Persians, everyone wakes up hungover and eats all the fried
food in the Arabic cookbook, including Tunisian *brik* and Egyptian *sambouseks* (stuffed pastries) with a shot of our traditional fig
liqueur, *boukha*, as a sort of hair of the dog.

I went to all the guests and asked if they would like anything. I didn't eat a thing because I was too busy serving people,
to the bewilderment of the non-Arabs and to the pride of my
grandparents and their Arab friends. For us, to be a good host
is the most noble worldly pursuit. No one needed to tell me to
greet my guests. Like learning cooking from Daida, I understood what needed to be done when the time came. This was
as it had been in our family for generations, spanning thousands
of miles across North Africa. Only, if we were back in the Arab
world, I would have been married, probably to a female cousin,
not long thereafter.

In between the temple service and the *hafla* (party) that night,
Oscar and I napped on a single bed while Daida and Nadia
sang folk songs and prepared traditional Tunisian cakes, as the

Boukhobza women in Mahdia had done as they prepared break fasts during Ramadan for the Ben Rhomdane family. The room was dark. I thought of how Oscar had passed down to me the wisdom his father had passed down to him. He had taught me who I am spiritually and ethnically, much as he complained that I was nowhere near as obedient as he or any Jewish Egyptian kid had been in Alexandria. Lying on that bed, both of us were elated and exhausted. I reached over and took Oscar's hand. *Rouhi*, he said, my soul. And we slept.

Oscar died in 2004 in a Catholic hospital not far from our home. Daida, with her characteristic North African mysticism, said she saw his spirit leave his body like a breath of smoke coming from his mouth. She swore she saw it.

At the hospital, around the corner from his room, was a statue of a mournful Virgin. How beautiful, it seems to me now, that she was there—a Jewish Palestinian woman in whiteface. The Madonna may be foreign to us in our spiritual practice, but she is also a Jewish Arab.

Michael Moore's *Fahrenheit 9/11* came out not long after Oscar died, and with it images of the bombardment of Iraq. Democracy had been a pretext to advance a neocolonial footprint in the Middle East much as the colonial Europeans in North Africa peddled rights for women and minorities. Nadia and I sat spellbound in the movie theater as we watched an Iraqi woman wail in Arabic in footage from the carnage wrought by the George W. Bush administration. It was a form of Arabic that was more similar to Egyptian Arabic than Daida's Tunisian Arabic. Without Oscar, we almost never heard Arabic in the home anymore.

Without Oscar, Daida had no one to speak Arabic with beyond *HamdelA* and *insha'Allah* to us. We mostly only spoke French in our home by that time. But as we listened to that woman yell through tears for what had been taken from her, we began to cry at the destruction of this world, Oscar's world.

Where did Oscar go after he died? To our home in Los Angeles? To Palestine, to Paris, to the Bronx? Or was he once more riding the trains in Egypt, that foppish man in the photos of his youth, his tarboosh-topped head bobbing back and forth on his way to Tanta and Mansoura? Since Oscar's death, I've spent a lot of time looking for him, even in the most mundane shit I do, like buying a can of Sahara-brand *foul mudammas* for breakfast. Maybe it's not healthy to dwell too long in the realm of the dead. But I was born in these memories. There's not much more left to me beyond this.

I dreamt of Oscar years after his death. He was sitting in a chair in a bazaar in Egypt—not in Alexandria, not anywhere in particular, for I'd not yet been to Egypt or to any Arab nation at that stage. *I'll be waiting*, he said.

Roughly a year after the dream, in 2008, my college's financial aid department mistakenly deposited three times the sum they needed to into my bank account. I never kept track of those deposits and would eventually have to repay the excess. But it seemed I had some extra money, and I found a ticket on Emirates from Beijing, where I was studying abroad, to Cairo and a cheap hotel in Giza, on the outskirts of the city near the pyramids. From there, I would head to Alexandria to visit rue Zahra (now Ismail Eid Street) and the graves of Oscar's mother and grandparents. But Daida and Nadia insisted, over the phone from Los Angeles, that it would be dangerous for me to go to Egypt. Since Oscar had left, there had been a series of terrorist attacks at tourist sites, fatal terrorist shootings in Cairo targeting tourists in 1996 and 1997 and bombings, for example. That was why every time Oscar suggested that we go, we didn't. I said I wouldn't tell anyone there I was Jewish. But they'd know, Daida insisted. I'd say the wrong thing, and they'd know Oscar wasn't a Muslim or Coptic Egyptian, but a Jewish Egyptian. After so long away, they had bought into the Western conception of our homelands as dangerous, unpredictable, pitiful places.

I didn't care for my safety. If I did, I would never have con- templated going at all, having seen only what I'd read in the American news. But I had fallen into such a depression over the loss of my grandfather, and even Daida and Nadia agreed that I should go—to see the land where Oscar had lived, to see if I could find him there. So I went.

On the first day I was there, after hearing that I had been raised by an Egyptian grandfather, a hotel worker in Giza com- mented, in French, that I had an Egyptian face, which, whatever it means, pleased me. I asked him where the nearest souq was, knowing nothing of Cairo and recalling my dream. Surprised by my ignorance, he said Khan el Khalili, the sprawling world- famous bazaar, and so, on my first evening in Egypt, I took a cab there, only to have it break down on the way. The driver entreated me to chant with him *Bismillah il-rahman il-rahim* (In the name of God, the most compassionate and most merciful), as he tried to restart the ignition. Steam began to emerge from the hood of the car, so I hitched a ride the rest of the way with two young men from Aswan, both unemployed and in town to make mischief. They asked if I had met any porn actors in China, since so much of the porn they saw came from Asia (from Japan, mostly; porn is illegal in China). I told them I had not.

Before entering the market, I visited the Al-Hussain mosque, which is adjacent to the market, and I sat on the floor and watched the faithful come and go. There was a festival in progress, with a parade taking place outside, where many vendors were selling blue metal Hands of Fatima, inscribed with *Mohammed Rassoul Allah* (Mohammed is the Prophet of God). These amulets, the food they sold there, and the faces of the pious—with the exception of the blood blisters on their foreheads that are distinctly Muslim—all reminded me of my family.

I entered the market, where I bought a scarf like one that had belonged to my grandfather. Oscar would have bought yams here, so I bought one, lightly caramelized, seasoned with a sprinkling of coarse salt, and cooked in an oven made out of a sawn-down metal trash can with a pot on top. With my scarf in one hand and my yam in the other hand, I wandered, and as dusk turned to night, I realized I was walking in circles. The alleys emptied as people retreated into their homes above and behind the stalls until it was just me, the stray cats, and the faint light of the moon. I searched in vain for the exit, thinking, I don't know this place. I am not from here. Oscar wasn't there. In that moment, I hated him for it.

Finally, the marketplace expelled me into a main street, with green neon lights and crowded pastry shops, which reminded me of Lina, the woman Oscar had fallen in love with before leaving Egypt.

In the days that followed, I walked along the Nile as Oscar had. I saw the opera house where the stars of his youth performed. I visited El-Geniza Synagogue, where Oscar attended high holiday services some years with his cousins. This was the spot where, according to Jewish Egyptian lore, the pharaoh's daughter had found the baby Moses, and the building's interior was decorated with the same inlaid mother of pearl that I'd seen on jewelry boxes in Arab American homes. El-Geniza is preserved with great care by the few remaining Jewish Egyptians in Cairo and by the Egyptian government, but it is now empty of its community, and while I was there, a band of tourists who were easily identifiable as a group of Christian Evangelists from the United States passed through, taking pictures, standing where my grandfather had stood.

I started talking with the woman who was selling souvenirs inside the synagogue: a few guidebooks and Egyptian-styled mezuzot, their small cases bearing the prayers that Jews fix to our doorways. She asked whether I was Jewish Egyptian. I said no, almost reflexively. I'm not a religious person, I told her. I would have liked to pray in that place, but I felt that I couldn't. As I left, I passed a poor woman outside selling water from the well beneath the Geniza. It was holy water she said, for this was where Moses—Moussa in Arabic—became royalty.

The Geniza is located in a part of town called Old Cairo, in close proximity to a Coptic church and a mosque, Amr ibn al-As. At the mosque, I found a perfect calm and none of the tourists from before, but as I sat there, in the quiet shade, looking onto the beautifully lit courtyard and its well, flanked by a few of the poor who sleep there, I felt myself collapsing inside.

I felt as though there were no future for me past that moment. I must have been very visibly unhappy because the taxi driver who picked me up from the mosque asked me what was wrong. My Arabic and his English were not strong enough for me to tell him exactly what I felt, but I told him as best I could that my grandfather, who was the only father I'd ever known, had meant to show me this place, and he was dead. The man took me to his family's restaurant and he and his wife fed me falafel for an hour or so and returned me to Giza, where he refused to accept any payment.

In every generation, it is required that we see ourselves as leaving Egypt, the Passover Hagadah ceremony reads, and I wanted out of this place of my grandfather's ghosts. I called my mother, and we decided I should leave Egypt immediately. I canceled my hotel in Alexandria. I tried to move up my flight back to Beijing, but nothing was available out of Cairo. Instead, I would have to take a bus to Borg el-Arab airport, which according to the concierge was north of Cairo, near Alexandria—a journey that Oscar would have taken.

From Cairo, the bus passed through a desolate landscape dotted with small clusters of homes, places of worship, and markets as we approached Borg el-Arab. We turned into the small airport's parking lot, and I knew I would miss almost everything I'd come to see—Alexandria. But perhaps that's not all that bad. The real Alexandria would not have been the Alexandria I'd hoped to see.

The first leg of the flight would take me to Dubai, then back to Beijing. At Borg el-Arab, an Egyptian woman wearing a large puffy white dress and a great deal of makeup waited in the sweltering heat at the small airport for a wedding that would apparently take place just hours later in the Gulf. I imagined how she felt on our flight; I, too, felt trapped in my own skin like she was trapped in all those gigantic ruffles and lace. I sat looking at the walls of that airport, adorned with posters of the Egypt that Oscar had cherished, scenes in Tanta and Mansoura that I would never see, and I thought, per Thomas Wolfe, you can't go home again.

I would never go back to Egypt. I watched Egypt from afar in the American and European news, which seemed to fixate on Egypt because of its proximity to Palestine. Egyptians didn't matter, it seemed, in the coverage of the Arab Spring that continued a struggle that had started long before. The unspoken question was not the fate of the most-populous Arab country, but whether an Egyptian nation beholden to the will of its people would allow Palestine to remain colonized. It is indeed a question that remains unanswered.

I had a brief stint working in Paris, but I wasn't making ends meet and I was fed up with France and its postcolonial complexes, so I quit.

On my last day there, I walked the long stretch from Belleville to Porte de Clichy, and for the first time in a long time, I spoke North African Arabic with the people in the communities I found there. For the first time, I had someone other than Daida make me a *sandwiche Tunisien*, a tuna sandwich on French bread with Tunisian condiments, such as spicy harissa paste and *slata mechouia*, a pickled slaw. I struck up a conversation with a Jewish Tunisian man, who was unemployed and sitting on the bench outside a kosher Tunisian restaurant. "How beautiful that all the Tunisians stay together," I said. "Jews and Arabs."

The man looked at me long and hard. "What is an Arab?" he asked—a question I would ask myself continually over the next few years. "In the United States, maybe it is different, but here in France, I am an Arab." He proceeded to explain the politics that prevented Muslims from integrating into French society and prospering. At the time, I was too young and embarrassed to continue the conversation. I bid him good day and continued on my trek. I bought Daida a box of *makrouds* in a beautiful box, as well as a Hand of Fatima and a small Tunisian flag, and I booked a flight out of France, to Germany, via Casablanca in Morocco.

Casablanca was quieter than Cairo, but equal to it in its hospitality. The very cells in my body seemed to recognize the air there. I felt it embrace my skin. I had only a few hours in town, so I went to the Hassan II Mosque, and there, looking out into the darkening lapis sky and listening to the waves crash against the back wall of the mosque, it recalled to me Daida's stories of her family home in Mahdia. I had never fully believed that there were houses built to embrace the waves on the Mediterranean, but here in Casablanca, where the second-tallest minaret in the world juts into the sky, the city meets the water, and the sound of the waves that had put my grandmother to sleep so many nights cleansed my mind.

I kept going back to different Arab cities in North Africa, the Levant, and the Gulf, and every time I went to an Arab country,

I felt at peace, so much so that when I'd return to the West, I'd feel rejuvenated and more ready to handle things about life there that, even born there as I was, are totally foreign to me.

When Al Jazeera America launched and I was hired as a reporter, I was excited to be part of what I saw as a rebranding of Arabs in the American consciousness, not as enemies but as people actively participating in the country's Fourth Estate. I was one of a handful of people of Arab origin there.

Many of the friends I made there were Arab American, and from them I learned a great deal of what modern Arab American-ness meant. At one point, I had the chance to go to Qatar for a month. The company sent me with a Christian Palestinian supervisor who would become a brother to me and who continues to instill in me the notion that, despite ongoing colonial machinations, Arabs are a beautiful people in the sum of our talents and shared legacies. In his undying hope for life and dignity for Palestine, I found something of Oscar's search for dignity around the globe. In him, I found things I had been ill-equipped to find on that first trip to Egypt. Together, we traveled to different parts of the Gulf when we were not working, and that was invaluable to me—to share in seeing the space that, if only in the abstract, gave birth to the Arab people.

But I never told him I was Jewish. In fact, I found myself in an almost exclusively non-Jewish Arab circle at the time, and I never told any of them that I was anything but Arab. On occasion, I did let people think I was Muslim. To my mind, I was uncertain that I could let them know that I was Jewish and continue to share with them fully in the Arab legacy that reminded me of Oscar and Daida and of how they had raised me. It pained me to imagine the unavoidable day when I would need to tell them that I had lied about myself.

There was never any suggestion that I would be discriminated against for my faith. I was also never ashamed of my faith and prayed regularly. But I was living a double life. Often, over drinks, they would say things like, "Did you know Jerry Seinfeld is half Syrian?" and through my inebriation, I would wonder if they were hinting that they had known I was Jewish all along—that they had perhaps Googled the last name Hayoun and discovered that it's very typically Jewish Arab (although I have encountered several Muslim Hayouns, likely originally from the same village in eastern Morocco). The next day, I would realize that I was just being paranoid, but I knew that someday we'd have an uncomfortable conversation over why I had chosen to withhold something so integral about myself.

In Qatar, I had an opportunity to fly directly to Alexandria for almost no money at all and in just a few hours. But colleagues at the Al Jazeera headquarters in Doha warned against it. Al Jazeera journalists had been locked up in Egyptian prisons, so it would be unwise, they said. I found myself once again so close to visiting Alexandria, but it seems I'll never see it.

There hasn't been a newsroom I've worked in, including Al Jazeera in the United States, where I didn't overhear or witness anti-Arab or anti-Muslim sentiment: jokes about Arab accents and jokes about misogyny in Arab culture at a time before the #MeToo movement recognized strikingly similar trends in the West; white feminists neglecting the existence of Arab feminists or the existence of any indigenous Arab women's rights movement; and Zionists dehumanizing Palestinians and Arabs and negating their history.

Israel takes its image in the United States very seriously, and, like many international governments, Tel Aviv spends enormous sums directing Washington's foreign policy through public relations. You have only—at least while some transparency reigns in U.S. government—to log on to the Justice Department's FARA.gov to see exactly how much money Israel and its allies spend on lobbying. In the first half of 2018 alone, the World Zionist Organization in the United States spent nearly $2 million reimbursing what it describes as "young emissaries from Israel" who, per their description, promoted the study of Jewish history and Zionism and disseminated information on Israel to Jewish American communities.[3] That's only a fraction of the overall sum spent by Zionist groups pushing that ideology in the United States. According to the Center for Responsive Politics research group's OpenSecrets.org publication citing justice department statistics, Israel and nongovernmental pro-Israel organizations spent $16,945,473 lobbying in the United States—a figure that includes contacts with politicians and the press. That's hundreds of thousands more than China, then the United States' largest trading partner, and more than double the amount Mexico, among the United States' top three trading partners, spent that year.

In 2018, Israel enshrined into law the state's Jewish identity, effectively making Palestinians with Israeli papers second-class citizens in a state governed by leaders who continually denigrate Arabs and launch deadly attacks that kill peaceful protesters and civil society in Gaza. Promoting Israel's image abroad effectively promotes the debasement, subjugation, and slaughter with impunity of Arabs.

There are organizations in the United States not officially tied to Israel or support for it that appear to sway our media conversation on Arabs. The Washington-based Middle East Media Research Institute (MEMRI), for instance, has come under fire for cherry-picking videos that would sour U.S. opinion of Arab and Muslim societies and publicizing them widely across platforms.[4] The press has also called the group's translations and overall accuracy into question.[5] MEMRI's founding president, Yigal Carmon, was a high-ranking Israeli intelligence officer.[6] The videos frequently feature a hardline Muslim cleric saying something that would incense a great many international Arabs and Muslims. If the viewer has no knowledge of those societies beyond those videos, they risk viewing the Arab and Muslim worlds as monoliths instead of a large mass of human beings that, like Americans, suffer the presence of some hardline whack jobs.

And then there are a great many American journalists who, without any apparent help from Israel or Israeli organizations, write in the style of the French North African Orientalist travel logs we have discussed. In 2018, the *New York Times*' Thomas Friedman wrote a characteristically broad-strokes, derisive, condescending piece entitled "Crazy Poor Middle Easterners" that advanced a particular mainstream U.S. media narrative of the Middle East as a uniformly self-destructive place, provoking little ire or bewilderment—certainly not enough to keep him from writing more racist trash—from a public accustomed to the denigration of all classes of people of color.[7]

Israel also boasts an online army that goes after its opponents, although it is often perplexing to me that governments with such boundless resources don't have more sophisticated weaponry in their arsenal than Twitter trolls, bloggers with sites that look like they haven't been revamped since the 1990s, and petty op-eds in sympathetic media. Still, whether they're directly employed by the Israeli government or merely sympathetic to its causes, they will stop at nothing to tear down their opponents. For instance, after I had interviewed Palestinian rights advocate Ali Abunimah for an article on Palestine, self-professed Zionists on Twitter called me an Islamic fundamentalist belly dancer with a pen on the internet—more whimsical than offensive, perhaps. I could only ever aspire to be so adept at multitasking.

The pettiness rooted in racism isn't only for online trolls, though. When a Palestinian teenager, Ahed Tamimi, was jailed in February 2018 for slapping an Israeli soldier and that arrest drew attention to scores of similar child imprisonments, Israeli authorities suggested that she and her family were not truly Palestinian or Arab because she had light skin and blond hair.[8] Despite the fact that many Arabs, especially Palestinian Arabs, have fair skin and blond hair, this was part of Israel's push to imply that third parties had inserted themselves into the Palestinian-Israeli conflict. Attacking Tamimi's fair skin, for all the millions in aid received by Tel Aviv annually, had been the best the Israeli government's spin doctors could do.

Predators in the wild who find themselves cornered stop at nothing to defend themselves. As Israel and its supporters find themselves without an argument for their continued offensives against the Palestinians, their desperation may be an indication that the end of their colonial tyranny is nigh.

Senegalese president and poet Léopold Sédar Senghor, in a 1966 speech, defined Negritude as "the totality of the values of the Black World, as they are expressed in the life and in the life's work of the Black People." In a similar vein, Arabness, or Arab-etude, is a total sum of the intellectual, cultural, and spiritual labor of the Arabs, celebrated in reaction to their denigration by the white supremacist West. An Arabetude movement would reclaim a much broader Arab legacy that has been lost. Arabness is a shared set of historical experiences: it is the thirst for life and dignity that unites me, Daida, and Oscar to our ancestors and to the many Christian and Muslim Arabs who continue to actively search for this legacy or are in a position of self-hatred so deeply rooted in their psyches by the colonizers of the last two centuries and of today.

It would be a mistake to read this work as simply that of a Jewish man reclaiming Arabness. It is the work of an Arab American man of Jewish faith taking a stand for his world—the Arab world and the human world—from an Arab American perspective. View it as the stone I throw in a fight for dignity that began long before my grandparents. The fight is for their legacy and that of all the generations that came before. A legacy that belongs to those to come.

My grandmother began this project with me. For two years, we discussed and refined the ideas behind this book. We are the coauthors of this book. So too is Oscar, even after death. He seemed to know it was coming, or he would have never urged me so often to read about his life and to contemplate what it had all meant.

Even before we began to think of this work, my grandmother and I shared news about Tunisia: the outpouring of support when its native Jewish Tunisian son, Yoav Hattab, was killed in an attack at a kosher supermarket in Paris in January 2015.[9] We shared pride in Tunisia's undying support for the Palestinians, for the way that in North Africa, the Tunisian, Algerian, Moroccan, and Mauritanian flags are flown beside the Palestinian flag. Where the idea of Arabness once frightened her, in her old age she often declared her Arabness with pride. What is Arabness, she would say, other than the act of belonging to the Arab nations?

For Daida, Arabness was an exaltation of what we have been made to see with shame for so long. It was a mandate. Other modern definitions of *Arab* were less meaningful to us than this living breathing thing we were. Was it a language? Was it a common history? It is more than that. Arabness is a choice to belong with other Arabs.

I am Daida. I am Oscar. I am all Arabs. I am Tunisia, Egypt, Morocco, Algeria, Palestine, and all adjoining nations that identify as Arab. I am the wealth of love I feel for the people of those nations.

Daida died knowing this book to be her final blow against the colonial establishments under which she had been made to bow. In response to the rise of more kinds of white supremacy, she would like me to say, without shame or confusion, that we remember when we were Arabs, and we will be Arabs in the future still.

Months after Daida's death, Nadia and I went to Tunisia for the first time. As a journalist, I had frequently interviewed Tunisians about Tunisia and I had traveled all over the Arab world but not to Daida's home. The street names had changed after independence, as had the layout of the city, so we had to get an old colonial map of her neighborhood, Lafayette, and match the streets to current maps. Daida had drawn pictures of Tunisia, of the places she had taken me in her stories. I had seen photos, too, including one of Daida in a horse-drawn carriage on her street—rue Beulé, now nahaj Libya (Libya Street)—with her mother, aunt, and cousins. Much in the way it was hard to write about her life until it had ended, it was hard to return to Tunisia when Daida physically could not because of her health and old age.

Nadia had never been to an Arab country. She said she had always anticipated she would go, but it never happened. As we passed a billboard advertising a brand of couscous, she found herself staring. When she was young, couscous had been the strange rice only her family ate, and here, in a place where she remarked that people "look like me," it was marketed everywhere.

The cab driver spoke to us in Arabic. We replied, with as many words of Tunisian dialect as we could think of, that we were visiting my grandmother's old home, in Lafayette. "You are Jewish Tunisian?" he asked, and when we said yes, he reached into his glove compartment and brandished a stick of *adamhot*, Tunisian fish eggs in a waxy cylinder, a traditional treat thought to originate in the Jewish community, often served with *boukha*. The conversation turned to the greats of Jewish Tunisian history: Habiba Messika, Georges Adda, and René Trabelsi, a Jewish Tunisian politician and businessman who has long been active in the Tunisian government and all-important tourism industry. The cab driver understood full well why we had come. We had come home, he observed. When he dropped us off directly on Daida's street, I embraced him as though he were my uncle.

The buildings perfectly resembled those in Daida's drawings, a bright white with a turquoise trim. From there, we walked through the streets Daida would have walked, toward the Bab el-Bahar gate. Daida would have crossed through the Bab el-Bahar into the Tunisian sector, as we did now, and as we walked, the sun's light reflecting off the white buildings revived us. We heard people use words we hadn't heard in some time. Our family had not been in Tunisia for more than half a century, and on that day, it was as though we—all those who came before, my grandparents, my mother, and I—were picking up where we had left off.

ACKNOWLEDGMENTS

Thank you, in no logical order and with immense love, God, Nadia, Jed Bickman and family, Ed Maxwell/Amy, Ben Woodward, Ellen, Sharon, Emily, Liana, Laila, Brian, Syeda, The New Press, Max, Courtney, Aziza, Yaqoub, Viviane, Iris, Kamouna, Sami, Guigui, Ba Kiki, Ma Julie, Rachel, Max, Youssef, Moussa, Liz, Fernando, Magz, Fanon, Nadeem, Kiese, Khaled, Souleyma and Osama, Diana, Halali, Said, Assidon, Halevi, Matsuoka, Redfern, Ben Slimane, Warda, Abdel Halim, Lulu, Rosy, Tanya, Hal, Dorothy, Alejandra, Meiling, Cappuccino sandwich stall at TUN, Aminah, Leah, President Hannah, Keren, Molly, Pierce, Abergel, Boyle Heights, UCLA, the Los Angeles Public Library system, Pacific Standard, Cardi B, AJAM/AJE friends, *Vancouver Observer*, Linda and Jenny, La Plaza de Cultura y Artes, Little Tokyo, Tijuana, El Yogurt Place, Chinatowns, Koreatown, the Hills, Sara, Amel, Ali,

American Chordata, Manu Chao, Blondie, Dalida, Miranda
July, Maheen, Raina Rai, Maria, Abderrahim and brother, Bay
Ridge, Steinway, Sunset Park, Stevie Nicks, the Aterciopelados,
Mon Laferte, Metric, Santigold, Beach House, Future Islands,
Erika/Max, Asmahan, Darwish, the Golden Girls, Jennie and
family, Olivia and family, Michael and family, the Serenity
Prayer, Faye Wong, Lin Qingxia in *Chungking Express*, Espacio
1839, Birrieria de Don Boni, Beijing, Sister Helen, Rev. Cor-
ral, Buñuel, Cynthia, Almodovar, Cecilia Roth, McNamara,
Riva, Moreau, Gallery Ishq, Beinin, Shabi, Shohat, Shehnav,
Smooha, Gottreich, Serfati, Hadj, Adda, Messika, Somekh,
Silver, Ai Weiwei, Ahmed, Brighton Beach, Kashkar Cafe,
Anadyr, Swartz, Guth, Asian Americans Advancing Justice, the
ACLU, Yolanda, Xavier, Teresa and family, Su Xiaoxiao, Bitar,
Kevin, Dream Team LA, the Korean restaurant waitress from
Lanzhou who moved to Hangzhou, Mirbeau, Khaled, Alex-
ander, Moustafa, Elaine, Vilkomerson, JVP, SJP, Kinokuniya,
Ting, Nawal El-Saadawi, Pati, Choumicha, Elle, Aparna Nan-
cherla, Submedina, Yoko Ono, *Diary of a Chambermaid*, *All
About My Mother*, *The Discreet Charm of the Bourgeoisie*, *Enchanted
April*, *Eternal Sunshine of the Spotless Mind*, *Hiroshima mon amour*,
Jules & Jim, *Masks*, Fumiko Enchi, *Midaq Alley*, Mahfouz, *Like
Water for Chocolate*, Laura Esquivel, Ros, Natalia Lafourcade,
Abdel Wahab, Charlotte and Serge Gainsbourg, Ryan, Flush-
ing, 1st Street, Joni Mitchell, Lexis, Marri, Alexandra, Jordan,
Samia, Amira, "Aïe mourir pour toi," Rashida, Ilhan, Alexan-
dria, Ginsburg, Stora, Kalin, America Ferrera, Wafa, Kareem
and family, Big Arc Chicken, Zard, "Veridis Quo," Montreal,
Monarca, Tracee Ellis Ross, "Hikoukigumo" by Yumi Arai and

the vibe of it, Ireland, ZPH, Nola, Aubrey Plaza, Jim Carrey, Aznavour, Aidy Bryant, Santa Cecilia Restaurant, Tracy Enid Flick, Parm, Salt & Straw, Kate McKinnon, Julia Louis-Dreyfus particularly in the Soup Nazi episode but also always, Tanoreen, Janelle Monae, Yevie, Sabah, Keri Russell's performance in *The Americans*, Muni, Alex Borstein's performance in *The Marvelous Mrs. Maisel*, Allison Janney, Zhou, Shen, Signoret, Montand, Big Boi, Yinhe, Saffron & Rose, the clothes lama, freedom of expression as guaranteed by the U.S. Constitution, dissent, compassion.

NOTES

Introduction

1. A recent fond recollection—one that honors the Jewish Egyptians of this generation and styles them after the classic Egyptian film stars—is the 2015 Egyptian television drama *Harat el-Yahud* (The Jewish Quarter), which you can watch online (in Arabic, unsubtitled) here: "مسلسل حارة اليهود - الحلقة الاولى | Episode 01—Haret El Yahud," *Mehwar Drama*, YouTube, June 17, 2015, https://www.youtube.com/watch?v=FomD2T3jwfA&list=PL9 _Ibxv4hPa1p_ihPOL5zxU44m6VOGgRw.

2. Niveen Ghoneim, "Magda Haroun: The Egyptian Jewish Community's Vibrant Past and Macabre Present," *Cairo Scene*, February 2, 2014, http://www.cairoscene.com/In-Depth/Magda-Haroun-Egypt-Jewish -Community-s-Vibrant-Past-and-Macabre-Present.

3. For research refuting the existence of race—although not racism, which certainly exists—as a scientifically valid means of studying humanity as well as the way race has and can be used to kill, see Dorothy E. Roberts, *Fatal Invention: How Science, Politics, and Big Business Re-create Race in the Twenty-first Century* (New York: The New Press, 2012).

4. "AAA Statement on Race," American Anthropological Association, May 17, 1998, http://www.americananthro.org/ConnectWithAAA /Content.aspx?ItemNumber=2583.

5. Elie Barnavi and Miriam Eliav-Feldon, *A Historical Atlas of the Jewish People: From the Time of the Patriarchs to the Present* (New York: Schocken Books, 1992), 54.

1: Origins

1. "Histoire de la Kahina (Dihya)," AmazighWorld.org, November 17, 2013, http://www.amazighworld.org/history/index_show.php?id=4133.

2. Genesis 25:13; Šawqī Abū Kạlīl, *Atlas on the Prophets Biography: Places, Nations, Landmarks: An Authentic Collection of Information on Prophet's Seerah with Maps, Illustrations and Pictures* (Riyadh: Darussalam, 2004), 54.

3. Genesis 29:35; Élie Barnavi and Miriam Eliav-Feldon, *A Historical Atlas of the Jewish People: From the Time of the Patriarchs to the Present* (New York: Schocken Books, 1992), 20–21.

4. Barnavi and Eliav-Feldon, *A Historical Atlas of the Jewish People*, 74; Dhu Nuwas, Zur'ah Yusuf Ibn Tuban As'ad Abi Karib, JewishEncyclopedia.com, http://www.jewishencyclopedia.com/articles/5159-dhu-nuwas-zur-ah-yu-suf-ibn-tuban-as-ad-abi-karib#ixzz0U8jvonQE.

5. Norman A. Stillman, *The Jews of Arab Lands: A History and Source Book* (Philadelphia: Jewish Publication Society of America, 1979), 4.

6. Maurice Eisenbeth, *Les juifs de l'Afrique du Nord* (Algiers: Imprimerie Carbonnel, 1936, Reedition by the Cercle de Généalogie Juive et la lettre Sépharade, Paris), 7.

7. Ibid.; Aly Tewfik Shousha, "Cholera Epidemic in Egypt (1947): A Preliminary Report," Bulletin of the World Health Organization 1.2 (1948), 353–81.

8. Joel Beinin, *The Dispersion of Egyptian Jewry: Culture, Politics, and the Formation of a Modern Diaspora* (Cairo: American University in Cairo Press, 2005).

9. Bension Taragan, *Les communautés israélites d'Alexandrie: Aperçu historique* (Alexandria: Les Editions Juives d'Egypte, 1932), 9.

10. Ibid., 22.

11. Ibid., 24.

12. "A Taste of Karaite Judaism in 30 Minutes or Less (Part 1)," YouTube, November 24, 2013, https://www.youtube.com/watch?v=iRb7DhWS6Z8.

13. Taragan, *Les communautés israélites*, 26.

14. Ibid.

15. Ibid., 29.

16. Benjamin Roger, "Y a-t-il encore des juifs au Maghreb?," JeuneAfrique, April 26, 2013, https://www.jeuneafrique.com/171077/societe/y-a-t-il-encore-des-juifs-au-maghreb/?=togo.

17. Saad Salloum, "Iraqi Jews Organizing to Regain Citizenship," *Al-Monitor*, September 1, 2018.

18. This section's biographical account of Qaid Nassim is heavily influ-

enced by Gilles Boulu, "Recherches sur les Scemamas ou Samama de Tunis," March 2005, http://www.shjt.fr/wp-content/uploads/2010/07/etude-Gilles -Boulu-Scemama.pdf.

19. References to de Flaux's writing in this section are from Armand de Flaux, *La régence de Tunis au dix-neuvième siècle* (Paris: Chez Challamel Aine, 1865), 70–71.

20. Paul D'Estourelles de Constant, *La conquête de la Tunisie* (Paris: Université du Québec à Chicoutimi/Plon, 1891), 56.

21. This and other details of what transpired between Nassim and the Italian authorities in Italy are from Général Hosaïn, "Lettre du Général Heusseïn au collège de la défense du gouvernement tunisien, dans loaffaire du caïd Nessim Samama: Traduction de l'arabe," Gallica/Bibliothèque Nationale de France, January 1, 1878, http://gallica.bnf.fr/ark:/12148/bpt6k840323b.

22. Ibid.

23. Fatma Ben Slimane, "Définir ce qu'est être Tunisien," *Revue des Mondes Musulmans et de la Méditerranée*, May 26, 2015, http://remmm.revues.org /9005.

24. Details of Elmaya Shemama's efforts to inherit Nassim's ill-gotten fortune, particularly the discredited fatwa from Sousse, are from Fatma Ben Slimane, "Définir ce qu'est être Tunisien," *Revue des Mondes Musulmans et de la Méditerranée*, May 26, 2015, http://remmm.revues.org/9005.

25. Général Hosaïn, "Lettre du Général Heusseïn au collège de la défense du gouvernement tunisien, dans l'affaire du caïd Nessim Samama: Traduction de l'arabe," Gallica/Bibliothèque Nationale de France, January 1, 1878, http:// gallica.bnf.fr/ark:/12148/bpt6k840323b.

26. Email correspondence with Osama Abi-Mershed, October 8, 2017.

2: The Nation

1. J. I. Enright, "The Pellagra Outbreak in Egypt," *The Lancet* 195, no. 5045 (1920): 998–1004, doi:10.1016/s0140-6736(01)08063-1.

2. Joel Beinin, *The Dispersion of Egyptian Jewry: Culture, Politics, and the Formation of a Modern Diaspora* (Cairo: American University in Cairo Press, 2005).

3. Patrizia Di Bello, Shamoon Zamir, and Colette Wilson, *The Photobook: From Talbot to Ruscha and Beyond* (London: I.B. Tauris, 2012).

4. Lyrics noted from: "Hbibi Lawel—Habiba Msika—Par Jalel Benna," YouTube, January 10, 2014, https://www.youtube.com/watch?v=ksKKB 0LhQf0.

3: The Rupture

1. This discussion of French and its prevalence in Egypt is influenced by Lanver Mak, *The British in Egypt: Community, Crime and Crises 1882–1922* (London: Tauris Academic Studies, 2012), 87.

2. Doha Chiha, "La francophonie en Egypte: Aperçu historique," *Cahiers de l'association internationale des études francaises*, March 15, 2016, http://www.persee.fr/doc/caief_0571-5865_2004_num_56_1_1527.

3. Encyclopdie de la Francophonie, "Les écoles françaises en Égypte à la fin du XIXᵉ siècle (document historique)," http://agora-2.org/francophonie.nsf/DocumentsEgyptes_ecole_francaises_en_Egypte_a_la_fin_du_e_siecle_document_historique_par_Louis_Malosse.

4. Ibid.

5. Information on École Harouche found in "Les écoles juives," *ASPCJE*, aspcje.fr/notre-histoire/organisation-ommunautaire/les-ecoles-juives-en-egypte.html?showall=1.

6. Joel Beinin, *The Dispersion of Egyptian Jewry: Culture, Politics, and the Formation of a Modern Diaspora* (Cairo: American University in Cairo Press, 2005), 49–50.

7. Annie Goldmann, *Les filles de Mardochée* (Paris: Denoel/Gonthier, 1979), 34–35.

8. Goldmann describes this opposition: ibid., 24–25.

9. Shimon Shamir, *The Jews of Egypt: A Mediterranean Society in Modern Times* (Boulder, CO: Westview Press, 1987), 53, 68.

10. Rodrigue explains how the Jewish French involvement in the Algerian colonies suited their own domestic interests in Aron Rodrigue, *French Jews, Turkish Jews: The Alliance Israélite Universelle and the Politics of Jewish Schooling in Turkey, 1860–1925* (Bloomington: Indiana University Press, 1990), 1–9.

11. Simon Schwarzfuchs, *Les juifs d'Algérie et la France (1830–1855)* Jerusalem: Institut Ben-Zvi, 1981), 67.

12. Rodrigue, *French Jews*, 8–9.

13. Ibid., 73.

14. Schwarzfuchs, *Les juifs*, 150.

15. Ibid., 102.

16. Frantz Fanon, *The Wretched of the Earth* (New York: Grove Press, 2011), 7.

17. Schwarzfuchs, *Les juifs*, 84.

18. Ibid., 100.

19. Ibid.

20. Ibid., 119–20.

21. Ibid., 151–52.

22. Ibid., 148.

23. Sarah Taïeb-Carlen, and Amos Carlen, *The Jews of North Africa: From Dido to de Gaulle* (Lanham, MD: University Press of America, 2010), 35–36.

24. Viviane Lesselbaum-Scemama, "Les relations judéo-arabes en Tunisie de 1857 à nos jours: Le pacte fondamental," *Harissa*, June 3, 2016, https://harissa.com/news/index.php?q=article%2Fles-relations-jud%C3%A9o-arabes-en-tunisie-de-1857-%C3%A0-nos-jours-le-pacte-fondamental-par-viviane-l.

25. For one such description, see Paul Pérez, "Jacques Hassoun, de mémoire . . . ," *Travailler, Penser, Créer*/Dailymotion, June 6,2018, www.dailymotion.com/video/x21bycy.

26. Rodrigue, *French Jews*, 1–4.

27. Ibid.

28. Quoted from information on École Harouche found in "Les écoles juives," *ASPCJE*, aspcje.fr/notre-histoire/organisation-communautaire/les-ecoles-juives-en-egypte.html?showall=1.

29. Bension Taragan, *Les communautés israélites dLAlexandrie: Aperçu historique* (Alexandria: Les Editions Juives d'Egypte, 1932), 83.

30. Ibid., 85.

31. Ibid., 103.

32. Rodrigue, *French Jews*, 1–4; "Notre histoire," AIU, http://www.aiu.org/fr/notre-histoire-0.

33. Take, for example, the "Appel de 1860," Alliance Israélite Universelle, https://www.aiu.org/fr/appel-de-1860.

34. *General Instructions* cited from André Kaspi, Valérie Assan, and Michel Abitbol, *Histoire de l'alliance israélite universelle, de 1860 à nos jours* (Paris: Armand Colin, 2010), 231–32.

35. Ibid., 454.

36. Ibid., 42.

37. Robert Estoublon, and Marcel Morand, *Revue algérienne, tunisienne et marocaine de législation et de jurisprudence*, vol. 12 (Algiers: L'École de Droit d'Alger, 1896), 197.

38. Chouraqui's writings on Jewish North African identity taken from André Chouraqui, *Between East and West: A History of the Jews of North Africa* (New York: Atheneum, 1973), 135.

39. Ibid., 184–86.

40. Note the blatant omission of the Arabs in the mention of North Africa's "Semitic strains." The identity that helps to inspire in Chouraqui's former Algerian compatriots a sympathy for fellow Arab Palestinians is the single North African identity that Chouraqui ignores.

41. Chouraqui, *Between East and West*, 184–86.

42. Ibid., 174.

43. Ibid., 142.

44. Ibid.

45. Ibid., 112.

46. Ibid., 185.

47. Ibid., 181.

48. Rodrigue, *French Jews*.

49. For another family's recollection of the *Leil Kibur*, see CCEJTV, "Tu sais que tu es juif tunisien si," YouTube, December 30, 2013, https://www.youtube.com/watch?v=7uoJm4H7ptE&t=391s.

50. Shamir, *The Jews of Egypt*, 170, 266.

51. For an example of the French use of the term *indigenous Israelites*, see Victor Piquet, *La colonisation française dans lAfrique du Nord: Algérie—Tunisie—Maroc; avec 4 cartes hors texte* (Paris: A. Colin, 1912), 354.

52. Lanver Mak, *The British in Egypt: Community, Crime and Crises 1882–1922* (London: Tauris Academic Studies, 2012), 87.

53. British preference for Copts and simultaneous self-seclusion from Coptic and other indigenes discussed in ibid., 54–68.

54. This paragraph on Egypt's census from: Shamir, *The Jews of Egypt*, 42–46.

55. Quotes in this paragraph all from: Schwarzfuchs, *Les juifs*, 152.

56. Ibid., 87.

57. Ibid.

58. Ibid.

59. For descriptions of this "false integration" into French and European sectors of the colonial cityscape see: Viviane Scemama-Lesselbaum, *"Le Passage": De la hara au Belvédère: histoire dune émancipation* (Lyon: Cosmogone, 2000), 37.

60. Maurice Eisenbeth, *Les juifs de l'Afrique du Nord* (Algiers: Imprimerie Carbonnel, 1936, reedition by the Cercle de Généalogie Juive et la Lettre Sépharade, Paris), 7.

61. Goldmann, *Les filles de Mardochée*, 108.

62. Ibid.

63. "Habiba Msika—Patrie: Les martyrs de la liberté," *Harissa*, https://harissa.com/news555/fr/Habiba-Msika-Patrie-Les-martyrs-de-la-liberte.

64. Biographical details of Georges Adda's life taken from "Tunisie: Décès de Georges Adda," *Business News*, September 9, 2008.

65. Excerpt from documentary with following quote available at "GEORGES ADDA le patriote Tunisien," Dailymotion, July 14, 2008, http://www/dailymotion.com/vidio/x64fpn.

66. "Abu Nazzara Zarqa. 1879. Paris, 1879," Abou Naddara Collection, http://kjc-sv016.kjc.uni-heidelberg.de:8080/exist/apps/naddara/journals.html?collection=%2Fdb%2Fresources%2Fcommons%2FAbou_Naddara%2FJournals%2F1879.

67. Reeva Spector Simon, Michael Menachem Laskier, and Sara Reguer, eds., *The Jews of the Middle East and North Africa in Modern Times* (New York: Columbia University Press, 2003), 99; Anna Della Subin and Hussein Omar, "The Egyptian Satirist Who Inspired a Revolution," *New Yorker*, July 10, 2017.

68. Ibid.

69. Michael Haag, *Vintage Alexandria: Photographs of the City, 1860–1960* (Cairo: American University in Cairo Press, 2008), 64.

70. Ofer Aderet, "The Great Mosque of Paris That Saved Jews During the Holocaust," *Haaretz*, November 27, 2013.

4: Exile

1. Descriptions of hostility between Alliance and Zionism heavily influenced by: Esther Benbassa, "L'Alliance israélite universelle et les sionistes en Orient," *Pardès* 12 (1990): 190–95; and Aron Rodrigue, *French Jews, Turkish Jews: The Alliance Israélite Universelle and the Politics of Jewish Schooling in Turkey, 1860–1925* (Bloomington: Indiana University Press, 1990), 126–31.

2. Benbassa, "L'Alliance israélite universelle," 194.

3. Leah Garrett, *A Knight at the Opera: Heine, Wagner, Herzl, Peretz, and the Legacy of Der Tannhäuser* (West Lafayette, IN: Purdue University Press, 2012), 89–90; Rodrigue, *French Jews*, 127, 200.

4. Rodrigue, *French Jews*, 127.

5. "Appel de 1860," Alliance Israélite Universelle, http://www.aiu.org/fr/appel-de-1860.

6. Benbassa, "L'Alliance israélite universelle," 193–94.

7. Ibid., 195.

8. Discussion of Zionism in Tunisia influenced mainly by Paul Sebag, *Histoire des juifs de Tunisie: Des origines à nos jours* (Paris: Éd. LHarmattan, 1991), 205.

9. Ibid., 206.

10. Bension Taragan, *Les communautés israélites d'Alexandrie: Aperçu historique* (Alexandria: Les Editions Juives d'Egypte, 1932), 124.

11. Ibid., 124.

12. Ibid., 124–29.

13. Ibid., 124.

14. Isaiah Friedman, *Germany, Turkey, and Zionism 1897–1918* (New Brunswick, NJ: Transaction Publishers, 1998), 95–100; Taragan, *Les communautés israélites d'Alexandrie*, 26–27.

15. Joel Beinin, *The Dispersion of Egyptian Jewry: Culture, Politics, and the Formation of a Modern Diaspora* (Cairo: American University in Cairo Press, 2005), 270.

16. Ibid., 270–71.

17. Ibid., 121–22.

18. For more on the Shomer Hatsair in Egypt, see ibid., 121–26.

19. Gudrun Kramer, *The Jews in Modern Egypt, 1914–1952* (London: Tauris, 1989), 180–81; Joel Beinin, *Was the Red Flag Flying There? Marxist Politics and the Arab-Israeli Conflict in Egypt and Israel, 1948–1965* (London: Tauris, 1990), 56–57.

20. Steven S. Carol, *From Jerusalem to the Lion of Judah and Beyond: Israel's Foreign Policy in East Africa* (Bloomington: IUniverse, Inc., 2012), 328.

21. Tom Segev and Arlen Neal Weinstein, *1949: The First Israelis* (New York: Henry Holt, 1998), 106–7.

22. Rufus Learsi, *Fulfillment: The Epic Story of Zionism* (New York: Herzl Press, 1972), 403.

23. Tom Segev, "Now It Can Be Told," *Haaretz*, January 13, 2018.

24. Abbas Shiblak, *Iraqi Jews: A History of Mass Exodus* (London: Saqi, 2005), 156.

25. Segev and Weinstein, *1949*, 167.

26. Shiblak, *Iraqi Jews*, 156, 164.

27. Ibid.; Michael J. Fischbach, "Claiming Jewish Communal Property in Iraq," Middle East Research and Information Project, www.merip.org/mer/mer248/claiming-jewish-communal-property-iraq; Segev.

28. Colin Shindler, *A History of Modern Israel* (Cambridge: Cambridge University Press, 2008), 94.

29. "Israel Honors 9 Egyptian Spies," *Ynetnews*, March 30, 2005, www.ynetnews.com/Ext/Comp/ArticleLayout/CdaArticlePrintPreview/1,2506,L-3065838,00.html.

30. Beinin, *The Dispersion of Egyptian Jewry*, 31–33.

31. Ibid., 244–45.

32. Cole C. Kingseed, *Eisenhower and the Suez Crisis of 1956* (Baton Rouge: Louisiana State University Press, 1995), 69.

33. Nadéra Bouazza, "Les dernières juives d'Egypte, des dinosaures malgré elles," *Slate* (French), December 17, 2014; "Egypt Places Jewish Leaders in Concentration Camps; Deports Others," Jewish Telegraphic Agency, November 26, 1956, https://www.jta.org/1956/11/26/archive/egypt-places-jewish-leaders-in-concentration-camps-deports-others.

34. FLN: Lettre aux Israélites d Algérie, Algeria-Watch.de, www.algeria-watch.de/farticle/1954-62/israelites.htm.

35. Ethan B. Katz, *The Burdens of Brotherhood: Jews and Muslims from North African to France* (Cambridge, MA: Harvard University Press, 2015), 174–75.

36. HIAS, "History," www.hias.org/history. Frédéric Abécassis, Questions About Jewish Migrations from Morocco, Q HAL Archive ouverte en Sciences de l Homme et de la Société, June 2012, halshs.archives-ouvertes.fr/file/index/docid/778664/filename/NEW_DIASPORAS._THE_JERUSALEM_WORKSHOP._JUNE_2012.pdf.

37. Ibid.; Rebecca Pierce, "Interview with Reuven Abergel," Jewish Voice for Peace, YouTube/Palestine Diary, May 6, 2011, www.youtube.com/watch?v=suUTEcoN6R; for more on the Moroccan government's involvement in Operation Yakhin: Tad Szulc, *The Secret Alliance: The Extraordinary Story of the Rescue of the Jews Since World War II* (London: Pan, 1993).

38. Ephraim Kahana, *Historical Dictionary of Israeli Intelligence* (Lanham, MD: Scarecrow Press, 2006), xxv–xxvi.

5: Darkness

1. "Saint-Chamas (13250): Résultats de l'élection présidentielle 2017," *L'Express*, May 7, 2017, https://www.lexpress.fr/actualite/politique/elections/presidentielle-2017/resultats-elections/ville-saint-chamas-13250_13092.html.

2. Freya Kamel and Jane A. Hoppin, "Environmental Health Perspectives," May 20, 2004, https://www.ncbi.nlm.nih.gov/pmc/articles/PMC1247187/#b126-ehp0112-000950.

3. "El-Soud ela al-hawia (1978)," IMDB, www.imdb.com/title/tt0332022.

4. "Al So3od Ela Al Haweya Movie—الهاوية الى الصعود فيلم," MelodyEntInc/YouTube, December 5, 2016, www.youtube.com/watch?v=7Gjw3qo0XXE.

5. Alfred-Maurice De Zayas, "The Illegality of Population Transfers and the Application of Emerging International Norms in the Palestinian Context," *Palestine Yearbook of International Law Online* 6, no. 1 (1990): 45, doi:10.1163/221161491x00012.

6. Eve Spangler, *Understanding Israel/Palestine: Race, Nation, and Human Rights in the Conflict* (Rotterdam: Sense Publishers, 2015), 155–56; for a denial of claims of ethnic cleansing in Ramleh and elsewhere, see Jack L. Schwartzwald, *Nine Lives of Israel: A Nation's History Through the Lives of Its Foremost Leaders* (Jefferson, NC: McFarland, 2012), 63.

7. Tom Segev, *1949: The First Israelis* (New York: Free Press, 1998), 157.

8. Ibid., 156.

9. Sammy Smooha, *Israel: Pluralism and Conflict* (London: Routledge and K. Paul, 1978), 88.

10. Ibid., 88–89.

11. Rachel Shabi, *We Look like the Enemy: The Hidden Story of Israel's Jews from Arab Lands* (New York: Walker & Co., 2008), 197.

12. Frantz Fanon, *Les Damnés De La Terre* (Paris: La Découverte/Poche, 2002), 42–43.

13. Frantz Fanon, *Wretched of the Earth* (New York: Grove/Atlantic, 2007), 5.

14. "ג'ו עמר לשכת עבודה," Elroy Shukrun/YouTube, November 18, 2011, https://www.youtube.com/watch?v=NVzEmGq_wC8.

15. Jonathan Cook, "Israel: DNA Tests May Provide Answers on Missing Babies," Al Jazeera, February 8, 2018.

16. "Exposed: Medical Experiments on Missing Yemenite Children," *Israel Hayom*, June 14, 2017.

17. Edward Said, "Edward Said: Diary: An Encounter with J-P Sartre," *London Review of Books*, June 1, 2000.

18. Rachel Holman, "Remembering the Paris Massacre 50 Years On," France 24, October 18, 2011, http://www.france24.com/en/20111017 -france-algeria-war-of-independence-fln-protest-paris-maurice-papon -government.

19. "יודילוביץ', מרב, ארי קטורזה. "חיים חפר: המרוקאים - לא מפותחים July 6, 2002, https://www.ynet.co.il/articles/1,7340,L-1933394,00.html.

20. Shlomo Swirski and Etty Konor-Attias, "Israel: A Social Report 2016," Adva, January 2017, http://adva.org/wp-content/uploads/2017 /03/SocialReport2016-EN.pdf.

21. Haviv Rettig Gur, "Study Finds Huge Wage Gap Between Ashke-nazim, Mizrahim," *The Times of Israel*, January 29, 2014.

22. Educational statistics from Or Kashti, "Study: Mizrahi-Ashkenazi Higher-ed Gaps Wider Than Ever," *Haaretz*, April 10, 2018, https://www.haaretz.com/israel-news/.premium-study-mizrahi-ashkenazi-higher-ed-gaps-wider-than-ever-1.5419232.

23. Tom Mehager, "Why Mizrahim Don't Vote for the Left," *972 Magazine*, January 24, 2015, https://972mag.com/why-mizrahis-dont-vote-for-the-left/101769.

24. "Netanyahu Apologizes for Comment Disparaging Mizrahi Jews," *Haaretz*, January 15, 2018, https://www.haaretz.com/israel-news/netanyahu-apologizes-for-comment-disparaging-mizrahi-jews-1.5450174.

25. Rachel Shabi, "Understanding Israel Through Its Marginalised Mizrahi Jews," *TRT World*, August 11, 2017, https://www.trtworld.com/opinion/understanding-israel-through-the-marginalised-mizrahi-jews-389035.

26. Sigal Samuel, "When Israelis Kill Innocents for the Crime of Looking Arab," *The Forward*, October 19, 2015, https://forward.com/opinion/322883/when-jews-kill-innocents-for-the-crime-of-looking-arab.

27. Leeor Ohayon, "Stop Blaming Mizrahim for Everything Wrong in Israel," *972 Magazine*, March 26, 2015, https://972mag.com/stop-blaming-mizrahim-for-everything-wrong-in-israel/104859.

28. Quotes taken from: Rebecca Pierce, "No Man's Land," Jewish Voice for Peace, YouTube, June 6, 2017, https://www.youtube.com/watch?v=I0uSQA1TMbw&t=161s.

6: Memory

1. Sherifa Zuhur, *Asmahan's Secrets: Woman, War, and Song* (Austin: University of Texas Press, 2000), 1.

2. Monique Parsons, "Muslim Women Challenge American Mosques: 'Now Is the Time,'" NPR, January 15, 2014.

3. "Supplemental Statement: World Zionist Organization, American Section Inc.," FARA, July 23, 2018, https://efile.fara.gov/docs/2278-Supplemental-Statement-20180723-29.pdf.

4. Brian Whitaker, "Selective Memri," *The Guardian*, August 12, 2002.

5. Brian Whitaker, "Arabic Under Fire," *The Guardian*/Wayback Machine, May 7, 2007, https://web.archive.org/web/20070517124655/www.commentisfree.guardian.co.uk/brian_whitaker/2007/05/arabic_under_fire.html.

6. "Yigal Carmon—President and Founder of the Middle East Media Research Institute (MEMRI)," House.gov, 2016, https://docs.house.gov/meetings/FA/FA00/20160706/105161/HHRG-114-FA00-Bio-CarmonY-20160706.pdf.

7. Thomas L. Friedman, "Crazy Poor Middle Easterners," *New York Times*, September 5, 2018.

8. Jonathan Ofir, "Stop Talking About Ahed Tamimi's Hair," *Mondoweiss*, January 17, 2018, http://mondoweiss.net/2018/01/talking-about-tamimis.

9. Elodie Auffray, "Yoav Hattab, 'une perte énorme' en Tunisie," *Libération*, January 10, 2015, http://www.liberation.fr/planete/2015/01/10/yoav-hattab-une-perte-enorme-en-tunisie_1178078.

ABOUT THE AUTHOR

Massoud Hayoun is a journalist based in Los Angeles. He has reported for Al Jazeera English, *Pacific Standard*, Anthony Bourdain's *Parts Unknown* online, *The Atlantic*, Agence France-Presse, and the *South China Morning Post*. He speaks and works in five languages and won a 2015 EPPY Award.

PUBLISHING IN THE PUBLIC INTEREST

Thank you for reading this book published by The New Press. The New Press is a nonprofit, public interest publisher. New Press books and authors play a crucial role in sparking conversations about the key political and social issues of our day.

We hope you enjoyed this book and that you will stay in touch with The New Press. Here are a few ways to stay up to date with our books, events, and the issues we cover:

- Sign up at www.thenewpress.com/subscribe to receive updates on New Press authors and issues and to be notified about local events
- Like us on Facebook: www.facebook.com/newpressbooks
- Follow us on Twitter: www.twitter.com/thenewpress

Please consider buying New Press books for yourself; for friends and family; or to donate to schools, libraries, community centers, prison libraries, and other organizations involved with the issues our authors write about.

The New Press is a 501(c)(3) nonprofit organization. You can also support our work with a tax-deductible gift by visiting www.thenewpress.com/donate.